THE PHILOSOPHY

OF MUSIC

To Michael

THE PHILOSOPHY
OF MUSIC

Theme and Variations

AARON RIDLEY

EDINBURGH UNIVERSITY PRESS

© Aaron Ridley, 2004

Edinburgh University Press Ltd
22 George Square, Edinburgh

Transferred to digital print 2004

Typeset in Bembo
by Koinonia, Bury
Printed and bound in Great Britain by
Marston Book Services Limited, Oxford

A CIP record for this book is available from the British Library

ISBN 0 7486 1162 2 (hardback)
ISBN 0 7486 0902 4 (paperback)

The right of Aaron Ridley to be identified
as author of this work has been asserted
in accordance with the Copyright, Designs
and Patents Act 1988.

Contents

Contents

Preface

It is more or less impossible, once one has finished something like this, to work out quite how much one owes, for what, and to whom. But I am wholly certain that the following people have all, in one way or another, contributed significantly to whatever virtues the present book has: Maria Alvarez, Nick Cook, Peter Lamarque, Jerry Levinson, Denis McManus, Alex Neill, David Owen, Tony Palmer and David Pugmire; I am especially grateful to Alex Neill and David Owen, both of whom gave me constant and invaluable help throughout. Any imperfections that remain are, of course, attributable to bad advice from the same people. I must also acknowledge the Arts and Humanities Research Board for funding the period of research leave during which the book was completed, and the proprietors and staff of the Avenue Bar in Padwell Road for (again) providing the environment in which the vast majority of the work was actually done. At Edinburgh University Press I would like to thank Jane Feore, who commissioned the book, and Jackie Jones, Carol Macdonald, Mareike Weber and Nicola Wood for their patience and professionalism in seeing the project through. Finally, I would like to thank my wife, Ann, for recreating the half-remembered – or perhaps just imagined – painting by Feininger that appears on the front cover, as well as for letting me run off with her original for my office wall.

Some of the material in this book has previously been published elsewhere: versions of parts of Chapter 3 in M. Kelly (ed.), *Encyclopedia of Aesthetics* (Oxford University Press, 1998) and the *Richmond Journal of Philosophy* (2002); a short version of Chapter 4 in *The Journal of Philosophy* (2003); and an ancestral version of some pages of Chapter 5 in the now defunct first edition of A. Neill and A. Ridley (eds), *Arguing About Art: Contemporary Philosophical Debates* (McGraw-Hill, 1995). My thanks to those concerned for permission to make use of the relevant material here.

Aaron Ridley
Southampton, 2003

Introduction

Music from Mars

['T]he things of the highest value must have another, *peculiar* origin – they cannot be derived from this transitory, seductive, deceptive, paltry world, from this turmoil of delusion and lust. Rather from the lap of Being, the intransitory, the hidden god, the 'thing-in-itself' – there must be their basis, and nowhere else.' This way of judging constitutes the typical prejudice that gives away the metaphysicians of all ages. (Friedrich Nietzsche, *Beyond Good and Evil*)

This book is animated by one fairly simple conviction – that music is part of life. It's a rotten slogan, but it does capture pretty well what I mean. To anyone who loves music, musical experience occupies a position right at the centre. It isn't filed away in some self-contained compartment to be visited from time to time when circumstances allow. In the form of themes running through one's head, sometimes for days; of pianos one can't quite walk past without brushing the keys; of snatches overheard, familiar but unplaceable, music can permeate the experience of even the least musical-seeming moments. Nor is music a lot less conspicuous in the experience of those who are indifferent to it. Next-door's radio, TV signature-tunes, church bells, muzak in shops, someone whistling, passing car stereos, telephone answering machines, juke boxes, advert jingles, buskers: there's plenty out there to be indifferent to. Whether welcome or not, music and musical sounds are ubiquitous; and that, certainly, is an aspect of what my slogan was meant to capture. But it has a wider point too. As part of life, music also shares some of life's basic characteristics and conditions. It is, for instance, historical through and through. Musical sounds change: where now we have computers, once we had crum-horns, and before that lyres and monochords. Musical roles change: music's place in tribal dancing is different from its place in Christian ritual, and neither is the same as its place in the Albert Hall, at Groucho's or at Yankee Stadium. Conceptions of music change: we have had Pythagorean metaphysics, the harmony of the spheres, devotional music, music as ornament, music as high art, *volkisch* music, protest music, commodity music. The point of music, what has counted as music and how it has been heard and thought about – all these have changed; which means that if the music and musical experiences we have now are to be understood, they will have to be understood, at least in part, historically – as the complex products of accretion, assimilation, atrophy and decay. Its historicity dovetails with another of music's life-like traits: its embeddedness. In common with everything else, music occupies a conceptual space, not in a vacuum, but at the interstices of an indefinitely large and shifting set of other concerns, each of which it conditions and is conditioned by. Thus, through dance, music is tied reciprocally to sex and sociality; through hymns and chants to the health of the soul; through nursery rhymes to play; through marches to the army; through anthems to solidarity; through proportion to mathematics; through the *chantier* to work; through dirges to death; and so on. It is this embeddedness that gives music much of its richness, as well as accounting, through the fluctuating composition of its conceptual environment, for all of its history. I am convinced that any attempt to understand music which tries to suppress this about it – the fact that it is embedded and historical – will be thin and unsatisfactory at best, and almost certainly worse than that. Hence my insistence, with apologies duly offered, that music is part of life.

I

No one, I think, would disagree with any of what I've just said. Indeed, it was pretty well continuously platitudinous. But one's practice can be out of kilter, to various degrees and in various ways, with what one would, at some level anyway, concede to be obviously true. And I think that the way that much recent philosophy of music has been done is out of kilter with precisely the platitudes that I have mentioned. I know from my own case that this fact can be quite hard to spot. But I used to think, at clear variance with the banalities set out above, although not obviously at variance with prevailing philosophical practice, that the best way to get at the truth about music must, in effect, be to separate it off as much as possible from everything else and to investigate it in what might be called its 'pure' state. Music needed to be disembedded, I thought, and approached *for itself*; it needed to be taken in isolation from what, a moment ago, I called its 'conceptual environment'. And this determination – to achieve for music a state of maximal purity – extended even into the issue of what *sort* of music I should investigate. The following remarks from Eduard Hanslick's seminal book of 1854, *On the Musically Beautiful*, struck me as self-evident: 'If some general definition of music be sought,' said Hanslick, 'something by which to characterise its essence and its nature, to establish its boundaries and purpose, we are entitled to confine ouselves to instrumental music. Of what *instrumental music* cannot do, it ought never be said that *music* can do it, because only instrumental music is music purely and absolutely.'[1] So I determined not only to divide music off from the rest of the world, but to divide it off, too, from singing and dancing, and from marching and from anything else that could not be described as 'music purely and absolutely'. In this way, I confidently expected, music – freed from every contaminating influence – would yield up its secrets. The fact that it never did, particularly, I was willing to attribute to my own incompetence. More disturbing was the fact that I didn't find very believable some of the things that other people were coming up with, either. And once I'd noticed and been bothered by this, the whole approach started to seem problematic. There is something very odd, after all, about the way in which so much philosophy of music has so often been done. To try to isolate music entirely, to try to leech or prise out of it its context-laden character, and indeed the very nature of one's own context-laden engagement with it, is rather like trying to pretend that music had come from Mars – that it had suddenly appeared on one's desk from nowhere, a perfectly formed but wholly mysterious phenomenon of which one knew precisely nothing. Which, as I say, is odd, given how far from the truth that picture is.

That philosophers of music have carried on with this exact assumption in mind is, of course, an overstatement. But I shall persist with the overstatement for the moment. It captures something that has been true of much recent philosophical practice, and by overstating it I hope to be able to make clear, albeit in exaggerated form, what the motivations for it might be and what the effects of it threaten to be, and in fact often have been.

Why, then, has the picture I've mentioned been found even slightly seductive? I think I can answer this, schematically at least. Reflection on my own prior (if thoughtless) attachment to it suggests that the picture owes its appeal to two factors, one methodological, the other theoretical. They're complementary, but I'll take them in turn. The methodological attraction derives from a particular way of taking a particular model of intellectual enquiry, and hence from a particular conception of objectivity.

3

The model itself is broadly scientific. Suppose you want to find out about the effects of pressure on the boiling point of water. You make sure your water's as pure as it can be – you distil it. You make sure your temperature and pressure gauges are operating to suitable standards. You conduct your experiments using a variety of different sorts of container. You make every effort to collect and to interpret your results without prejudice. In short, you do whatever you can to isolate the phenomenon you're interested in from external interference – from impurities in the water, from eccentric thermometers, from expanding vessels, from bias. Only thus can you hope your findings to be *about* the effects of pressure on the boiling point of water (and not, say, about dodgy thermometers or about your own private expectations). Accept this for a moment as a fair, if skimpy, sketch of one aspect of scientific method. The conception of the object of enquiry it presupposes is evident: the object is conceived of as isolable, as ideally (if never in practice) instantiating a closed system, as insulated entirely from extraneous influence. In the relevant sense, then, the object is conceived of as Martian; and scientific objectivity consists in finding out things about objects from Mars. A scientifically objective finding is thus one that is maximally independent of the vagaries of time and place, of equipment and methods and, above all, of what one might term the human element – prejudices, feelings, wants, needs. And this is just as it should be. My sketch of scientific method has been a caricature, but not a hostile one; for it is precisely these ways of thinking that have underwritten the phenomenal success of science in the modern age. But the conception of objects and of objectivity it presupposes has snares in it nonetheless.

There is an entirely harmless way in which the model I've described can be applied to non-scientific forms of intellectual enquiry. If construed simply as an injunction to exclude the irrelevant, to ensure that one's attention really is focused on the object that interests one, then the model is not merely harmless but indispensable to any form of enquiry worth the name. But, construed thus, the issue of what is and what is not irrelevant in any particular case is left open. The vagaries of time and place may be irrelevant to the physicist investigating liquids, for instance, but they certainly won't be to the cultural historian with an interest in, say, nationalism. The cultural historian will exclude certain sorts of factor as irrelevant, the physicist will exclude others. The snares only begin to tighten when the model itself is construed more tightly – specifically, when it is taken as an injunction to rule out not merely the irrelevant, whatever in a particular case that might happen to be, but to rule out precisely the factors that natural science rules out. When the model is construed in this way, the result is scientism – the belief that the standards appropriate to the natural sciences are equally appropriate to every other type of enquiry.[2] And this belief is just false. Science, as I've mentioned, standardly and properly attempts to exclude the human element, things like feelings, wants and needs. But if what I want to find out is how to make a good tzatziki, the subtle inter-relations between my cucumber, garlic, olive oil and yoghurt and questions of human preference and response are central. I could, to be sure, rule them out: in which case I might hope to discover something about the chemistry of Greek food. But if I do do this, I certainly won't find out what I wanted to know about tzatziki – which is why cookery isn't a branch of science.

Or take an example discussed by Roger Scruton. Sex, he notes, became discussable only once an overtly science-like approach to it was adopted, with the result that:

> modern discussions of [sex] have been conducted in a 'scientized' idiom which, by its very nature, removes sex from the sphere of interpersonal relations ... Freud's shocking revelations, introduced as neutral, 'scientific' truths about the human condition, were phrased in the terms which are now more or less standard. According to Freud, the aim of sexual desire is 'union of the genitals in the act known as copulation, which leads to a release of the sexual tension and a temporary extinction of sexual instinct – a satisfaction analogous to the sating of hunger.' This scientistic image of sexual desire ... seems to me ... entirely false, and could become true only by so affecting our sexual emotions, as to change them into emotions of another kind.[3]

By adopting such language, sex is presented as 'a relation between aliens' and in 'redescribing the human world in this way, we also change it'. The world we concoct instead has no place in it for such commonplace observations as that:

> sexual behaviour has to do with courtship, desire, love, jealousy, marriage, grief, joy and intrigue. Such excitement as occurs is excitement of the whole person. As for the sexual organs, they can be as 'excited' (if that is the word) by a bus journey as by the object of desire ... [Thus scientistic] language is opaque to *what is wanted* in sexual desire; it reduces the other person to an instrument of pleasure, a means of obtaining something that could have been provided equally by another person, by an animal, by a rubber doll or a piece of Kleenex.[4]

What Scruton says here is surely precisely right. One need do no more than reflect for a moment on the dreadful scientised language of the Kinsey report, for instance, to realise that nothing said in it could possibly have any bearing on the topic alleged to be at issue.

The problem in the sexual case is the same as in the cookery case. By importing a narrowly scientistic model of enquiry into an area where it has no place, the object of enquiry is falsified and the 'objectivity' thereby secured is entirely spurious. A good meal is not a piece of complex chemistry – indeed it is not *that* sort of object at all. It is, rather, a balance of tastes and textures, properly pitched to the occasion and pleasing to the eye; it is a product of skill and care offered by host to guest – entertainment as much as nutrition, an expression of culture as much as of hunger. This is the sort of complex object that any real enquiry into cookery would have to focus on; and its results would be objective precisely to the extent that it did not disregard the kinds of factor that would be irrelevant to the natural sciences. And the same with sex. The object descried by scientism would be recognisable as human sex only to a sociopath and its findings thought 'objective' only by someone who didn't know what that word meant.

Objectivity is a matter of getting the object right. If the object of enquiry is historically constituted, as for instance nationalism is, then objectivity depends on not ruling out the vagaries of time and place. If the object is culturally constituted, as to different degrees sex and cookery are, objectivity requires the human element. The error of scientism is to imagine that because water, say, lacks a history or a culture in the relevant sense, and because science attempts to factor such things out accordingly, objectivity must by its very nature be ahistorical and acultural. But that is to mistake one injunction for another. One should exclude the irrelevant, by all means; but one shouldn't therefore exclude it by irrelevant standards of relevance.

Thus the scientistic misunderstanding of the scientific model of enquiry confuses objectivity with scientific objectivity, and supposes the latter to exhaust the former. In doing so, it fosters a false conception of the sorts of object that can be investigated objectively. Such objects, scientism suggests, are stripped to their bare essentials: they are divested of every contingency, plucked free of history and culture, disentangled from any merely human concern and polished up to a state of immaculate purity. But of course these sorts of objects are the proper objects of science, not of intellectual enquiry as such. Polish up sex or cookery in this way and you've nothing recognisable left. They are not merely 'entangled' in history, culture and the rest of it, they are partly made up of those things and their 'bare essentials' include them. Cookery without culture is no more cookery than water without hydrogen is water. The urge, then, to construe any proper object of enquiry as a Martian object of immaculate 'purity' is a more or less inevitable corollary of bad methodology, of taking a method proper to one sort of enquiry for the essence of good method everywhere. The mistake here is obvious, even banal. But it is very easy to make all the same, particularly given the deservedly high regard in which science is held, and it would be a brave person who, hand on heart, could swear that philosophers, for instance, have been immune to its charms. Certainly I don't think that philosophers of music have been immune.

So part of the explanation of why the music-from-Mars picture should have been found even slightly tempting lies, I'm sure, in doubtful methodology: the (perhaps half- or un-conscious) misapplication of scientific criteria of relevance and a correspondingly partial conception of objectivity together issue in a way of thinking about objects which is liable to misrepresent (at least some of) them systematically. Of course, it *may* be true that music is best investigated when thoroughly disembedded, polished up and isolated. But if so, that is an interesting fact about music; it is not a precondition of objective musical enquiry as such. So one would need other reasons than this to think of music as Martian.

II

This is where the second, theoretical, part of the explanation comes in. A certain picture of music has, as Wittgenstein might have put it, held us captive – or at least it has insofar as we have been analytic aestheticians. The picture or theory of music in question lies behind Walter Pater's famous remark that all art aspires to the condition of music.[5] What Pater meant by this was that the other arts were becoming more and more self-contained. Poetry was becoming more concerned with its own internal qualities than with saying things about the world (e.g. Baudelaire), the novel more bound up with its own language and form than with psychology (e.g. Flaubert), painting more obsessed with its own nature as painted surface than with the things actually depicted there (e.g. Cézanne). It doesn't matter for present purposes whether Pater was right about this (although his view is much what one might expect from someone looking in the second half of the nineteenth century towards France). What matters is the conception of music he presupposes: that music is the self-contained art *par excellence*. Music, one is given to understand, exhibits naturally the qualities to which the other arts aspire.

It doesn't trouble with the world outside itself; it doesn't depict or say things or bother itself with psychology; its proper subject-matter is, simply, itself – and its glories are the glories of form, design and structure, unsullied by any content not wholly its own. Thus for Pater, music is *sui generis*, self-sufficient – in a word, autonomous.

And not only for Pater. The view that music is essentially autonomous has been popular for more than a hundred and fifty years. But it wasn't always so. Lydia Goehr's excellent book, *The Imaginary Museum of Musical Works*, shows in detail how it came to enjoy such prominence. Goehr is interested in the emergence (in about 1800) and the effects of what she calls the 'work-concept'. In thinking of pieces of music as 'works', she suggests, we have become accustomed to suppose that 'that the tonal, rhythmic, and instrumental properties of works are constitutive of structurally integrated wholes that are symbolically represented by composers in scores', such 'works' continuing to exist indefinitely after their composition.[6] The work-concept, then, enshrines a way of thinking about pieces of music which conceives of them as stable objects whose essential characteristics are those capable of symbolic representation in musical scores. Such a conception is clearly consonant with the conception of pieces of music as autonomous. If a work is, essentially, the structure of sound notated in a score, then its point or meaning must, essentially, be a function of the properties of the structure notated there: the work must, that is, be autonomous. And, as Goehr shows, these two conceptions did indeed emerge together. Before the late eighteenth century, music had not been grouped with the fine arts at all. It had, rather, been seen as a comparatively lowly activity whose service to political, religious or social ends was performed chiefly with the help of words (i.e. not through its own resources). Thus much of music's 'meaning had come from 'outside' of itself'.[7] But then, for complex reasons, the fine arts themselves began to be reconceived. Rather than seeing the significance of the fine arts as lying in their 'service to particularized goals of a moral or religious sort', Romantic theorists argued that it lay in the ability of the fine arts 'to probe and reveal the higher world of universal, eternal truth. This ability originates, according to Gustav Schilling, in "man's attempt to transcend the sphere of cognition".' Under this conception, music not merely became 'more closely … allied to the other fine arts', it came to be seen as exemplary of them: for 'instrumental music, without particularized content', that is, without words, seemed:

> the most plausible candidate for being the 'universal language of art'. Such music provides a direct path to the experience of a kind

of truth that transcends particular natural contingencies and transitory human feelings. Schilling made the point again: 'No aesthetic material is better suited to the expression of the ineffable than is sound.'

Thus the Romantic argument involved a '*transcendent* move from the worldly and particular to the spiritual and universal' and a '*formalist* move which brought meaning from music's outside to its inside.'[8]

The conflation or intertwining of these two moves resulted in a highly peculiar position: music's significance was now all its own, but the 'purely musical, in these terms, was now synonymous with the moral, the spiritual, and the infinite in its uniquely musical form'. Therefore 'matters in relevant circumstances considered extra-musical could in other circumstances be regarded as purely musical', so that theorists came to 'accept a double-sided view of musical meaning, that it be transcendent, embodied spirituality and purely musical at the same time. In sum, the new romantic aesthetic allowed music to mean its purely musical self at the same time that it meant everything else.'[9] Clearly such a position was unstable (not to say unintelligible). But its long-term effect was to move the idea of the *autonomous* musical *work* to the centre of the conceptual stage, so that when the Romantic aesthetic finally collapsed it was the transcendent move that was repudiated, leaving the formalist move (which shifted musical meaning from the outside in) in place. By the beginning of the twentieth century, then, the view that pieces of music were essentially those autonomous structures of sound capable of being symbolically represented in scores was firmly entrenched.

A host of points emerge from Goehr's account, but I'll highlight only two. The first is that there is nothing 'natural' or self-evident about the claim that music is autonomous: there had been music for centuries before anyone got round to having the idea, and there is no reason at all to suppose that every piece of responsible thinking about music must be conducted in its terms. The other is that the concept of musical autonomy became voguish at precisely the point and for many of the reasons that art as a whole was being rethought (i.e. that the fine arts were being romanticised); and this suggests that its prominence may not be due entirely to any insights it embodies about music. What the concept did make possible, however, was the rise of a new, positivist style of musical analysis, one that could 'claim to be 'enlightened' and therefore uninfluenced by 'external' − sociological, political, and historical − considerations'.[10] Once it had been decided that pieces of music were essentially autonomous structures of sound, after all, it seemed evident that the analysis of those structures would reveal the innermost truths about music; and it seemed, moreover, that if one got one's analysis right, those truths should be demonstrable. Thus the study of music promised to take a scientific turn; and this was a turn which, in view of the prestige of science, served further to entrench the conception of music that made it possible. Much of the last hundred years or so bears witness to the inspirational power of this prospect. Great schools of analysis grew up, quarrelled with one another, split and regrouped; ever more technical means of probing musical structures were devised; and ever wider gaps opened up between what the analysts said music was all about and what ordinary listeners actually heard.[11]

The problem, in hindsight, was that the decision to regard music as essentially autonomous really was just that − a decision. It certainly wasn't a discovery about the essence of music, although it allowed discoveries about music to be made; which means that the presumption, until recently hegemonic, that valuable truths about pieces of music were to be had *only* through the analysis of structure was baseless. No one sensible doubts the capacity of technical analysis to reveal truths about music. But there is every reason to doubt that the truths of analysis are the only ones there are − and this precisely because there is every reason to doubt that music really is, in the relevant sense, autonomous.

Philosophers of music have been a good deal slower to pick up on this than musicologists have. Musical autonomy is still, for philosophers, a more or less holy cow, their dominant attitude to music being, as Goehr puts it, one of 'apriorism and ahistoricality';[12] and the picture that holds them captive is, again, of music as Martian − as immaculate, disembedded and cut off from the rest of the world; as, in Peter Kivy's words, 'a quasi-syntactical structure of sound understandable solely in musical terms … and making no reference to anything beyond itself'.[13] I said earlier that the methodological and the theoretical reasons that philosophers have had for thinking of music in this way were complementary. It should now be clear why. For if one adopts a model that construes the proper object of enquiry as maximally disembedded, and if one simply presupposes that music is, essentially, autonomous, one is going to have an uphill struggle to avoid the conclusion that music is, indeed, best investigated as if it had appeared on one's desk from nowhere. The theory reinforces the method. Or, to put the point the other way: if one is committed to the view that pieces of music are essentially structures of sound, and if one adopts a method of studying them that enjoins the excision of everything else as irrelevant, it is unlikely that one won't find oneself confirmed in the conviction that music is, indeed, autonomous. The method reinforces the theory. So perhaps 'complementary' was overly generous. The relation between the two seems a lot closer than that – and this, in the end, is the conclusion that I draw.

The habit of thought that I have described is endemic, too. It would be invidious to illustrate the point by picking on anyone but myself, so I'll offer just one example of the habit at work. Here I am, in a study of musical expression, setting up my discussion as if the *fact* of musical autonomy were beyond question: 'For what could it be,' I asked, 'in a mere series of noises – blown, struck, plucked, sung, bowed – which has the power to put one in mind of, even in a state of, passion?'[14] A 'mere series of noises', note – that is, mere ordered sound – here offered on page one as a perfectly uncontentious and neutral characterisation of the phenomenon at issue. Certainly I never got round to *arguing* that a piece of music was, essentially, a series of sounds, or might best be seen as such; I didn't see the need to. The picture held me captive. And here, from the same study, is what one might generously call a methodological remark:

> If we concentrate on songs, for example, or on music accompanied by long explanatory texts, or by actions on stage, we risk mistaking the expressive effects of words or actions for the effects of musical dynamics. We do better, then … to concentrate on pure instrumental music, with as little extra-musical expressive import as [possible].[15]

Again, this just struck me as obvious: polish up music, I thought, so that everything 'extra-musical' is excluded, and the truth is bound to shine through. No argument offered. Plenty of people have found plenty of things wrong with what I wrote. But no one, in my hearing at least, has pointed out that my theoretical and methodological commitments were a bit too close to one another for comfort. Nor, in the event, is that surprising; for in the quoted passages I was doing little more than mouthing the clichés of recent musical aesthetics.

III

The habit of thought I've described is not so much an intellectual position as an intellectual condition, a syndrome. Call it – still in a spirit of overstatement – autonomania. The autonomaniac begins by assuming that music is, essentially, pure sound, and then sets about investigating it in accordance with a method which reinforces that assumption. His conclusion, not surprisingly, is that music is much as Pater had supposed it to be. This restricts quite sharply the sorts of things that the philosopher can hope to be interesting about. Specifically, it restricts him to just a single aspect of music: its character as sound-structure. And on this, as one might expect, autonomanic aesthetics has been good. Just as technical analysis has taught us a lot about intra-musical relations, so analytic philosophy of music has taught us a lot about the ways in which those relations feature in our musical experience. The problems start only when attention is directed elsewhere.

Attention often is directed elsewhere, however. For, by no coincidence, many of the traditional problems in the philosophy of music revolve around music's relations, not to itself, but to the rest of the world. What is music's relation to the emotions? What, if anything, does it mean to say that music can express them? What is music's relation to objects and events? What, if anything, does it mean to say that music can represent them? And so on. The reason that questions such as these have attracted so much attention is self-evident. First, there is the undoubted fact that most people who are not philosophers of music do routinely and unreflectingly take it for granted that these relations are real, and even central. What could be more obvious than that Tchaikovsky's *Pathétique* ends in despair, or that the *William Tell* overture has galloping horses in it? Why, if such relations weren't obvious, would marketing people put the music they do into adverts, or film-composers use the *Marseillaise* to refer to the French? These pre-theoretical assumptions are interesting, and naturally invite investigation. But investigating them becomes urgent when one assumes, as many philosophers of music have, that music is *essentially* autonomous; for, by these lights, the sorts of things that non-philosophers say and assume about music are utterly mysterious. How could it possibly be true that a pure sound-structure ends in despair? Or that a mere sequence of sounds is a horse or a Frenchman? How, if music's most significant relations are all internal, are these allegedly extra-musical relations possible at all? Such are the challenges that analytic aesthetics has set itself. That it is supremely ill-equipped to meet them, however, is no less clear than the reasons for those challenges being posed in the first place. For the questions are effectively foreclosed. Once one has decided that pieces of music are most illuminatingly to be seen as pure sound-structures, disembedded and self-sufficient, very few options remain. One is obliged either to deny that these alleged extra-musical relations are real; or to admit that they're real, but to deny that they're important; or, darkly suspecting them to be both real and important, one is obliged to square the circle and show

how something can be essentially related to the world at the same time as it is essentially autonomous. And these alternatives have indeed absorbed a non-negligible proportion of the philosophical energies that music has attracted, with expectedly drab results.

My point, then, is not that it is wrong to think of music as sound-structure. Music no doubt is that, among other things. The mistake is to assume that music is *essentially* sound-structure; that its character as structured sound is its true, real, ultimate nature. For that might very well be false. And if it is false, one is going to be left up a gum tree – either denying things that are true, or else desperately trying to re-embed something that one has already characterised in such a way as to make it logically unembeddable. Nor do I want to suggest that every autonomanic conclusion about music's extra-musical relations is wrong. It may be, for example, as many philosophers have said, that music is incapable of representation, or is very bad at it. But if that is the case, the reasons for it are going to be rather richer and more interesting than that music is, somehow by definition, autonomous. The point I want to make is more modest: it is simply that we do ourselves a disservice if we decide before we start what sort of thing we're going to find in the end, especially if we don't notice that that's what we've done. We pre-empt ourselves and limit what we can discover. Above all, though, we risk mystifying the object of our enquiry, representing it to ourselves in such a way that almost anything that anyone has ever wanted to say about it becomes, at best, baffling, and more usually nonsensical. The pretence that music is from Mars, I suggest, constitutes just such a mystification.

We ought, Goehr suggests, 'to think about music, less as excused and separated, and more as inextricably connected to the ordinary and impure condition of our human affairs'[16] – to think of pieces of music, not as autonomous patterns of sound, but perhaps rather as patterns of sound that are (to some degree or other, but always to *some* degree) embedded in the rest of the world, shot through with history, their significance quite as likely a function of culture as of structure.[17] This is a baggy conception of music, certainly. But it has its strengths. For one thing, it manages, as the autonomanic conception does not, to encompass the sort of thing that people actually listen to and care about, the sort of thing one goes to concerts to hear or blocks one's ears to shut out. And, as a corollary of this, it doesn't foreclose any questions. What one should say about musical expression, say, or about representation, isn't legislated in advance, and so – ideally – one's chances of saying something interesting or true about them should go up a bit. Certainly that is my hope in this book. So I adopt a baggy musical ontology both as a preliminary gesture of hostility towards Mars and all his works and also for the goods that I believe it ought to be able to deliver. I also, in due course, suggest that any more grandiose ambition for musical ontology should be shelved, preferably indefinitely.

IV

It is time now to rectify the overstatement that I introduced at the beginning of section I, and which has shaped, or at least amplified, the discussion since then. The music-from-Mars picture has, in fact, held no philosopher of music that I can think of captive for the whole of the time, and it has detained some of them hardly at all. Nor, correspondingly, is the condition of captivity – a condition that I have called 'autonomania' – anything like as ubiquitous or as evenly distributed as I have implied. But the picture and the condition are none the less real for that, and in inflating them I have tried to indicate as clearly and as graphically as I can why the one is to be resisted and the other, where it has taken hold, to be shaken off. It is a principal aim of this book, moreover, to show how even quite high levels of alertness may be insufficient to keep the picture and its attendant condition at bay, and to suggest how subtly they can lurk in, and warp, even the most innocent-seeming passages of philosophical argumentation.

The strategy in what follows is simple enough. The book contains five chapters, each of them divided into two parts. The first part of each chapter is intended both to set the scene, by introducing significant themes and topics, and to offer a brief overview of the philosophical literature relevant to the argument of the second part; the second part of each chapter is where the meat is. In Chapter 1 I explore a case in which, autonomanic prejudices suspended, the notion of musical under-standing is illuminated by consideration of what it is to understand words. In Chapter 2 I ask what might be meant by the claim that music can be representational when one doesn't just assume that pieces of music are, essentially, mere structures of sound. In Chapter 3 I turn to musical expression: what, I ask, is to be said about expressiveness if we don't arbitrarily presuppose that purely instrumental music is para-digmatic? In Chapter 4 the argument against ontology is offered, by way of an enquiry into musical performance. And in Chapter 5 I turn to the question of profundity: how, if the conclusions of previous chapters are right, might a piece of music be said to be 'profound'?

I have drawn heavily on Lydia Goehr's work in this introduction, so I ought probably to register at least one aspect of the present book that would not win her approval. Goehr is keen to point out that there are plenty of categories of music on which the work-concept has no purchase, or should be permitted no purchase: jazz, for instance, or folk music, or any music composed before 1800. Her view is that this fact, together with the shortcomings of the work-concept itself, indicates that one ought not, when doing musical aesthetics, to concentrate on individual, canonical pieces of 'classical' music as if they somehow exhibited musicality as such, or somehow showed music in its native state.[18] So she can scarcely be expected to applaud my decision to build each chapter of this book around a single, canonical piece of 'classical' music. I offer no apologies for doing so, however. I agree with Goehr that the 'work-concept' is apt to be unhelpful. It is, after all, part of the autonomanic package. But nothing follows from this about the propriety of talking about specific pieces of music, just so long as those pieces of music are not construed, *a priori*, as structures of pure sound. And of course I have no intention of construing them in that way. Nor does the fact that there are categories of music (jazz etc.) that resist formal notation much bother me; this book isn't about them. I choose individual pieces of 'classical' music, then, partly because I like them (and it may be that one writes better about the things one likes), partly because the sort of philosophy of music I want to move away from concentrates on them (so the contrast with autonomanic aesthetics should be clearer) and partly because, as I have suggested, there is no reason not to.

But there is a wider point as well. Too often in the philosophy of music the terms of debate have been set, not by any particular perplexity prompted by any particular piece of music, but by issues and positions which have their real currency elsewhere in philosophy. When the philosophy of music is pursued in this spirit, the result is usually a kind of applied philosophy of mind, or applied metaphysics, in which actual pieces of music function as little more than illustrative examples. I think that music is more interesting than that. Indeed, I think that unless one sets out *from* particular, concrete pieces of music one's chances of saying anything of interest about music, let alone of interest to other areas of philosophy, is much reduced. So each of the chapters in this book is built, more or less closely, around a single piece of music (as it happens, a canonical 'classical' one), in an attempt to address the questions that it, specifically, raises. Of course this strategy could easily misfire – not everyone, for instance, might think the pieces I've chosen perplexing or interesting in the way that I do. But that's a chance I'll have to take. If I pull it off, the proof will be in the puddings that follow. If not, my apologies.

NOTES

1. Eduard Hanslick, *On the Musically Beautiful*, trans. G. Payzant (Indianapolis, IN: Hackett, 1986), pp. 14–15. I return to this passage at some length in Chapter 3.
2. For a discussion of some aspects of scientism, see Tom Sorrell, *Scientism* (London: Routledge, 1995).
3. Roger Scruton, *An Intelligent Person's Guide to Philosophy* (London: Duckworth, 1996), pp. 127–8.
4. *Ibid.*, pp. 134–5.
5. Walter Pater, 'The School of Giorgione', in A. Phillips (ed.) *The Renaissance: Studies in Art and Poetry* (Oxford: Oxford University Press, 1986), p. 86.
6. Lydia Goehr, *The Imaginary Museum of Musical Works* (Oxford: Oxford University Press, 1992), p. 2.
7. *Ibid.*, p. 152.
8. *Ibid.*, p. 153.
9. *Ibid.*, pp. 156–7.
10. *Ibid.*, p. 6.
11. A point made forcefully by Nicholas Cook in his *Music, Imagination and Culture* (Oxford: Oxford University Press, 1990), pp. 1–9.
12. Goehr, p. 5 (see Note 6).
13. Peter Kivy, *Music Alone* (Ithaca, NY: Cornell University Press, 1990), p. 202.
14. Aaron Ridley, *Music, Value and the Passions* (Ithaca, NY: Cornell University Press, 1995), p. 1.
15. *Ibid.*, pp. 104–5.
16. Goehr, p. 286 (see Note 6).
17. For a very striking account of the effects of culture on the significance of one piece of music, see Nicholas Cook, *Beethoven: Symphony No. 9* (Cambridge: Cambridge University Press, 1993).
18. Goehr, chapter 9 (see Note 6).

1

Understanding

> If a man finds that the cadences of an Apache war-dance come nearest to his soul, provided he has taken pains to know enough other cadences – for eclecticism is part of his duty ... let him assimilate whatever he finds highest of the Indian ideal, so that he can use it with the cadences, fervently, transcendentally, inevitably, furiously, in his symphonies, in his operas, in his whistlings on the way to work, so that he can paint his house with them ... this is all possible and necessary, if he is confident that they have a part in his spiritual consciousness. With this assurance his music will have everything it should of sincerity, nobility, strength, and beauty, no matter how it sounds. (Charles Ives, *Essays before a Sonata*)

PART 1. BACKGROUND

A spokesman for Tessa Jowell, the UK Culture Secretary, recently announced that 'Noise is noise. It doesn't matter whether it's Tchaikovsky or a power drill',[1] so bearing witness to the sad fact that philosophical conclusions can sometimes fail to make it into the political mainstream. The *apparatchik* was wrong, of course; and a fair amount of ingenuity has gone into explaining, not only why noise is sometimes not merely noise, but why, in fact, it is sometimes music. Much of the attention that this issue has received takes its lead, in spirit at least, from R. G. Collingwood, who noted that a musical concert is, in one respect, rather like a scientific lecture. 'The lecture,' he says:

> is not a collection of noises made by the lecturer with his organs of speech; it is a collection of scientific thoughts related to those noises in such a way that a person who not merely hears but thinks as well becomes able to think those thoughts for himself.

Similarly, he suggests:

> what we get out of [a] concert is something other than the noises
> made by the performers. In each case, what we get out of it is
> something ... which will remain forever inaccessible to a person
> who cannot or will not make efforts of the right kind, however
> completely he hears the [noises] that fill the room.[2]

In each case, the difference that Collingwood is marking is the difference between the person who *understands* what he is hearing, and the
person who does not. To the person who doesn't understand the lecture
– that is, who doesn't understand it at all, not a word of it – it might as
well be in Chinese; indeed it might as well be a power drill. For him, it is
mere noise (made, as it happens, by the lecturer's 'organs of speech'). And
likewise for the uncomprehending concert-goer: he hears a lot of noise,
perhaps, as a cat or a dog might, but for him it signifies nothing. As *music*,
it passes him by completely.

If the person who understands the lecture understands the scientific
thoughts that it elaborates, then what is it that the person who understands a piece of music understands? A representative and plausible answer
to this question is offered by Roger Scruton:

> There are certain basic perceptions involved in hearing music, and
> these are crucial to understanding it. For example, there is the
> hearing of movement – as when one hears a melody, theme, or
> phrase, move from one note to another. There is the hearing of
> tones as opposed to the hearing of pitched sounds ... the hearing
> of rhythm (as opposed to temporal sequence); the hearing of
> harmony, as opposed to aggregates of tones, and so on. All of these
> experiences are basic, in that a person who did not have them
> would be deaf to music. And all other musical experiences depend
> upon them: for example, the hearing of melodies would be impos-
> sible without the hearing of musical movement, the hearing of
> counterpoint impossible without the hearing of harmony ... I have
> made various distinctions – between hearing a sound and hearing
> a tone [etc ... – and these] distinctions ... lie *in* the experience [of
> listening to music].[3]

Scruton's point, then, is that the primary objects of musical understanding are, as one might put it, 'purely' musical – musical movements,
rhythms, harmonies and so on. It is things of *this* sort, therefore, that
feature in the experience of a person who understands what he is
hearing when he listens to a piece of music, and which are absent from

the experience of someone for whom Tchaikovsky might just as well be a power drill.

This answer has won widespread acceptance, even if there has been relatively little enthusiasm for Scruton's further contention that, because notions such as musical 'movement', and 'highness' and 'lowness' of pitch, appear to be metaphorical, musical understanding itself must be essentially metaphorical. Just as the baby is thrown out with the bath water when one attempts to analyse out what is metaphorical in a metaphor, so, he suggests, the attempt to state literally what one understands when one understands a piece of music suppresses precisely those features of what one has understood that made one's understanding of it musical in the first place.[4] This claim – that the experience of music is irreducibly metaphorical – has been rejected by, among others, Malcolm Budd, on the grounds that 'unless the underlying point of a metaphor is understood its characterisation as a metaphor is unrevealing.'[5] Budd's point, here, is not that metaphor might not feature in one's experience of music, but rather that, if it does, whatever is metaphorical about it can always be analysed out. In a more positive vein, and consistently with the first part of Scruton's position, Budd argues that what is given in one's musical experience, and so is understood in it, is, because irreducibly perceptual (rather than metaphorical), impossible to specify without reference to the object of that experience, which is to say, without reference to the music itself.[6] This ties musical understanding intimately to its object, and explains why – as Donald Ferguson has shown – the competent listener may have to be attentive to every change of motion and tension in a piece of music, since those changes, in shaping the listener's experience, also shape his understanding.[7] In all of these ways – and more; the list could be extended immoderately – philosophers of music have sought to analyse and to underline what I have called the 'purely' musical character of musical understanding, a mode of understanding focused exclusively on intra-musical relations.[8]

Two things emerge clearly from these discussions. The first is that the *objects* of musical understanding, which is to say, pieces of music, are standardly taken to be unique individuals – or, perhaps better, to be individuals whose claim on our understanding resides, at least partly, in their uniqueness, in the ways in which their properties are peculiar *to* them. The second thing to emerge is the degree of practice and cultivation of ear that understanding such individuals is taken to involve. Close attention – to nuance, to detail, to the finest gradations of tempo and phrasing – stands out in every account. And this is salutary. It reminds us of something important and true: that listening to music is not a passive exercise, as being subjected to noise is, but an activity. Therefore, like any activity, it is something one can get better at (by making what Collingwood calls 'efforts of the right kind'). The burden of this last point is not that musical understanding – as understood by philosophers of music – depends on formal musical training, or that it is somehow the natural preserve of experts. If that were the point, then the philosophical analyses which made it would be more or less worthless. They would tell us of 'musical understanding' only in a special, atypical sense, leaving it entirely open what the rest of us might mean when we say that we understand a piece of music, or say we understand one better now than we did before. No, the *kind* of understanding that these philosophers have described is – and must be, if what they have to say about it is to be of any moment – standard for engaged and interested listeners as such, not merely for some unusual minority of them. Thus it is an upshot of these analyses that they underline, not the esoteric and mysterious nature of a 'purely' musical understanding, but its ubiquity and ordinariness.

In Part 2 of this chapter I presuppose a conception of musical understanding much like the orthodox conception sketched out above. In the course of my argument, however, I give reasons to think that the emphasis on uniqueness that comes with that conception ought not to be overdone, and corresponding reasons to doubt that the ubiquity of 'purely' musical understanding, although real enough, should be taken to entail its exhaustiveness. Individual musical works may be less utterly singular than the orthodox position suggests, in other words, and an understanding of them *may* go beyond what is grasped in a 'purely' musical take on them – certainly to the extent that such a take is focused on those intra-musical relations that individual musical works, uniquely, exhibit. I also try to say something about one very striking and peculiar piece of music.

PART 2. *CENTRAL PARK IN THE DARK*

Charles Ives (1874–1954) wrote *Central Park in the Dark* in 1906, at the age of thirty-two, although like much of his music it was not performed in his lifetime. It is one of the first of Ives's works to exhibit his mature musical manner, as well as being one of the first and most striking works of American modernism. Ives's music characteristically functions through juxtaposition – of the traditional and the experimental, of the new and the second-hand, of the artsy and the folksy – to produce results poised in bizarre equilibrium between outright originality and outright pastiche.

Central Park has all the hallmarks. It begins with a hushed and strictly atonal murmur of strings, shifting softly and intertwining but heading, it seems, nowhere in particular. This opening is a radical one. For one thing, Ives's atonalism here predates Schoenberg's much more famous break with tonality by two or three years, which is a remarkable fact when you stop to think about it; and for another, the flavour of Ives's opening anticipates (although for obvious reasons it couldn't have influenced) Bartok's altogether better-known version of the same sort of thing – his so-called 'night music', as heard, for instance, in the third movement of *Music for Strings, Percussion and Celesta* (1936). So a fair bit happens early. Not much else happens for a while, though, until, at length, the brass enter with distant little parping noises. Then there is a snatch of piano music. And then, behind the overlay of string sounds, some rag-time music strikes up, becomes gradually louder and louder until it finally swamps everything else – and the piece ends. Those are the bare outlines of what we hear. But it is hard to know what to make of it all. At one level, perhaps, there is no problem. *Central Park in the Dark* is a record or evocation of the sounds that someone might hear when walking in Central Park in the dark; and in this much one might decide that Ives had composed a piece of musical representation, and leave it at that. But at another level, the piece, like many of Ives's, has a disconcerting quality. There's an inconsistency of style (which style here is Ives's?), of inventiveness (that rag-tune can't have taken a lot of inventing), of tone – of what, above all, one wants to call musical *language*. Hearing *Central Park* is a little like hearing a poem which veers from high seriousness via burlesque to doggerel of the most derivative sort, and it poses similar problems to the listener. How is one to understand, in either case, what one is hearing? This is the central problem that Ives's music seems to me to raise, and the remainder of this chapter is devoted to it. Before beginning, though, a couple of caveats. First, if the reader shares nothing of my perplexity at Ives's music, quite a bit of what follows may seem rather pointless – but that can't be helped; and second, and whether or not my perplexity is shared, what follows is bound to seem unduly round-about. I don't really get back to Ives until the final section. But I think I know what is disconcerting about the music, and the route that I follow in attempting to explain it is as direct as I have been able to make it; so bear with me.

I. Music and Words

It is possible that what I've said has already raised the odd eyebrow, if not an actual hackle. To liken a piece of music to a poem, to want to call something a musical *language* (with that emphasis), is to play fast and loose with one of the several orthodoxies of analytic aesthetics – in this case, the one that says that music and words are simply too unlike to be worth comparing (unless, of course, the point of the comparison is to show just how unlike they are). But I want to disturb that orthodoxy here, at least a little. Wittgenstein once remarked, although not in the hearing of most philosophers of music, that 'understanding a sentence is much more akin to understanding a theme in music than one might think';[9] and the corollary of this, if it's true, is that understanding a theme in music may be much more akin to understanding a sentence than most philosophers of music, at any rate, have been willing to concede. I am convinced that this thought – the thought that music and language might indeed be mutually illuminating – deserves to be given much less short shrift than it generally is, not least since its effect, if one takes Wittgenstein seriously, is to show just how hard questions of meaning and understanding turn out to be, whether in or out of music.

But of course one needs to be careful. Wittgenstein was sometimes wrong, and attempts to understand music in terms of language hardly have a glittering track-record of success. Deryck Cooke, whom it is both customary and useful to mention at this point, unwittingly showed in his book *The Language of Music* just how much can go wrong when one tries, as he did, to identify the musical equivalent of a linguistic vocabulary.[10] His failure was due partly to mistakes he made on the musical side of the parallel; but was due, too, for reasons I'll go into in a moment, to a naivety about language. But a single failure doesn't show much about what can and can't be done, and one would certainly want a more solid reason than this before drawing the sort of sharp line between music and language that subsequent philosophers of music have drawn. More solid, or solid-seeming, reasons have duly been given, however, of which the best worked-out of the recent ones are Stephen Davies's. Music, he says, cannot, as a point of principle, resemble language in any relevant way, because the relevant way would be this:

> Meaning E: Arbitrary Meaning Generated within a Symbol System: For meaning E, a symbol or sign has meaning as an element or 'character' in an arbitrary symbol scheme that provides rules for the generation of meaning by the appropriate uses of these elements. Linguistic meaning is of meaning E.[11]

22

The idea here, which derives from linguistics, is that words have the meanings they do, first, by belonging to a system of symbols by which, second, their proper deployment in the production of meaningful utterances is determined. Proper deployment, for Davies, is secured by 'rules for the generation of meaning'. So these rules define the system of symbols and govern the meaningful manipulation of the individual symbols or 'elements' it comprises. Musical meaning, by contrast, is not of type E. Music cannot be construed as a 'Symbol System' in the relevant sense.[12] Hence, Davies says, music is not and cannot be meaningful in the way that language is meaningful.

Does this give us cause to draw the line? I think we should grant Davies his claim that musical meaning is not of type E, and for much the reasons he gives. But if he's right in his larger claim – that the failure of music to exhibit meaning E rules out any relevant parallel between music and language – then the Wittgenstein remark I quoted a moment ago must be pretty thoroughly off-beam. Understanding a sentence could hardly be less akin to understanding a theme in music, if Davies is right, since understanding a sentence, on his account, is a matter of understanding a meaning of type E – a type of meaning which, according to him, music cannot have.

Before we conclude that Wittgenstein is wrong and the kind of position outlined by Davies is right, however, we should ask what the point of Wittgenstein's remark actually is; for here the plot begins to thicken. Part of what Wittgenstein is doing is objecting to a popular conception of linguistic meaning, one according to which the meaning of a sentence is a compound made up out of the independently and antecedently meaningful words it comprises. Thus, on this conception, the meaning of the sentence 'The chair is blue' is simply an additive function of the meanings of the words 'the', 'chair', 'is' and 'blue'. The words themselves are the basic units, or 'atoms', of meaning, while sentences and other complex expressions mean what they mean in virtue of the atoms arranged within them. According to meaning-atomism, then, understanding a sentence is a matter of analysing it into and understanding its consituent parts.

Wittgenstein's remark about understanding a theme in music cuts directly against this picture of meaning, and does so, moreover, in a way that shows precisely what is wrong with Deryck Cooke's attempt to identify the musical equivalent of a linguistic vocabulary. Cooke's idea was that short musical phrases – patterns of just a few notes – had stable expressive meanings, so that the expressive sense of any extended sequence of notes, for instance of a theme, was a function of the independently and antecedently meaningful phrases it comprised. To understand the 'language of music', in Cooke's view, was therefore to understand the expressive meaning of each of those short phrases from which musical works are built up; and the result was to be a kind of musical dictionary. Cooke's labours were heroic, without doubt. But they were also futile. For he underestimated disastrously the extent to which the expressive significances of his basic phrases were sensitive to musical context. A descending minor triad, for instance, supposed (according to Cooke's dictionary) always to be expressive of 'passive sorrow', is in fact capable, depending upon the context it appears in, of expressing more or less anything. And this is exactly the feature of musical meaning that Wittgenstein wanted to draw attention to: its extreme context-dependence. The significance that the individual phrases have in a particular musical theme is a function, not of their own invariant meanings, which one as it were adds up as one listens along, but of one's hearing them as parts of that theme. Just as individual notes have no independent significance (if the theme in which a C appears is in G, it will function as the fourth degree; if in A-flat, it will be the third; and when heard as part of the opening fugue of Beethoven's C-sharp minor quartet, it won't be a C at all, but a B-sharp), so, in the case of a theme, the meaning of the individual parts (the constituent phrases) is a function of the meaning of the whole, and not the other way around. Meaning-atomism, in music at any rate, is certainly false.

It is Wittgenstein's claim that just the same goes for words, and for the same reasons. When one understands a sentence, he suggests, one doesn't merely grasp some additive compound of independently meaningful atoms. Rather, one understands words as meaning what they do because of the contexts – for example, the sentences – in which they appear and function. Meaningful parts get their senses from meaningful wholes, and not vice versa. It doesn't always feel like that, of course. Indeed it often seems thoroughly natural to suppose that words really are the basic building-blocks of meaning from which intelligible sentences are constructed (hence the popularity of meaning-atomism). But the reason it doesn't always feel like that, if Wittgenstein is right, is that we are highly practised language users who are, as a result, highly proficient at contexts. Take again the sentence 'The chair is blue'. The sentence is, as it stands, entirely ambiguous: it could mean that a certain piece of furniture is a certain colour or it could mean that a certain person presiding over a meeting or organisation is feeling a bit low. Taken by itself, the sentence might mean either or neither of these. The only way to grasp its meaning in any particular case is through context. If 'The chair is blue' is offered in response to a question about interior design, one will not understand the remark to refer to the mental state of the person with the casting vote. We all know this, and know it without having to think about it, which is why the role of context in our ability to understand what is said to us is, because ubiquitous, also inconspicuous. But the basic point is crucial. We don't resolve the ambiguity by inquiring more closely into the meaning of the word 'chair', say, as we would if meaning atomism were true; we resolve it by understanding the context in which that word appears. By itself, 'chair' can mean more or less anything (a person, a thing, something settled by a stipulative act you weren't present at) or nothing. And one can invent contexts in which the meaning of even the most innocent-sounding words or phrases becomes different or problematic. It is because he didn't see this that Cooke, starting out with a plausible, but false, conception of linguistic meaning (atomism), constructed a 'language of music' that was false without even being plausible. He got language wrong, and so got music wrong too.

Thus 'understanding a sentence is much more akin to understanding a theme in music than one may think'. In terms of Wittgenstein's philosophical logic, the point of emphasising the role of context is to show that atomistic conceptions of meaning – conceptions like Cooke's which construe complex meanings as built up out of basic meaning atoms – are a non-starter.[13] And in terms of the things we say we understand, the point of the remark is to show how the falsity of meaning atomism may be more easily spotted in music than in language. The tactic of comparing music to language, then, can go either way. It can create confusions, as with Cooke, or dispel them, as with Wittgenstein.

Several things follow from this. First, it follows that it is a mistake to assume that we have – or could have – a reductive, atomistic theory of linguistic meaning, such that music could match or fail to match its constraints. Second, because in the foregoing it was music that shed light on language, it follows that it is a mistake to presuppose that musical meaning is somehow and automatically *more* mysterious or less well understood than other kinds of meaning. This presupposition, which has been almost a badge of office among philosophers of music, is, evidently enough, part of the music-from-Mars picture. Under its aegis, music is treated as a brand new, extra-terrestrial candidate for meaningfulness whose status needs to be settled, as it were, from scratch. And from this perspective, the temptation arises to ask whether music is assimilable to something else, to something this-worldly and so, presumably, not mysterious at all. Is music meaningful in the way that the weather is meaningful (philosophers ask)? In the way that a rash is meaningful? In the way that pictures are meaningful? In the way, above all, that *language* is meaningful? And almost always the answer is 'no' – which leads, by no coincidence, to the 'solution' that we are so often offered, namely, the postulation of a variety of 'meaningfulness' that is wholly and ineliminably musical. But this is pure hubris. However much the determination represented here may look like a high-minded refusal to beg any questions (by putting music to the most *stringent* of tests), it is in fact nothing of the sort. For, as we have just seen, such stringency isn't available even in what is meant to be the paradigm case – language. The third and final thing that follows from Wittgenstein's remark is that any style of musical analysis that is implicitly or explicitly atomistic cannot be a style of analysis that will succeed in laying bare what we understand when we understand a piece of music.

We don't understand linguistic meaning as well as philosophers of music are given to suppose, then, and we're a good deal more at home with musical meaning than they imply. Nor, as we have seen, is there any principled reason to suppose that neither can shed light on the other. So I intend to press on with the music/language parallel, and to do so with the continued assistance of Wittgenstein.

II. Paraphrase

The question we began with, remember, was how to understand *Central Park*; and so far we can answer no more than that we shouldn't, indeed couldn't, understand it in accordance with the tenets of meaning atomism. Which is hardly world-shaking. But we can go further. Wittgenstein is concerned, as we have seen, to draw attention to the importance of context to our capacity to understand. But he is also concerned to make a point about the concept of 'understanding' itself; and it is this point that I now want to explore.

Wittgenstein's claim, in a nutshell, is that the concept of 'understanding', as it applies to language, is made up of two aspects: one having to do with the paraphraseable, the other with the non-paraphraseable, uses of words. In order to see what he is getting at, however, we will have to do some work on the notion of paraphrase – a notion which, perhaps oddly, turns out to be tricky to handle. The difficulty stems in part from the sheer range of things that might count as paraphrases. At the extremely minimal end of the range, one might describe as paraphrase the substitution of a word by a synonym (e.g., of 'feline' by 'cat-like'). Or, more elaborately, a paraphrase might involve someone stating a point he has stated before, but now from a quite different perspective. And more elaborately still, a paraphrase might consist in something like a full-blown analysis or explanation, as when someone attempts to produce an exegesis of or commentary upon a complicated text or position. Each of these senses of paraphrase clearly involves a quite distinctive kind of effort directed at a quite distinctive kind of end, both effort and end becoming more interesting as the paraphrase itself becomes more elaborate. But the most elaborate paraphrase presupposes the possibility of the less elaborate; and the possibility of paraphrase of any degree of elaboration depends upon the minimal, substitutional sense with which we started. In what follows, then, I will be dealing primarily with that minimal sense of paraphrase, for two reasons. First, it is sufficient to show what Wittgenstein was getting at; and second, even the minimal sense turns out to be quite tricky enough.

The sense of paraphrase at issue, then, turns on the substitution of certain words by others, such substitutions having their most natural place, one might suggest, in routinely instrumental contexts. If I have the practical need or desire to get you to turn up at a certain time and place I might not, within limits, much mind which form of words does the trick. I use one form ('See me here at midday'), but I might just as well have used another ('Meet me here at noon'). The paraphraseable use, then, suggests words wielded like tools, and wielded in that way when the context they're used in is already understood *instrumentally*. Thus, one might say, the paraphraseable use of words is words used, and understood to be being used, to achieve an end which is specifiable independently of the means by which it is brought about. The best example of (minimal) paraphrase I know would appear to bear this out. George, in Kingsley Amis's *Ending Up*, has had his memory for everyday common nouns almost eliminated by a stroke, with the result that he is, on his own diagnosis, a complete pain to live with and to talk to. So he determines to make amends to the rest of the household by adopting a new and more fluent language of 'periphrasis'. What he comes up with sounds like this:

> '[T]his thing here is very manageable apart from putting in new pieces, and of course much easier for me than using the old way. Most of the writing stuff used to go over my hands or what I was wearing or the things on the bed rather than on what I was supposed to be doing …' [Later,] anxious not to appear sullen or bored, he said 'I was reading where a chap wrote this morning … about those four young swine who broke into the place to rob it, but there was hardly any money in where they keep the money, because the boss had just been and paid it in, so they hit him with

a tightening-up affair and the iron business for the fire and so on, and took the money in what he was wearing and how you tell the time and even his smoking stuff. What can you do about people like that?'[14]

Paraphrase here becomes surreal – but it works. And part of the reason it works, of course, is that we are so used to working for ourselves, to filling in context and to understanding the imperfect, ungrammatical kinds of sentence that so much writing and almost all conversation actually consists of.

So one might accept an account of (minimal) paraphrase built about the idea, not merely of intersubstitutability, but of *instrumental* intersubstitutability. Indeed I think one should accept such an account – but not without noticing its limits and difficulties. I characterised instrumentality, a moment ago, as the use of means to achieve independently specifiable ends. But this is clearly problematic, certainly in the case of words. Suppose I want to you to understand that a chair is heavy. I say 'That chair is heavy.' You don't see what I'm getting at, so I say 'That thing you're about to lift up is not at all light.' What exactly is the independently specifiable end I'm trying to achieve here? Presumably, it's to get you to understand something – that a certain piece of furniture is relatively weighty. But notice: *any* attempt to specify what it is that I want you to understand inevitably involves me in further paraphrase, for instance in talk of the 'relatively weighty' quality of a 'certain piece of furniture'. So it would seem that the analysis of paraphrase in terms of instrumental intersubstitutability is circular: paraphrase presupposes instrumentality, the analysis suggests, but then instrumentality turns out to presuppose paraphrase.

This point can be brought out in another way. Suppose we ask what it means for two expressions to be instrumentally intersubstitutable. An obvious and plausible answer would be that they both say the same thing, but say it in different ways. But now if we ask *what* it is that they both say, we run into the same problem: no answer can be given which isn't itself just another 'way' of saying the 'same' thing. It is impossible, in other words, to specify what it is that two expressions have in common without producing a third expression said to have it too. And if we try to say precisely what that third expression shares with the original two, we find we need a fourth expression, and so on. But if the 'same thing' that an expression and its paraphrase say in different ways cannot be specified without saying the 'same thing' in still another way, paraphrase again appears to presuppose itself.

It is important not to misconstrue the point of this. The point is not to suggest that the very idea of paraphrase is incoherent, and should somehow be done without. It couldn't be done without. It is entirely integral to our concept of understanding that someone who understands something can say what it is that he's understood in a different way. Nor is the point to mark off the sense of 'instrumentality' as it applies to language from any other sense. It might, for instance, be thought that in the realm of non-linguistic tools – that is, of actual bits of equipment – none of the same conundrums arises. But they do. If I want to raise a heavy weight, I might use a lever or a pulley. Either tool will achieve my end. But since my end is to *raise* the weight, that is, to lift it in some way, that end cannot be specified entirely independently of the means (tools-for-raising) by which it is to be brought about, even if levers or pulleys, specifically, need not feature in the specification. 'Pure' instrumentality – that is, the use of means to achieve ends that are specifiable altogether independently – doesn't exist, in or out of language. Which is hardly surprising: for the very idea of an 'end' to be achieved through the use of 'means' would be unintelligible, in any intelligible instance of tool-use, were the end not conceived at least partly as the product of end-producing means. That we can use tools at all depends on this.

So we can distinguish two senses that might be attached to the claim that instrumentality involves the use of means to an independently specifiable end. The stronger sense, the sense characteristic of what I have called 'pure' instrumentality, construes 'independently specifiable' as meaning specifiable independently not only of any particular way of doing what is to be done, but of ways of doing what is to be done in general, *tout court*. This sense, I have suggested, is not intelligible. The weaker sense, by contrast, is fine: here 'independently specifiable' means only that what is to be done can be specified independently of any particular way of doing it. This is the sense in which paraphrase, and indeed all tool-use, is instrumental. I can specify what two instrumentally intersubstitutable expressions have in common, what they both say, by offering a third expression, distinct from either, which says the same thing. That I can do this is what makes paraphrase possible. What I cannot do, however, is to specify what it is that two instrumentally intersubstitutable expressions say in different ways without offering to say the same thing in some way or other. And that I can't do this is what makes paraphrase problematic.

The problem, as we've seen, is that paraphrase seems to presuppose itself; the capacity to understand something as a paraphrase seems to depend on the capacity to offer further paraphrases. This is why the aspect of the concept 'understanding' relevant to understanding paraphrase is indeed, as Wittgenstein says, only an aspect, and not the concept itself. How, then, is the circle to be broken, or at least prevented from turning indefinitely? Let's go back to the earlier example. Suppose I've tried 'That chair is heavy', 'That thing you're about to lift up is not at all light', 'That piece of furniture is relatively weighty' – all without success. You still don't understand what I'm saying. The only thing I can do is to keep on saying the 'same thing' in different ways until either we give up, and conclude that this is a thought which for some reason is beyond you, or else, at last, some particular way of saying it does the trick. 'No feather, that rocker', I say, and understanding suddenly dawns. The meaning you've now understood is no longer deferred; no further paraphrases are needed. What you've done is to have understood a particular phrase, not in virtue of the paraphraseable content it shares with other phrases, but simply as a phrase which says what *it* says. Meaning has here been earthed, and the circle of deferral broken. This second aspect of the concept 'understanding', then, the aspect relevant to the non-paraphraseable use of words, turns out to be essential to the understanding of paraphrase as well. If all understanding were merely understanding of paraphraseable content, after all, understanding itself could never begin: there would be no way to break into the endless circle of deferral. But once earthed, in the non-periphrastic grasp of a particular expression, understanding becomes possible – and so, as a corollary, does paraphrase. If you've understood 'No feather, that rocker' you'll now be able to offer paraphrases of it, to say the same thing in different ways.

III. Paraphrase and Art

Wittgenstein links the non-paraphraseable use of words to poetry, and more generally to the aesthetic: here we understand 'something that it expressed only by these words in these positions'[15] – that is, we understand the words not as instrumentally intersubstitutable for others, or not primarily, but simply as saying what they say. In *Culture and Value* Wittgenstein makes the point like this:

> [Y]ou might say: the work of art does not aim to convey *something else*, just itself. Just as, when I pay someone a visit, I don't just want to make him have feelings of such and such a sort; what I mainly want is to visit him.[16]

My visit, that is, has no primary point on top of its character as a visit: it is not understood if it is construed instrumentally, as paraphraseable. And similarly with our understanding of facial expressions: 'It is possible,' Wittgenstein says – meaning possible but not natural – to say:

> 'I read timidity in this face' but at all events the timidity does not seem to be merely associated, outwardly connected, with the face; but fear is there, alive, in the features. If the features change slightly, we can speak of a corresponding change in the fear ... But *what* fits *what* here?[17]

– the answer being, of course, that talk of *fit* here is simply out of place. The fear isn't understood, when the face is understood, as something above and beyond the face itself, any more than I see some paint and a man as somehow matching up with one another when I understand a picture of a man as a man. Faces and pictures *'live* for me', Wittgenstein suggests,[18] precisely when the question of 'fit' drops out. Poetic language lives for me when its paraphraseable content does not obtrude as something different from, and hence as something that might be said to match up to, the actual words that I hear or read. Hence a poetic sentence could not 'be replaced by any other. (Any more than one musical theme can be replaced by another.)'[19]

Aesthetic contexts, then, offer some paradigmatic cases of this use of the notion of 'understanding'. But that such a use is not confined to the aesthetic is something we have already seen: for the very possibility of ordinary, instrumental uses of paraphrase turns out to depend on it. This is why Wittgenstein insists that the uses of the word 'understanding' relevant to the paraphraseable and to the non-paraphraseable uses of words do not indicate two different meanings of the word 'understanding' (i.e. two separate concepts). Rather, he says, 'these kinds of use of 'understanding' make up its meaning, make up my *concept* of understanding.'[20] Both aspects are essential, then, to the experience of words and sentences as meaningful – to the experience of being at home in a world made articulate by (among other things) language. The indispensability of the non-paraphraseable aspect we have already seen. If I cannot experience language as living for me – that is, as not, primarily, instrumental – I will not be able to grasp it instrumentally, either. Words, in their paraphraseable aspect, would be merely a code to which I lacked the key, and among which, like some unnaturalised extra-terrestrial, I'd be reduced to a futile rooting around for 'matches' that I'd have no capacity even to recognise as such if I stumbled across them. But the indispensability of the paraphraseable aspect is no less clear. If I cannot grasp words as tools

– that is, as instrumentally intersubstitutable – then the same thing said by different words, and the different things said by the same words in different contexts, would be bound to elude me; which is to say, given that meaning atomism is false, I would never be able to understand what they meant (I'd be reduced to parroting). Another way of making this point is to say that you'd rightly doubt that I had understood a poem if I could give you no idea whatever of its paraphraseable content – even when we both agree that paraphraseable content, that is, the question of *fit*, or *match*, is not what we are interested in when we read a poem as a poem. Both uses of the word 'understanding' are essential to understanding, then; and neither use is available, even in principle, to someone for whom the other is not.

This is rather an important point. If Wittgenstein is right – and I hope I have said enough to suggest that he is – then the symbiotic relation between the two uses of 'understanding' will be characteristic, not only of understanding as it applies to language, but of understanding full stop. Usually, of course, one sense will be more salient than the other. The soldier who loses himself in contemplative admiration of the expression given to an order by his commanding officer will shortly find himself pulled up. The student who insists that Juliet might just as well have been called a heavenly body as the sun could, even today, be marked down. It is from context that we gather which aspect of understanding is summoned to the fore, what the appropriate mode of attention is. But behind even the most unambiguous and soldierly attention to the paraphraseable use of words lies a grasp of their non-paraphraseable use; and even the real student of poetry, despite his disdain for questions of 'fit', must have something to say about why Juliet is the sun and not, for instance, a side of pork. If the meaning of something is what one understands when one understands it, then understanding, no less than meaning, resists atomisation: the two uses of the term are utterly interdependent.

It will come as no surprise to learn that I want to apply this point to music – to identify, as far as it is possible to prise them apart, senses of musical understanding to which the notion of paraphrase is irrelevant, and senses to which it is not. For if understanding sentences and themes in music are indeed akin, as Wittgenstein suggests, one ought to expect to find here, as with words, both senses operating together – in fact to find that, together, 'these kinds of use of "understanding" make up its meaning, make up [the] *concept* of [musical] understanding.' Before proceeding, however, it may be helpful to introduce some rather less cumbersome terminology. We speak of understanding a sentence 'in the sense in which it cannot be replaced by any other': this sense I shall call 'internal', to register the fact that what is grasped in it is, because 'expressed only by these words in these positions', understood as internal to *this* particular arrangement of words. 'We [also] speak of understanding a sentence in the sense in which it can be replaced by another which says the same': I shall call this sense 'external', to mark the fact that what is grasped in it is, because 'something common to different sentences', not understood as internal to any one specific formulation.[21]

Little resistance is to be expected to the postulation of an internal sense of musical understanding. Many of the examples that Wittgenstein offers to bring out what he means in the linguistic case are drawn from music; and it is more or less a cliché in aesthetics that part of what makes a work of art a work of art is its resistance to paraphrase, the fact that just *these* effects or meanings cannot be secured in any other way. In music, the point seems clearer, perhaps, than anywhere else. One need only reflect on the oddness, for most purposes, of claiming that Mozart's Divertimento K.563 would be instrumentally unchanged if the blithe theme from its first movement were replaced with the blithe theme from the first movement of his Quintet K.515 to appreciate the reality of music's non-paraphraseable aspect. Indeed, one need only imagine thinking of the blitheness of either theme as being something above and beyond the musical phrases in which it lives – and which the blitheness somehow 'matches' – to see how naturally the internal use of the word 'understanding' is brought to bear. Nor is it contentious to remark how even quite small changes to a theme, changes which one wouldn't think would make much of a difference, can sometimes alter its character quite markedly (as, for instance, when the syncopated rise of a major sixth that introduces the final phrase of the *Ode to Joy* theme is got wrong). Where every distinction apparently makes a difference, the prospect of paraphrase appears remote.

This kind of point is, as noted in the Background part of the present chapter, precisely the kind that philosophers of music have always wanted to make, and they have made it well and persuasively. Of interest to me here, though, is the way in which the work that has been done on musical understanding has also tended to take its purview – which is to say, internal understanding – to be the whole vista. One does not, after all, have to deny flatly that an external understanding of something is possible in order to show that an internal understanding is possible too, and is possibly more important. Yet such a denial is quite standard. Partly this is because of the cliché mentioned earlier. Art, by definition, resists paraphrase; therefore to understand a work of art as a work of art is to understand it internally; therefore no aesthetically pertinent sense can be attached to the notion of external understanding. This thought is honourably motivated, no doubt. It is certainly true that resistance to paraphrase is a highly significant feature of works of art (as Wittgenstein's use of them to show what he meant by internal understanding illustrates). But to resist paraphrase is one thing, to repel it altogether is quite another. If you say you understand a poem, and yet refuse to provide me with any idea at all of what it says, then I'll doubt that you really do understand it. In this much, it is axiomatic that whatever can be understood can also be paraphrased. Suppose you grant this, and do grudgingly produce a paraphrase. You are now, I would say, exhibiting your external understanding of a work of art. But you demur; you admit that you are exhibiting an external understanding, but deny that this understanding is an understanding of the work of art *as a work of art*. What made the poem memorable, beautiful, you say, has been entirely lost. Therefore it is no longer the *poem* that is the object of your under-standing. But there is no reason to accept this. If it is not the poem you're understanding externally, what is it? The thought expressed in it, perhaps? But to say anything like that would be, first, to set up a very odd sort of distinction between the poem and what it expresses, and, second, to concede that the thought expressed by a poem is, indeed, externally understandable – which is all that I require. In fact, the whole response is confused. I can agree wholeheartedly that the paraphrase misses out or loses everything that made the poem worthwhile, but that is hardly surprising. The paraphrase is not, after all, the poem itself, and to expect it to share anything *other* than paraphraseable content with the poem, for instance interest or beauty, would be quixotic. (Thus a poem 'resists' paraphrase.) But then, in offering to paraphrase the poem, one is not offering to replace it with something just as good, or even with something of the same sort. One is offering merely to express one's understanding of what the poem says by saying it in a different way.[22] That it is the poem one is paraphrasing, however, is beyond doubt. Hence, in paraphrasing it, it is certainly one's understanding *of the poem* that one expresses. Therefore, when one does so, one shows that one understands a work of art (with or without italics) externally. And if one couldn't do this, then – for the reasons already given, indeed laboured over – one wouldn't be able to understand it internally either.[23]

There is, then, a perfectly straightforward sense in which the notion of external understanding applies in aesthetic contexts – a sense pre-supposed in all of our conversation about works of art, and by the very existence of art criticism. (By criticism, incidentally, I mean that old-fashioned activity, still practised in the odd last redoubt, of trying to get clear about how particular poems, paintings, pieces of music, and so on, achieve or fail to achieve what they do. I offer this clarification for students in Literature departments.) Nor are musical contexts an exception. I remarked earlier how odd it would be to think that the blithe themes from Mozart's Divertimento and Quintet could be swapped for one another. That oddness reflects the primacy of internal understanding. But the example also shows the external sense at work; for included in the paraphraseable content of either theme is the quality 'blitheness', a quality we can pick out in both pieces even when we agree that the blitheness of neither, understood internally, is anything above and beyond the phrases in which it lives. The capacity to offer descriptions and characterisations of pieces of music is, first, a condition of understanding them which, second, is satisfied only through an external grasp of what they do – a grasp which may be expressed in emotion-terms, say, or in the much more formal language of musical analysis.[24] It may even, in some cases, be expressed by dancing a jig.

In offering descriptions of pieces of music, we highlight qualities in them that other pieces of music might share (qualities such as being blithe, or in D major, or jig-worthy). We do not suppose that such descriptions can capture or exhaust what we have understood internally, any more than we ought to suppose that a paraphrase of a poem can exhaust or capture that. But we do suppose that our descriptions, the ones we are happy with at least, say something apt and true about the music in question; and in supposing this, we acknowledge both the fact of our external understanding and its role in our understanding of the pieces of music we say we understand. Thus we can and usually do do more, if asked what there is to be understood in a piece, than simply sit down and play it again, as Schumann is said to have done, even when we are perfectly clear that the external must always be 'earthed' in its complement, and that what we understand internally is almost always more significant than anything we can nail in a paraphrase.

IV. Paraphrase and Music

We understand sounds in and out of music externally in the appropriate contexts – woeful voices, cheerful voices, hunting horns, thunder, the thwack of bat on ball and more or less anybody's national anthem. Hunting horns are heard, by those who know what they are, as *hunting* horns, not simply as members of the brass family; their sound is inseparable from the thrill of the chase. Anthems are heard as patriotic. Indeed, to hear X *as* Y simply is, at one level, to hear externally: it is to hear X as having the paraphraseable content Y. We are thoroughly habituated, then, to an external grasp of the audible world, and anyone who wasn't would be, in a strong sense of the word having nothing to do with physiology, deaf. This is part of what I meant in the Introduction when I insisted that music is thoroughly *embedded*. Once one notices this, moreover – once one grants the existence of musical understanding in its external aspect – some potentially quite puzzling things become immediately clearer.

For example, I have always found Roger Scruton's claim, that a grasp of the dimension of music we call rhythm is a consequence of the experience of dance, extremely persuasive.[25] But then, somewhat uncomfortably, I've also always found persuasive Malcolm Budd's objection to that claim, that dance already presupposes music and hence already presupposes rhythm.[26] I think that the internal/external distinction offers a way through this dilemma. For if Scruton means that an internal understanding of rhythm is consequent on the experience of dance, his claim is viciously circular only if the understanding of dance embodied in that experience is itself internal. If, on the other hand, the relevant understanding of dance and hence of dance-music and hence of rhythm is fairly thoroughly external, that understanding may be presupposed quite harmlessly by the (internal) sense of rhythm that Scruton is interested in. Budd's objection has bite only if both rhythm and dance occupy the same side of the divide. And I think that a moment's reflection on recent dance-music will show that they needn't. Take hip-hop. Here it is the beat that counts above all, as those who manufacture it know perfectly well; and to this extent, the measure of the pointfulness of a particular piece of hip-hop music in the context of hip-hop dancing practices is the degree to which it is intersubstitutable for other pieces of music already having a place in the context of those practices. No doubt this way of putting the matter is too coarse. No doubt, either, that even this rude instrumentalism requires 'earthing' in at least a moment's internal grasp of a rhythm as a rhythm that calls for dancing. But to concede this is to say only that the symbiotic or dialectical relationship between the complementary senses of understanding is as alive in the understanding of rhythm as it is everywhere else; and this is merely what one should expect, not a withering objection to the thought that one's sense of rhythm might be cultivated through one's experience of dancing.[27]

So the acknowledgement of an external sense of musical understanding does some work here, even if only of a rather local sort. But it does more far-reaching work too. Were one, for instance, to insist that all musical understanding (properly so-called) is internal, one would find oneself stumped not only by many of the things one does in fact understand about pieces of music, but by things which composers *count* on one's understanding, and compose into their music accordingly. What I have in mind here is musical redundancy, passages of music which take up time without being meant to be especially noteworthy or striking. Such passages occur frequently, and for the good reason that composers understand their listeners. By providing zones of relatively low interest, high-interest material stands out more clearly by contrast; and it is part of the art of any composer worth his salt to know how and when to write music which, by not attracting the listener's attention unduly, allows his more interesting, or his more structurally important, ideas to be heard with their full weight. Nor is this any kind of condescension. It is not that the composer composes down to the level of his less gifted listeners.[28] It is, rather, that he recognises the management of background and foreground as integral to the composition of pieces of music capable of sustaining interest or of sounding well-structured. Where everything is of equal importance, nothing achieves salience; where everything lacks salience, nothing can be said to have been given structure. It is therefore a condition of his success as a composer that he be as adept at writing music which doesn't obtrude too much into the listener's consciousness as he is at writing music which leaves indelible traces there. Correspondingly, it is an essential aspect of competent listening that one can tell which bits are which (i.e. that one can hear background *as* background). Thus one usually misses the point if one accords as much significance to a few bars of sequential passage-work as to the principal themes it both links and, just as importantly, holds apart. One usually misses the point if one mistakes the accompaniment for the melodic line it supports. One usually misses the point if one hears preparatory, key-establishing chords as already part of what is being prepared for. And so on. Background/foreground relations, relations between the frame and what is framed, are as indispensable in music as they are in painting, and the understanding of the competent listener is built around those relations to whatever extent the composer's handling of them permits. When Tovey moaned (somewhere) that Liszt's *Les Préludes* consisted in a prologue to a prelude to an introduction to a preamble (or words to that effect) his complaint was that Liszt's music was all background, all frame and no action; and uniformity of uninterestingness is plainly just as lethal to salience, and hence to structure, as unalleviated interest. But the comparatively interesting does nevertheless require the comparatively uninteresting if it is to be possible at all.

The claim I want to make, of course, is that the aspect of under-standing relevant to background material, and hence indispensable to the understanding of pieces of music, falls primarily on the external side of the divide. To the extent that one hears background material as background, I suggest, one hears it as at least potentially replaceable by other material that would do the job (of being a background) equally well. In almost every piano sonata, for instance, where Mozart used the straight Alberti bass he could just as effectively have used one of its variants. Linking stretches of passage-work from more or less any Vivaldi concerto could, suitably transposed, function perfectly adequately in more or less any other Vivaldi concerto. Standard cadential figures are often interchangeable. And so on. Nor should this be thought surprising. Part of what it is to be an efficient background, after all, is to be unobtrusive in the relevant context; and unobtrusivenes is clearly best secured by lack of individuality. Therefore, in proportion as a musical passage functions as background, so it will exhibit little individuality – and so, in proportion, will be replaceable by other equally generic, equally unremarkable passages that are just as unobtrusive in context as the original. To be sure, one might *notice* if one patch of unobtrusive background were substituted for another in a very familiar piece. But to the extent that it really is background, one could have little reason other than pure habit for objecting to the change.

I don't want to overstate the case. My point is not that pieces of music standardly call for episodes of purely external understanding. First, it is very doubtful that there could *be* such a thing as an episode of 'purely external understanding', since, for the reasons I've given, the two senses of understanding – the external and the internal – go together with one another. And second, no piece of background is so perfectly character-less, no frame so entirely featureless, that it lacks individual qualities altogether. Nothing is ever, in the relevant sense, *merely* generic. There-fore the substitution of one bland accompanimental figure for another, even the blandest, is bound to make a difference of some sort, and this difference may well be one that the listener grasps internally. My point, rather, is that in understanding any piece of music in which certain passages are more salient than others, one understands the less salient passages – the background or framing material – more externally than one does the foreground, just because the background's comparative lack of salience is secured through its comparative lack of distinctiveness, of individuality, and because one understands this. To insist, then, that all musical understanding is thoroughly and undifferentiatedly internal would be to make altogether mysterious the commonplace fact that some passages in a well-structured piece of music are more significant, and need to be heard as more significant, than others. The truth, then, is that musical understanding involves both aspects of understanding – the internal and the external deployed together, but with a relative emphasis that shifts continually in response to context.

One might analyse entire pieces of music in terms of these shifts – a claim I make with some confidence, since people have in fact done so. The terminology is different, the burden of argument different, but in so-called 'semiotic' analysis the point is precisely to track and to account for the shifts in emphasis between the internal and the external in the understanding of someone who understands the music he is listening to. Robert Hatten, who is probably the most sophisticated exponent of this style of analysis, has written a book to show it at work.[29] His approach is derived, perhaps not altogether unexpectedly, from studies in linguistics, although the result of this, as he insists, is not to effect 'a "reduction" of music to language, or music theory to linguistics'.[30] Rather, it is to show that at least one concept that has been used to think about language has an analogous contribution to make to the study of music. The concept in question is 'markedness', which Hatten defines like this: markedness is:

> the valuation given to difference. Wherever one finds differentia-
> tion, there are inevitably oppositions. The terms of such oppositions
> are weighted with respect to some feature that is distinctive of the
> opposition. Thus, the two terms of an opposition will have an
> unequal value or asymmetry, of marked versus unmarked, that has
> consequences for the meaning of each term.[31]

Examples that Hatten gives from language include the opposition of the words 'cow' and 'bull', where '"bull" is marked for the distinction of gender' and '"cow" is unmarked.'[32] The point here is that the word 'cow', in most contexts, refers indifferently to male or female cows, whereas the word 'bull' always refers to the male. Thus there is an asymmetry between the two words: the marked word 'bull' has a more closely focused sense (in most contexts) than the unmarked word, 'cow'. This sort of opposition is known as 'privative': it signals the presence versus the absence of some particular quality, in this case maleness. The other sort of opposition that Hatten discusses is called 'equipollent'. Here the contrast is strictly symmetrical, as for instance in the pair 'male'/'female'. Neither term in an equipollent opposition is marked.

Asymmetrical oppositions are the more interesting; and it is these, primarily, that Hatten sets out to trace in Beethoven's music. A comparatively uncontentious example is the opposition in the Classical style between the major and minor mode, where it is the latter that is marked:

> Minor has a narrower range of meaning than major, in that minor consistently conveys the tragic, whereas major is not simply the opposite (comic), but must be characterized more generally as non-tragic − encompassing more widely ranging modes of expression such as the heroic, the pastoral, and the genuinely comic, or *buffa* ... [E]vidence for the stylistic encoding of a marked opposition is that ... the marked term will occur less frequently than the unmarked. This is true for minor vs. major in the Classical style, but not in the early Baroque, where minor does not consistently invoke expressive states within the realm of the tragic.[33]

Thus the minor/major opposition, which is marked in the Classical style, is equipollent in the Baroque. Hatten goes on to discuss a large number of other dimensions of markedness in Beethoven's style, including markedness of key relations, of material, of textures, of formal locations, of themes and styles, of sonorities and of 'tropes', hierarchically organised, and represented in tables of sometimes horrifying complexity. What Hatten wants to show is that 'stylistic competency', whether exhibited by composer or listener, involves an understanding of musical materials capable of being represented perspicuously in terms of marked-ness, the significance of markedness itself going beyond the 'purely musical' and extending into what Hatten calls the 'cultural universe of [the music's] conception'.[34] And to this end he offers exhaustive analyses of movements and complete works from Beethoven's last period, often, in my view, to compelling effect. The following passage, concerning the notion of what he calls the 'intentionally unmarked theme' − a theme or thematic idea whose point is to throw strategically more marked material into sharper relief − is especially relevant to my purposes.[35] The tail of the fugue subject from the first movement of Beethoven's Quartet Op.131, Hatten says, is unmarked:

> The trailing quarter notes, primarily stepwise and without any dynamic direction, seem merely to elaborate in conventional fashion a structural descent from [the fifth degree of the scale] to [the third]. This is a common underlying descent in fugue subjects ... By reason of its stylistic unmarkedness, its deployment after the notably marked head and its inherent lack of expressive focus, the subject tail can be used as a kind of background, setting in relief the appearance of more expressive material.[36]

Thus Hatten's notion of markedness is really a much more fine-grained version of what I have been calling salience – as it needs to be, if it is to do the analytic work he requires from it.

But the background/foreground relation is clearly central to Hatten's conception, as, by no accident, is the fact that unmarked material is material which, in context, exhibits generic rather than sharply distinctive qualities. That is why, despite differences in terminology, it is clear that Hatten's style of analysis is exploiting precisely the same basic facts about musical experience that I have been trying to highlight.[37] The results of Hatten's work are, I think, impressive; and their impressiveness, if what I've been arguing here is right, is due to his willingness to countenance, and then to exercise with great sophistication, a measure of external understanding in the analysis of various aspects of stylistic competence.[38]

In this section, then, I have tried to show that external understanding is integral to the concept of musical understanding. The internal sense may very well have the upper hand. Indeed, since pieces of music are works of art, and since works of art do indeed 'resist' paraphrase, it surely does have. But since nothing understandable is altogether unparaphraseable, the internal sense certainly doesn't have the field to itself. And it is in the understanding of background/foreground relations, I have argued, or in degrees of what Hatten calls 'markedness', that the interdependence of the internally and the externally understandable emerges most clearly. Wittgenstein was right about the concept of understanding as it applies to words, I think. The two sorts of use do indeed, together, make up its meaning. And so they do, too, when the understanding at issue is musical.

V. Understanding Ives

It is time, perhaps in fact high time, that I got back to *Central Park in the Dark*. Last heard of, it was being said to be impossible to understand in accordance with the tenets of meaning-atomism. Nothing since then should have changed our minds about that. But what we should now expect is that understanding *Central Park*, since *Central Park* is a piece of music, will involve at least some sort of interplay between the internal and external senses of understanding. And so indeed it does, in a very odd fashion. I remarked at the outset that Ives's music is disconcerting. Partly, as I said, that is due to its strange mix of styles; but it is possible now to be a good deal more specific. For the fact of the matter, if my experience of it is at all representative, is that in *Central Park* Ives has

41

written music which more or less reverses the usual order of priority between the internal and the external; and it is this, I think, that makes it disconcerting.

Let's begin at the beginning, with the atonal nocturnal murmuring. This is a highly distinctive sound, and at first, at least, it seems certainly to call for a reasonably internal mode of attention – though not perhaps an entirely internal mode, since the murmuring also has an air of scene-setting about it. One does expect the scene to be occupied shortly by some foreground. But it isn't. The murmuring just goes on. I surely can't be alone or deaf in thinking, after say twenty seconds of those chilly, shifting strings, that so long as a sound *of that general sort* were to keep going it wouldn't much matter whether the notes played were the ones that Ives actually wrote down. What was initially highly distinctive has become quickly generic, so that one can imagine other equally generic atonal weavings taking the place of the ones the orchestra in fact play, and taking their place just as effectively. By this point the balance of one's understanding has moved well over to the external side. Then some events do happen. There's a bit of parping and, presently, a snatch of piano music. These stand out, sure enough, simply by virtue of not being more of what we've been hearing so far. But – hand on heart – could you *really* say that it had to be just *those* parps, just *that* particular little wobble on the piano? I know I couldn't. For one thing, the atonal backdrop that has been so long in place ensures that the pitches at which the parping happens sound arbitrary. A tone or two up or down would make no difference. Nor is the snatch of piano in any way distinctive. It is just a hint of anonymous vamping, much like any other. What Ives has done, in other words, is to compose foreground that more or less defies the sort of understanding that one expects foreground to call for and to reward. He's written paraphraseable foreground against a paraphraseable background. (In fact, the effect of this, for me at least, is to refocus for a moment a more internal mode of attention on the 'backdrop': suddenly those nocturnal shiftings sound interesting again. What frames what here?) And then the rag tune strikes up – and turns out, as one might by now expect, to be so utterly faceless, so all-purpose in its basic idea and so thoroughly routine in its working out, as to be almost wholly unmemorable. Certainly it is less memorable than any comparably catchy piece of music I know. And so it goes on, getting louder and louder, until – in a veritable riot of banality – it ends, and with it *Central Park*. The main event, like nearly everything that has paved its way, has turned out to be of no interest at all.

This really is a remarkable piece of music – perhaps the most deliberately boring ever written.[39] One normally expects, after all, or at least hopes, that a composer will have some worthwhile or striking musical ideas to impart, and that one will understand these, if one does, internally – as unique, distinctive, individual. But here we have the opposite of that. Instead of comparatively paraphraseable passages setting off comparatively unparaphraseable ones, Ives gives us comparatively paraphraseable passages setting off passages more paraphraseable still, until, by the end, one is uncertain that anything in the entire work even resists paraphrase, let alone resists it stoutly. I remarked earlier that any composer worth his salt must be as adept at writing background music as he is at writing foreground. And what Ives has done here is to put on a virtuoso performance of background-composition – even showing how material that isn't already generic (the atonal string-patterns) can, in the right hands, be made so. It is a compositional challenge to which he rises masterfully. The corollary of this, of course, is that the listener is put through some unfamiliar paces. Instead of hearing the music with the balance of understanding tipped heavily to the internal, as would be usual, it is the normally relatively inconspicuous external side that comes to the fore, and relentlessly so. And this makes for hard work. For in prising apart the two complementary senses of 'understanding', and by reversing their standard weightings, Ives is forcing us to listen against the grain of our ordinary musical experience and to unlearn or to suspend some pretty central habits. That we can do this at all shows that understanding externally is indeed part of our standard musical competence, if standardly a recessive part. And that we are made to do it systematically is, I suggest, what makes listening to *Central Park* so disconcerting.

Such, at any rate, is my take on Ives's music. Ives has identified an aspect always latent in musical experience, and then highlighted and exploited it – quite deliberately and to great effect. To this extent, then, *Central Park* is quite as much a piece *about* musical understanding as it is one calling for musical understanding. And if the considerations I've offered here are plausible, what it confirms is that understanding pieces of music can be much more akin to understanding words than the sharp division usually set up between the two would suggest. Music *is* an art; and so, as with poetry, what is usefully paraphraseable in it is normally rather little. But if the sounds which music comprises could not, like the words in a poem, also be understood in another way – which is to say, externally – then, like words that actually repelled rather then resisted paraphrase, they could not be understood. That, I believe, is what this most thoroughly instrumental piece of music has to tell us, or remind us of. And this prompts a last thought about musical meaning. I mentioned earlier that a deafness to Wittgenstein's remark about themes and sentences has often led philosophers of music to conclude that music, if it is meaningful at all, must be meaningful in some purely musical way. But this, we can now see, is either trivial or false. It is trivial if it shadows the claim that language, understood internally, is meaningful in some purely linguistic way: everything understandable is meaningful in that sense (tools toolishly, pictures pictorially – etc.). And it is false if it depends on the view that, unlike linguistic understanding, musical understanding is internal through and through. I suspect that the false version is the one that people have had in mind. But to ignore the ubiquity of externally understandable sound, in music and out of it – and so to treat music as if it came from Mars and us as if we were musical parrots – is precisely to surrender all hope of making headway with the questions that interest us. We need to be less confident of our theoretical grasp of language, in other words, and more – that is, duly – confident of our understanding of music. That way we might actually come to understand better what it is that we're understanding when we understand anything at all, including themes and sentences.

A final remark. There may be a temptation to think as follows: if, as I've argued, internal understanding doesn't have the field to itself when it comes to understanding pieces of music, even though it does (normally) have the upper hand in the understanding of intra-musical relations, then perhaps the natural place to expect a reversal of emphasis, so that external understanding has the upper hand, is in the understanding of music's extra-musical relations, of its relations to the rest of the world. But this temptation, if it presents itself, should be resisted. Just as linguistic reference (to the rest of the world) must be 'earthed' in a moment of internal understanding, so music's relations to the rest of the world, if they are real, and if there is anything about them that requires to be understood, must be understandable internally – must be capable, that is, of sustaining a mode of understanding that does not consist simply and solely in some sort of casting about for 'fits' or 'matches'. This point will turn out to be quite important for the chapters that follow.

NOTES

1. Reported in *The Times*, 2 February 2002.
2. R. G. Collingwood, *The Principles of Art* (Oxford: Oxford University Press, 1938), pp.140–1.
3. Roger Scruton, 'Understanding Music', in his *The Aesthetic Understanding* (London: Methuen, 1983), p. 79.

4. *Ibid.*, pp. 80–94.
5. Malcolm Budd, *Music and the Emotions* (London: Routledge and Kegan Paul, 1985), p. 45.
6. Malcolm Budd, 'Understanding Music', *Proceedings of the Aristotelian Society*, Supplementary Volume, 1985.
7. Donald Ferguson, *Music as Metaphor* (Minneapolis, MN: University of Minnesota Press, 1960).
8. Other helpful discussions include: Michael Tanner, 'Understanding Music', *Proceedings of the Aristotelian Society*, Supplementary Volume, 1985; Stephen Davies, *Musical Meaning and Expression* (Ithaca, NY: Cornell University Press, 1995), chapter 7; Jerrold Levinson, 'Musical Literacy', in his *The Pleasures of Aesthetics* (Ithaca, NY: Cornell University Press, 1996); Levinson, *Music in the Moment* (Ithaca, NY: Cornell University Press, 1997); and Peter Kivy, *Music Alone* (Ithaca, NY: Cornell University Press, 1990), chapters 4–6. My own thoughts on the matter can be found in *Music, Value and the Passions* (Ithaca, NY: Cornell University Press, 1995), chapter 3.
9. *Philosophical Investigations* (1953), section 527. For a stimulating exploration of some of Wittgenstein's other remarks relating music to language, see Jerrold Levinson, 'Musical Thinking', in *Midwest Studies in Philosophy*, vol. 27, 2003.
10. (Oxford: Oxford University Press, 1959).
11. *Musical Meaning and Expression*, p. 34 (see Note 8).
12. *Ibid.*, pp. 39–49.
13. Which may well have repercussions for Davies's conception of linguistic meaning: the 'elements' or 'characters' on which his rules for the generation of meaning are supposed to go to work look uncomfortably like meaning atoms.
14. *Ending Up* (Penguin, 1977), pp. 100, 105.
15. *Philosophical Investigations* (1953), section 531.
16. *Culture and Value* (1980), 58ff.
17. *Philosophical Investigations* (1953), section 537.
18. *Ibid.*, Part II, section 205.
19. *Ibid.*, section 531.
20. *Ibid.*, section 532.
21. *Ibid.*, section 531. The labels 'internal' and 'external' are mine, not Wittgenstein's.
22. This seems an obvious point, but it is often missed. For a particularly clear case of someone missing it, see Peter Kivy, *Philosophies of Arts* (Cambridge: Cambridge University Press, 1997), p. 160, a case to which I return in Chapter 5.
23. For a related discussion, see Stanley Cavell, *Must We Mean What We Say?* (Cambridge: Cambridge University Press, 1976), pp. 74–86.
24. For discussion of the different ways in which such understanding can be expressed, see Michael Tanner, 'Understanding Music', *Proceedings of the Aristotelian Society*, Supplementary Volume 59, pp. 215–32, 1985, and Peter Kivy, *Music Alone* (Ithaca, NY: Cornell University Press, 1990), chapters 4–7.
25. Roger Scruton, 'Understanding Music' in Scruton, *The Aesthetic Understanding* (London: Methuen, 1983), pp. 77–101.
26. Malcolm Budd, 'Understanding Music', *Proceedings of the Aristotelian Society*, Supplementary Volume 59, pp. 233–48, 1985.
27. This is admittedly weaker than Scruton's original claim, as he states it himself. But I think that it gives him everything that he wants.
28. Although, as a matter of fact, 'composing down' is exactly how Schoenberg once described this, in his *Style and Idea* (London: Faber, 1975).
29. *Musical Meaning in Beethoven: markedness, correlation, and interpretation* (Bloomington and Indianapolis, IN: Indiana University Press, 1994).

30. *Ibid.*, p. 63.
31. *Ibid.*, p. 34.
32. *Ibid.*
33. *Ibid.*, p. 36.
34. *Ibid.*, p. 66.
35. *Ibid.*, p. 115.
36. *Ibid.*, p. 154.
37. Just to remind ourselves: my fundamental claim is simply that external as well as internal understanding is integral to the concept of musical understanding. This comes out in the way we understand relations between background and foreground. My claim is *not* that background material, say, is the exclusive preserve of external understanding – and nor could it be, since *everything* understandable is understandable in both ways.
38. Hatten is not unique in this, of course. Charles Rosen, for example, in his massively influential book, *The Classical Style* (London: Faber, 1976), emphasises the structural role of the anonymous 'filler'.
39. Although Robert Craft's claims on behalf of Brahms's *A German Requiem* can't be dismissed lightly. See Craft, *Prejudices in Disguise* (New York, NY: Knopf, 1974), pp. 176–9.

2

Representation

I ventured to say that some had tried in poetry, others in painting – I added
with some trepidation one or two musicians – to shake off the ancient dust
of tradition and it had only resulted in their being treated as symbolists or
impressionists – convenient terms for pouring scorn on one's fellows.
(Claude Debussy, *Monsieur Croche the Dilettante Hater*)

PART 1. BACKGROUND

For the greater part of recorded history, the thought that music is a
representational art of some sort has been taken for granted. In Ancient
Greece, for example, the various modes or scales were held to represent
(and to promote) various types of character: the Dorian mode, for
instance, was said to 'fittingly imitate the tones and accents of a man
who is brave in battle and in every difficult and dangerous task', while
the Phrygian mode was said to 'imitate a man in the actions of peace'.[1]
In the mediaeval period, the rhythms and intonations of plainchant were
held to represent the voice and soul of a man at prayer, while in the
eighteenth century it was widely thought that the 'proper role' of music
was to offer an 'artificial portrait of the human passions' and, more
generally, to 'imitate nature'.[2] This unanimity over music's representational capacities, if not always over the sorts of objects that music was
held to represent, is attributable, in large part, to the long hegemony of
the Aristotelian doctrine that *mimesis* – imitation – is the defining
feature of all the arts. If music was to be considered one of the arts,
therefore, and no one seriously doubted that it should be,[3] then by
definition it must be imitative or representational, the only matters
remaining for dispute being what, precisely, it was supposed to imitate or
represent, and how.

This consensus did not, however, survive the nineteenth century. This was due partly to the influence of Kant's radical new aesthetic formalism, and partly to the rise of purely instrumental music, from which the kinds of representational context provided by words, dance and stage action were largely absent. An intriguing snapshot of the consensus in mid-collapse, as it were, is provided by Eduard Hanslick's *On the Musically Beautiful*, the book which effectively inaugurated musical aesthetics in its modern form. In it, Hanslick insists sternly on 'music's inability to represent specific feelings',[4] but rather surprisingly allows that:

> The fall of snowflakes, the flutter of birds, the rising of the sun – these I can paint musically ... by producing audible impressions dynamically related to them. In pitch, intensity, tempo, and the rhythm of tones, the ear offers itself a configuration whose impression has that analogy with specific visual perception which different sense modes can attain among themselves ... Thus one can in fact portray an object musically. But to want to portray in tones the feelings which falling snow, a crowing rooster, or flashing lightning produce in us is just ridiculous.[5]

What makes this surprising is that one of the kinds of argument that Hanslick relies upon to discredit music's pretensions to represent specific feelings – namely, that to 'represent ... is to produce a clear and distinct content', and yet 'everyone differs' when it comes to saying what specific feeling a particular piece of music is supposed to represent – would presumably be just as effective against the thought that a piece of music might represent the fall of snowflakes, specifically, rather than of autumn leaves, say, or of leaflets dropped from a balloon – especially given that Hanslick expressly disallows appeal to 'pieces with specific titles or programs'.[6,7] Despite this uncharacteristic wobble, however, Hanslick is soon back to his official, formalist position, and indeed devotes the final chapter of his book to the claim that it is 'only by firmly denying any other kind of "content" to music' – that is, any content but purely 'musical content' – that we can 'preserve music's substance.'[8]

Hanslick's official position, that music is not in any significant sense a representational art, has, in due course, become philosophical orthodoxy, more or less wholly supplanting the Aristotelian consensus that preceded it. Few aestheticians today would argue that music is interestingly representational – except perhaps in the odd fringe or atypical case – and most of the energies that the issue has attracted have been devoted to explaining why not.[9] More specifically, most of those energies have been devoted to the defence or critique of the capacity of various general theories of representation to account for music's relative mimetic inertness in a perspicuous way.

The most exhaustive survey of the recent literature, as conducted by Stephen Davies, reveals two main sorts of position with respect to this issue – one drawing on the 'semantic' account of representation, the other on the 'seeing-in' account.[10] Both of these accounts, on Davies's reconstruction of them, specify the following three conditions as necessary for representation:

1. '*Intention*: It is a necessary condition for X's representing Y that X be intended to represent Y.'[11]
2. '*Medium/content distinction*: It is a necessary condition for X's representing Y that there be a distinction between the medium of the representation and the represented content.'[12]
3. '*Conventions*: Commonly (perhaps always), X represents Y within the context of conventions … so that recognition of Y in X presupposes the viewer's familiarity with those conventions and his viewing X in terms of them in perceiving Y in X.'[13]

The semantic account, but not the seeing-in account, also specifies as necessary the following condition:

4. *Thoughts*: It is a necessary condition for X's representing Y that X express thoughts about Y, and that an understanding of X involve an understanding of those thoughts.[14]

The seeing-in account, by contrast, specifies as necessary the following condition, not required by the semantic account:

5. '*Resemblance between perceptual experiences*: It is a necessary condition for X's representing Y that there be a resemblance between a person's perceptual experiences of X and of Y, given that the person views X in terms of the applicable conventions.'[15]

According to the semantic account, conditions 1–4 are jointly sufficient for representation; while on the seeing-in account, conditions 1–3 and 5 are jointly sufficient.

The various proponents of these accounts differ about which condition or conditions music fails to meet. So, for example, Roger Scruton, a defender of one rather heterodox version of the semantic account, holds that music cannot (in general) satisfy conditions 2–4, and so cannot, in any interesting sense, be regarded as a representational art.[16] Stephen Davies, by contrast, who favours the seeing-in account, argues that music can satisfy conditions 1 and 2, but expresses doubt about its ability to meet conditions 3 and 5. His conclusion – that music is not, in any interesting sense, to be regarded as a representational art – is thus the same as Scruton's, although they disagree about the necessity of condition 4, and disagree about music's capacity to satisfy condition 2. One might suppose from this that the negative conclusion that both of these (representative) figures reach about music's mimetic potential is therefore, at bottom, a function of their (shared) view that music cannot satisfy condition 3 – the condition that there be a background context of conventions against which music can be heard as being representational. One might suppose, that is, that the semantic and seeing-in accounts, for all of their local divergences, are essentially in accord, at least in this respect. But that turns out not to be quite right. For, as I will suggest in Part 2 of this chapter, the considerations, or alleged considerations, that Scruton and Davies offer for the claim that music cannot meet condition 3 are derived, respectively, from Scruton's adherence to condition 4 and from Davies's adherence to condition 5; which is to say, they reach their common conclusion for seemingly incompatible reasons. But even this isn't quite right. For when one looks more closely one finds, not so much that their reasons are 'seemingly incompatible', as I have put it, as that their reasons are only seemingly reasons. One finds, in fact, that their agreement about music's inability to satisfy condition 3 is really predicated on another agreement, prior and unspoken – namely, that music cannot, in any interesting sense, be a representational art. What looks like a dispute about the relative merits of the semantic and seeing-in accounts of representation, in other words, turns out, on inspection, to be little more than a collective exercise in autonomanic question-begging, a sort of smoke-screen behind which a common conclusion is presupposed only in order, by one means or another, to be 'demonstrated'.[17]

Not everything that has been written about musical representation is guilty of this sort of failing. Peter Kivy, for instance, steers clear of it in his account of the issues, and proposes an eminently modest and sensible position as a result.[18] So too does Jenefer Robinson.[19] But I have chosen to focus instead on Scruton and Davies for two reasons. First, the arguments and conclusions that they offer have been influential: if there is an orthodox, mainstream position on musical representation, then, in their slightly different ways, these two philosophers exemplify it. And second, they show – in a very direct fashion – just how powerful and systematic the grip of the autonomanic picture can be, and just how difficult the blandishments of that picture can be to resist. They show, in other words, just how hard it has sometimes become, in the wake of

Hanslick, to think clearly about music in the face of the temptation to assume, more or less unconsciously, that individual works must, essentially, be abstract structures of pure sound, bearing no connection to anything beyond themselves.

PART 2. *LA CATHÉDRALE ENGLOUTIE*

Claude Debussy (1862–1918) – who, together with Maurice Ravel, was the leading exponent of so-called musical 'impressionism' – published two books of twelve preludes for solo piano, the first in 1910, the second in 1913. *La Cathédrale Engloutie* (The Sunken Cathedral) is the tenth prelude from Book I, and is one of the best known of Debussy's piano pieces – perhaps because it is quite nearly playable, in some loose sense of that term, by less than transcendently gifted pianists. The title refers to an old Breton tale which tells how the cathedral of Ys, long ago submerged as punishment for the Godless ways of the populace, sometimes, on a clear morning, when the sea is translucent, rises briefly from the waves, as a reminder and warning, before sinking back into the depths. Debussy responds to this tale with all of the richness and colour that one would expect from him, deploying the full resources of his unique, and uniquely sonorous, pianistic palette. Hollow, watery parallel fourths evoke the *organum* of mediaeval plainchant; the waves part to rocking figurations in the bass; bells toll and chime, the metallic overlay of their harmonics unmistakable in this masterly reconstruction. It is difficult to imagine a more telling or apt portrayal than Debussy has produced here. The background to the composition is to be borne in mind, however. When Debussy was composing, the long-standing debate over so-called 'programme music' was still going on. At issue was the propriety, or otherwise, of music written to illustrate, or in some sense to be supported by, extra-musical textual narratives – a practice with a long history behind it, but made topical in the second half of the nineteenth century through the claims entered on its behalf by composers (and their supporters) such as Hector Berlioz and Franz Liszt. By the beginning of the twentieth century, however, it is fair to say that the anti-programme camp – the musical purists, as one might call them – were in the ascendant, a fact to which Debussy will have been sensitive. It is for this reason, one must suppose, that he made the following unusual decision: instead of having the title of each prelude printed, as would be normal, at the top of its first page, he had the title printed either at the end of the relevant prelude, or in the table of contents. The point, clearly enough, was to insist that even if some of his preludes – like *La*

Cathédrale Engloutie – did, as a matter of fact, have programmes, they could nonetheless function perfectly adequately, and be understood perfectly adequately, as stand-alone pieces of pure piano music. (From this point of view, I should no doubt have called this part of the present chapter 'Prelude X, Bk. I'.) What Debussy did strikes me as interesting; and it will be one of the concerns of this chapter to ask whether his decision to half-conceal (or half-acknowledge: one can look at it either way) the possibly programmatic character of certain of his preludes might not actually have had some philosophical point to it, rather then being, and as it might at first seem, no more than a rather transparent attempt to have his musical cake and eat it. It may be, in other words, that Debussy was right to want to have it both ways; and it may be that the philosophical point of his wanting to do so is one that should cause a certain discomfort to the musical purists (the autonomaniacs) he was seeking, in part, to appease.

I. Detachable Sounds

According to the position advocated by Roger Scruton – as briefly set out in the Background part of this chapter – Debussy's decision to put his title last was entirely redundant. Wherever he had put the title, *La Cathédrale Engloutie* would not have represented a sunken cathedral, since music simply fails to satisfy the conditions required for representation: it does not satisfy condition 2 (the 'medium/content distinction'), condition 3 (the 'conventions' requirement) or condition 4 (the 'thoughts' requirement).[20] Let's take these conditions in turn.

The point of the first of these conditions, which Scruton derives from consideration of visual depiction (on the reasonable grounds that paintings and drawings are capable of representing, if anything is), is as follows. One misunderstands a painting of a man, say, if one falsely believes that what one is looking at is a real human being, rather than a picture of one. Equally, since 'A varnished painting of a man is not a painting of a varnished man, however much it may look as though it were', one misunderstands the painting if one takes it to depict someone unusually glossy. An understanding of visual representation, therefore, depends upon the viewer's ability to see that a content is being presented *via* a medium (rather than being presented directly) and to distinguish features of that content from 'the peculiarities and conventions of the medium'.[21] And if this is what an *understanding* of representation requires, Scruton suggests, then, for any putative instance of representation, it must be possible to distinguish between the medium through which the representation is effected and the content that is represented there. The medium/content distinction is thus a necessary condition of representation.

On Scruton's view, as I have said, music cannot satisfy that condition. He considers cases in which a composer attempts to represent the sound that something makes, as Debussy attempts to represent the sound of a cathedral's bells. One would have thought, as Scruton notes, that if musical sounds are capable of representing anything, then other sounds should be it. But he holds that the nature of sound itself precludes this. Sounds, he says, unlike visual appearances, 'are individuals, with a history and identity separate from the objects which emit them', so that a sound is something that is 'detachable' and has an 'independent existence'.[22] The consequence of this, he suggests, is that when one attempts to represent sounds in music, the music:

> has a tendency to become transparent, as it were, to its subject. Representation gives way to reproduction, and the musical medium drops out of consideration … [S]ince there is nothing to music except sound, there ceases to be any *essential* difference between the medium of representation and the subject represented.[23]

The idea here would seem to be this. The sound of a cathedral's bells stands apart from the bells themselves, in a way that their visual appearance does not. The bell-sounds have a life of their own, and are identifiable independently of their source (the 'look' of the bells, by contrast, has no such 'independent existence'). And the same is true of the bell-sounds that Debussy coaxes from the piano: these, like the sounds of a cathedral's bells, stand apart from, and are identifiable independently of, their source. Both the putative representation, therefore, which is to say the bell-sounds emitted by the piano, and the putative subject of it, which is to say the bell-sounds emitted by a cathedral's bells, are free-standing individuals of precisely the same type; there is no distinction to be drawn between medium and content. Both are, quite simply, bell-sounds, and Debussy's piano-generated ones no more represent the sound of a cathedral's bells than the bell-sounds emitted by the cathedral bells themselves do. At best, as Scruton puts it, one bell-sound might 'reproduce' another.

Scruton's argument depends for its force on the claim that sounds are radically 'detachable' from their sources. And it is true, in at least some sense, that they are detachable. If I say 'There has been a noise in this room all afternoon, and I think that it is getting louder',[24] what I say makes perfectly good sense. I am picking out the noise as a free-standing individual, and I am identifying it quite independently of its source –

indeed, in most ordinary contexts, my words would suggest that I do not know what its source is. But being detach*able* in this sense is not the same as being actually (or necessarily) detached. If Scruton's argument were correct, after all, it would mean that I couldn't possibly hear an impressionist impersonating – representing – the prime minister's voice on the radio. All I could hear would be a (reproduction of a) prime-minister-voice, a free-standing individual of precisely the same type as the prime minister's own prime-minister-voice. But surely this is implausible. Specifically, it cannot be plausible to think that the mere fact that the sound of the prime minister's voice is 'detachable' from the prime minister himself should mean that that sound stands in no special relation to him – for instance, in the relation indicated by calling the sound a 'prime-minister-voice'. Rather, one should want to say that the content or subject of the representation is the (undetached) *voice of* the prime minister (and not, for instance, a sound that the prime minister, like the impressionist, might just happen to emit), and that the medium of representation is the impressionist's own voice. Indeed, to say anything else would be to show that one had failed to understand what one was hearing *as* an impersonation. (This is not to deny, of course, that one might mistakenly believe that one is hearing the prime minister himself. But, if one does believe this, that is not because the medium/content distinction is unsustainable in the case of sounds; it is because one hasn't realised what sort of programme one is listening to.)

It will be objected, perhaps, that this example is not analogous to the musical case, since speaking voices are more than mere sounds, and so may not be subject to the constraints (or freedoms) of noises emitted by bells or pianos. Scruton insists, after all, that it is precisely because 'there is nothing to music except sound' that 'there ceases to be any *essential* difference between the medium of representation and the subject represented'. But this is hardly a compelling response. First, the impressionist example does not depend upon the subject of representation being the prime minister's speaking voice. The subject could just as well have been his laugh, or his way of sneezing, and, for exactly the reasons given above, it would still be perfectly intelligible to distinguish the medium of representation (the sounds made by the impressionist) from the content of it (the laughing or sneezing *of* the prime minister). And second, it is not at all clear what more, on Scruton's view, there would have to *be* to music 'except sound' in order to establish an '*essential*' difference between medium and content. Certainly the extra ingredient had better not be the sort of independent meaningfulness (i.e. representational capacity) that speaking voices have. The issue, after all, is whether music *has* that capacity, and to conclude that it hasn't just because there is 'nothing' more to it than 'sound' would be the merest question-begging. But what else might Scruton have in mind? The impressionist example shows that the (bare) fact that the medium and content of a representation are both (exclusively) audible is insufficient to undermine any '*essential* difference' between them. And a moment's reflection on the actual differences between the sound of Debussy's piano chords, say, and the sound of real cathedral bells – differences far greater than would be found in any quarter-way decent radio-impression of a voice – suggests that the '*essential*' distinction between medium and content may be quite a good deal less imperilled in the musical case than it is in the impressionist's.

The foregoing indicates that Scruton's insistence that sounds are 'detachable' individuals is something of a red herring – a suspicion reinforced when one notices that the visual appearances of objects, which Scruton always contrasts with their sounds, are themselves rather more 'detachable' from their 'sources' than he says. As Stephen Davies has argued, 'the visual experiences of a train', say, and of:

> a hallucination of a train, of the image of a train reflected in a mirror, of a photograph of a train, and of a miniature model of a train might be phenomenally identical. How do we know that a painting producing such an experience represents a train, not a hallucination, a reflection, a photograph, or a miniature model, or merely a visual experience as of a train, or even a visual experience as of a picture of a train?[25]

Davies's point here, of course, is that, just as bell-sounds are 'detachable' from the bells or pianos that make them, so train-appearances may float free, as it were, of trains. Yet this fact hardly warrants scepticism about the medium/content distinction in the case of visual representation, and nor, he concludes, should the corresponding fact be thought to do so in the case of sounds. So, from the cathedral bell-like quality of Debussy's piano chords, there would appear to be nothing in Scruton's detachability considerations to disallow the thought that those sounds represent the sounds of cathedral bells. And Davies goes further – rightly, I think. Just as one should move, he says, 'from "the sound as of an X" to "an X's sound"', so, 'if the conventions do not disallow it, one should move from "an X's sound" to "the presence of an X"'.[26] One should conclude, that is, for all that anything has been shown to the contrary, that *La Cathédrale Engloutie* might represent, not merely cathedral bell-sounds, but cathedral bells.

There are good reasons to think, though, that Scruton's emphasis on the 'detachable' character of sounds may be misleading in a more far-reaching way, too. Consider again the case of a *really* detached sound, the sort of which one might say 'There has been a noise in this room all afternoon.' The experience that prompts the remark may be irritating, perhaps, but also – in most contexts – puzzling. 'Where is that noise coming from?' one might ask oneself, 'What's making it?' The fact is that one doesn't *understand* what one is hearing – and won't, until one has reattached the sound to its source. To understand a sound, then, in standard cases, is – inter alia – to know what's making it, indeed is to hear it *as being made by* what's making it.[27] And this suggests that the medium/content distinction can only really be at risk in the case of sounds, if it ever is, when the relevant sounds are not understood. It would seem, in other words, that this part of Scruton's argument against the possibility of musical representation must – if it is to have any chance of working at all – take as paradigmatic the experience of the uncomprehending listener; the person who, when listening to *La Cathédrale Engloutie*, doesn't understand, and *a fortiori* doesn't appreciate, the fact that what he is hearing is being played on the piano. The thought that such a person might also remain oblivious to Debussy's cathedral-effects is somehow not very disturbing.

II. Cryptographical Conventions

If Scruton's attempt to show that music cannot satisfy the medium/content condition of representation is not convincing, nor, it has to be said, is his attempt to show that music cannot satisfy condition 3, the 'conventions' requirement. Scruton simply assumes, without argument, that the relevant conventions would have to consist in a set of rules for mapping particular musical passages onto the bits of the world that they (allegedly) represent, so that music becomes a sort of code to be disencrypted. His conclusion – that such a translation schema would be theoretically possible, but that we don't have one, and that if we did it would alter the experience of listening to music out of recognition, so much so that we would no longer, in effect, be talking about *music* – is incontrovertible. But there is no reason at all to think that the relevant conventions must take this form. They don't, after all, in the cases of literary or visual representation; and the mere fact that music may not represent in the way that literature does, or that paintings do, hardly establishes that the option that Scruton discusses is the only one left. The 'conventions' requirement is a plausible one. It is plausible, that is, to think that a degree of acculturation, of familiarity with music and with the habits and expectations appropriate to it, should be integral to one's ability to understand whatever representational content music may have. But one would have thought that it might therefore be better to work backwards, as it were, from the (acculturated) experience of hearing a (putatively) representational piece of music, such as *La Cathédrale Engloutie*, and to try to work out what habits and expectations are actually in operation there, than to set up a straw cryptographer and knock him down.

III. Musical Thoughts

Scruton also holds, finally, that music cannot satisfy the 'thoughts' condition of representation. The point of this condition, briefly, is that a representation standardly expresses thoughts about its subject, and does so by depicting it as being this way rather than that. So, for example, Michelangelo's sculpture of David portrays him as noble and stern (rather than as wimpish, say); while Conrad's literary depiction of colonialism presents it as dehumanising (rather than as, say, spiritually elevating). To understand a representation must involve understanding the thoughts it expresses about its subject: just as one would miss much of the point of the *David* if one missed the nobility in it, so one would hardly count as having read *The Heart of Darkness* if one didn't detect a certain negativity in its take on the Belgian Congo. 'Even in the most minimal depiction,' Scruton suggests, for instance of an apple on a cloth, 'appreciation depends on determinate thoughts that could be expressed in language ... for example: 'Here is an apple; the apple rests on a cloth ...' Representation, in other words, is essentially propositional.'[28] In order to *be* a representation, therefore, something must at least be capable of expressing such propositions – of expressing thoughts about what it represents. And that, according to Scruton, is precisely what music cannot do.

He has two sorts of reason for claiming this. The first is that, even if music can, as it were, pick out a subject, it is unable to characterise it, to convey what he calls a 'completed' thought about it. So even if it were to be conceded that Debussy manages to imitate the sound of a cathedral's bells, his music can still say nothing 'determinate' about that sound, and so cannot be said to have represented it. Quite why 'Here is the sound of bells chiming; it gets louder and clearer and then falls away' cannot count as such a thought, Scruton doesn't say. And I am far from alone in doubting that there is anything much he *can* say about this. The problem, as Davies puts it, is that Scruton models representation too closely on linguistic assertion, a context in which a thought can be said to have been 'completed' when the (grammatically decent) sentence expressing it terminates in a full stop. And it is true that music doesn't have the capacity, in the relevant sense, to offer full stops or to 'complete' thoughts. But then nor does painting. 'Where is the thought expressed in a painting completed?' Davies asks.

> Pictures are said to be worth a thousand words just because there need be no end to the description of the way a subject is represented ... Therefore, that music fails Scruton's ['thoughts'] condition can hardly count against music's being depictive, since representational paintings fail the same condition in a similar manner.[29]

Indeed, as Peter Kivy puts it, if Scruton is to acknowledge the representational character of (some) paintings, as he clearly wants to, then his 'thoughts' hurdle is going to have to be set so low that music 'cannot fall below it, since, really, all the minimal claim to propositional content amounts to is what all representation possesses: a verbally expressible subject' – such as the sound of a cathedral's bells.[30] These considerations strike me as easily sufficient to discount Scruton's first reason for denying that music can satisfy his 'thoughts' condition.[31]

The second reason that he offers focuses, not so much on music's capacity or lack of it to express thoughts about its (putative) subject, as on the irrelevance of such thoughts as might be expressed to an understanding of the music in question. If it is true that one can *fully* understand a piece of music without understanding whatever thoughts it might (happen to) express, then the music's expressing those thoughts, if it does, must be a fact about it of no significance at all. If, therefore, those thoughts are representational, so that the music itself is to be considered representational, then that fact too is irrelevant to an understanding or appreciation of it. From this point of view, in other words, it might be true (1) that Debussy's piano chords represent bell-sounds, or even bells, and (2) that the thoughts expressed by those chords are 'Here is the sound of bells chiming; it gets louder and clearer and then falls away' – and *still* this would be a matter of complete indifference to anyone wanting to get the point of *La Cathédrale Engloutie*, a matter of as little aesthetic moment as the fact that the *Mona Lisa* weighs, well, whatever it weighs. This position is weaker than the one that Scruton defends, of course, since he denies (1) and (2). But even if he is wrong to deny (1) and (2), as the discussion so far suggests that he is, he still has this as a fall-back position, the claim that, musically, musical representation is irrelevant even if it is possible. And, indeed, this claim features rather prominently in his essay.

What, then, are Scruton's grounds for claiming that one can fully understand a piece of music without grasping or understanding such representational content as it might have? In the event, no grounds are actually given, but here are some characteristic remarks: 'a man may hear and appreciate 'representational' music *without* hearing' its representational aspect. To miss the representational aspect of a poem, by contrast, 'is not to appreciate the poem as poetry. An interest in poetry is not an interest in pure sound; a genuine interest in music, on the other hand, may by-pass its representational pretensions altogether.'[32] 'When a passage from [Debussy's] *Voiles* reminds me of drifting sails I do indeed hear an aspect of the music. But the *important* part of this aspect – the part that seems essential to a full musical understanding – can be perceived by someone who is deaf to the "representation".' Thus we 'can have considerable understanding of a 'representational' piece of music, while being ignorant of, indifferent to, or contemptuous towards, its representational claims … To understand a representational painting', by contrast, 'one must have some knowledge of the subject; but the same has never been honestly claimed for music.'[33] Leaving aside Scruton's mention of 'considerable' rather than full understanding, what we have here is a mere set of categorical assertions – about what a 'genuine' interest in music involves, and how that is different from a 'genuine' interest in poetry; about what is *important* or *essential* to musical understanding; and about what can 'honestly' be claimed for painting but not for music – all of them clearly dependent on a very particular and exclusive notion of what it is to understand a piece of music. Scruton is aware of this, of course, and what he has to say about it needs to be quoted at some length:

> But it will be asked: what is meant by 'understanding' here? And it might be thought that the claims I am making are purely legislative, and that I am simply trying to define away the possibility of musical representation. The objection is a welcome one, since it helps us to understand the point at issue. We are not concerned to show that music can or cannot represent objects. We are attempting to show rather that the question whether music is representational is a question about the *appreciation* of music, and not a question about music's structure. The question is: do we understand music in that way? It is clear that we could envisage definitions of 'understanding' music according to which music is interpreted as a kind of code … On such a view music would become an inherently information-bearing medium, and its capacity to represent the

world would hardly be disputed. I do not propose to argue for the notion of musical understanding that I am here assuming. My point is that we do have an intuitive idea of musical understanding, and that this idea reflects our experience of music as an aesthetic object. And according to this intuitive idea – with its emphasis on melody, harmony and auditory relations – there is little place for representation in the appreciation of music.

'Little place'? Like his earlier (apparent) concession that someone ignorant of a piece of music's 'representational claims' may have only a 'considerable' rather than a full understanding of it, this might seem to leave at least *some* place for representation. But no. The very next sentence abolishes even that: 'If we insist, nevertheless, that there is such a place' – that is, any such place at all – 'then we find ourselves imposing an idea of musical understanding that has no intuitive appeal, and which fails to reflect the activities of those who compose and listen to music.'[34]

The whole argument, then, is underpinned by Scruton's undefended 'intuitive idea' of musical understanding, an idea that is clearly a version of the one described in the Background part of Chapter 1, and of whose exhaustiveness the remainder of that chapter gave reason to be sceptical. Nor is it only this particular part of Scruton's argument that is underpinned by his 'intuitive idea': the whole of his case against musical representation is underpinned by it. The passage just quoted shows the role that it plays, as one half of a false alternative, in his attempt to show that music cannot satisfy condition 3, the 'conventions' requirement; and his (unconvincing) claim that music cannot satisfy condition 2, that there be a distinction between medium and content, is lent whatever appearance of plausibility it might have by the assumption that musical relations must all be 'auditory relations', rather than – say – relations between sounds and their sources. The lynch-pin of Scruton's entire position, then, is something that he does 'not propose to argue for', because it is 'intuitive'. Which would be fine, were it not for the fact that the 'intuitive idea' he depends upon is one that quite expressly rules out the possibility of musical representation in advance. If a 'genuine' and 'honest' interest in what it is '*important*' to understand in music is legislatively restricted to intra-musical relations, after all, the whole issue of extra-musical representation is foreclosed, whatever Debussy or anybody else might try to do about it.[35] This concludes my first case-study in autonomanic question-begging.

IV. Resemblances

The structure of Scruton's argument, as he presents it, is elusive. So, too, is the structure of Davies's. As I said at the outset, his overall position seems to be that music cannot satisfy the 'conventions' requirement of representation (condition 3) because it cannot satisfy the condition that, where X represents Y, there be 'a resemblance between a person's perceptual experiences of X and of Y' (condition 5 – hereafter, the 'resemblance' requirement). The principal clue that this is what he means is as follows: 'I have already suggested,' he says, 'that music does not satisfy [the 'conventions'] condition.' In the end, however, 'how one feels about music's success or otherwise in meeting' that condition 'is likely to be determined by its fate in meeting' the 'medium/content' condition and the 'resemblance' condition. 'Only if a case can be mounted for saying these conditions are satisfied by music is it appropriate to revise the reservations expressed about music's meeting' the 'conventions' requirement.[36] The 'reservations' that Davies refers to are insubstantially grounded, to say the least, and it is not perplexing that he should feel the need to bolster them.[37] One must suppose, therefore, that the roundabout route that he proposes is intended, inter alia, to do just that. I have already drawn upon Davies's excellent treatment of condition 2, the 'medium/content' requirement, and concur fully with the reasons that he gives for holding that music can satisfy it. His grounds, then, for thinking that music cannot finally meet the 'conventions' condition – and so cannot, in any interesting sense, be a representational art – must derive exclusively from the fact that music fails to satisfy the 'resemblance' condition. It is to this that I now turn.

The point of Davies's 'resemblance' condition is fairly self-explanatory. The experience of looking at one of Monet's paintings of Rouen Cathedral, for example, has at least something in common with the experience of looking at the cathedral itself – enough, at any rate, to allow one to recognise the cathedral in the painting. It is thus characteristic of a (visual) representation that someone who understands it can recognise what it's of. And this immediately seems to pose a problem for the possibility of musical representation. It is notoriously the case, after all, that – unprompted – more or less no one ever guesses correctly what a musical 'representation' is meant to be of. Listen to Debussy's prelude cold. The tolling of bells might come to mind, perhaps, but it is unlikely that anyone would guess that it was supposed to be coming from an underwater cathedral. Why not a cathedral shrouded in mist? Why not some sort of funeral procession? The fact is that – without the title – the subject of Debussy's 'representation' is pretty well unrecognisable. It is of course true that the same is sometimes the case with visual representation: few, without help from the title, would know what Mondrian's *Broadway Boogie-woogie* was supposed to represent. But this is an atypical instance, Davies suggests, trading for its possibility on a whole background of effortlessly recognisable visual depictions. In music, by contrast, (relative) abstraction would appear to be the norm, not the exception. So it is tempting to think that, for representation in any given medium to be possible, there must be at least *some* clear-cut cases – cases in which any competent person would be able to recognise, unprompted, what is being depicted. And it may be tempting to think that music cannot pass that test.

It clearly can, however. As Peter Kivy has put it, 'musical pictures, insignificant though they may be in Western music, are as readily recognisable without verbal aids as any representational painting. (No one fails to recognise the bird songs in Beethoven's *Pastoral*, or, I believe, the steam engine in *Pacific 231*.)'[38] And if *some* clear-cut cases are all that is required, this gives us everything we need. Davies, though, seems oddly disinclined to go along with this. 'In Beethoven's work, the clarinet's "cuckoo" and the oboe's ["quail"] are plain enough, but the subtle complexities of rhythm and timbre marking the nightingale's song are mostly lost to the flute', and even if someone did recognise it, they 'might wonder whether the aim is to depict *Luscinia megarhynchos, L. svecica, L. luscinia*, or *L. calliope*.' He also doubts that Honegger's steam engine is as unmissable as Kivy believes.[39] But this – once Davies has granted Kivy his cuckoo and his quail – is mere quibbling, and does nothing to undermine the fundamental point that Kivy is making. It may be true, of course, that clear-cut musical cases are quite rare, and this may suggest, as Kivy remarks, that musical representation is a relatively peripheral phenomenon, in Western music at least. But it certainly doesn't establish or even suggest that musical representation is a non-phenomenon.[40]

Much more interesting is the question of titles.[41] It is clearly true that *La Cathédrale Engloutie* only has any chance of representing the temporary resurfacing of a sunken cathedral if its title is taken into account. So what sort of contribution can a title make? Take again the case of *Broadway Boogie-woogie* – a painting that, without its title, looks like an abstract, but in which some rather sassy resemblances to a Manhattan street-plan can be recognised when the title is known.[42] Davies accepts – rightly, I think – that *Broadway Boogie-woogie* is a representational painting;[43] and he endorses several eminently sensible claims about the nature and function of titles, including: that a title 'must be conferred by the artist'; and that:

a work's title affects the work's properties, including those that are artistically important. The title is relevant not simply because it directs attention to properties that are present but might easily be overlooked but, further, because it establishes a context in which the work takes on its properties.[44]

Broadway Boogie-woogie is representational, therefore, because the title is Mondrian's own, is part of Mondrian's work, and because it 'directs attention' to resemblances between the painting and a Manhattan street-plan that 'are present but might easily be overlooked'.

One might have thought that this would pretty well settle the question of musical titles. If the title *Broadway Boogie-woogie* is allowed to do this much for Mondrian's painting, then surely Debussy's title can do the same for *La Cathédrale Engloutie* – namely, direct attention to resemblances (or to such resemblances as there are) between the music and the cathedral of Ys. But Davies suggests otherwise. 'I can concede the importance of titles and programs,' he says, 'while denying that program music is representational.'[45] His way of trying to make good on this claim, however, is far from convincing. He notes that 'the importance of the title does not usually consist in its making [a work] depictive where otherwise it would not be'; and also that it 'is rarely the case that a nonrepresentational painting would be made depictive had its title been different'.[46] These points are harmless enough in themselves, I think. But they do have the effect of changing the subject, an effect that becomes quite noticeable a couple of pages later on. Davies invites us to consider:

> the discovery that an abstract painting had a title other than what one had thought. If the title were found to be 'Study No. 15', one might expect to locate it in a series ... If the title were found to be 'Girl and Boy' and the painting features pink and blue, the associations of these colours might become important. If the title were discovered to be 'War', one might find in the work expressions of violence. In these cases the qualities one newly finds in the work are not properties one overlooked formerly but properties effected by the interaction between the work's title and its other parts.[47]

Davies's point, clearly enough, is that the mere addition of a title does not *create* depiction – that something abstract is not *made* representational (rather than expressive, say) just by adding a title to it. And no doubt he is quite right. But then it turns out that this is supposed to be the clinching argument against music's capacity to satisfy the 'resemblance' condition, an argument warranting the conclusion, apparently, that 'Music is expressive in character, rather than representational as pictures are, and sometimes the title of a musical work can be relevant to an appreciation of the detail of its expressive character.'[48] I'm sorry? (as one might want to say). Why are we suddenly talking about 'abstract' works, and about the impossibility of making them representational by adding titles to them? Whatever happened to the *Broadway Boogie-woogie* example? No one was talking there as if the title had somehow *created* the depiction. Rather, the idea was that Mondrian's painting simply *is* a representational work, and that knowing what its title is can help you to recognise what it represents: we emphatically did *not* begin by assuming that the painting was an abstract (an abstract work that needed – *per impossibile* – to be *turned into* a representation). So why are we now making that assumption in the musical case? Why, that is, are we supposed to accept that *La Cathédrale Engloutie*, for example, is properly to be thought of as akin to 'abstract' or 'nonrepresentational' paintings rather than representational ones? We have been given no reason to accept that. And yet it is only on this assumption that Davies can distinguish musical cases from visual ones such as *Broadway Boogie-woogie*. And it is only on this assumption – which is to say, on the assumption that music is a nonrepresentational art – that Davies is able to conclude that music is … a nonrepresentational art.

This blatant piece of question-begging constitutes, so far as I can see, Davies's principal 'argument' against the thought that music can satisfy the 'resemblance' condition of representation. It also, given the overall structure of his position, constitutes his principal, albeit indirect, 'argument' against the thought that music can satisfy the 'conventions' requirement, since music's 'fate' in meeting that condition was supposed to hang on its ability to meet the medium/content requirement (which Davies thinks it can) and the 'resemblance' requirement (which Davies has certainly not shown that it can't). I conclude accordingly: Davies's account of the issues makes no more headway than Scruton's in establishing that music is not, in any significant sense, a representational art – and fails to make it, moreover, in a strikingly similar manner.

V. Putting the Title Last

I think that I have established that none of the conditions of representation that Scruton or Davies talk about in any helpful detail, which is to say all of them except the 'conventions' requirement,[49] has been shown by them to be incapable of being satisfied by music. I would also want to cleave to my earlier, modest and informal, characterisation of the 'conventions' requirement, namely, that a degree of acculturation, of familiarity with music and with the habits and expectations appropriate to it, is likely to be integral to one's ability to understand whatever representational content music may have. And, in preferring Davies's thoughts about *Broadway Boogie-woogie* to his thoughts about pieces of music with titles, I would want to say, as well, that something's title can tip you off as to what it's about.

So what of *La Cathédrale Engloutie*? Scruton and Davies both make much of the fact that many (putatively) 'representational' pieces of music work perfectly well as stand-alone pieces of music, as pieces that can be understood and appreciated in a 'purely' musical way.[50] Debussy, as his decision not to put his title first might indicate, (rightly) thought that Prelude X, Bk.I passed that test. Scruton, Davies, Debussy and I can therefore be taken to agree, at least, that *La Cathédrale Engloutie* measures up as a piece of 'pure' music. But Debussy included the title. And his point, I take it, was to say, 'Sure, the piece makes sense by itself. That is registered by the fact that I didn't put the title at the top of the first page. But it can also be heard as, can be recognised as being about, the sunken cathedral of Ys. That is why the title is there at all.' His point, in other words, was that just because something is understandable in one way doesn't mean that it isn't to be, or can't be, understood in another. Which is surely true. And precisely the same sort of thing might be said about painting. When Clement Greenberg insisted, in his famous essay on Modernism, that 'the past' had appreciated the paintings of Leonardo, Raphael, Titian, Rubens, Rembrandt and Watteau 'justly', but – because it had focused on their representational rather than their formal properties – had given 'wrong or irrelevant reasons for doing so', he was making two sorts of point, one of them controversial.[51] The controversial point was that Modernism had shown that representation, although perfectly real, was 'irrelevant' to the appreciation even of pre-Modernist painting – that such painting could and should be understood and appreciated purely for its formal qualities. The other point was that, because the realisation of this 'had left most of our old *value* judgements intact',[52] the Modernist and pre-Modernist ways of understanding must at some level be complementary, for all their apparent incompatibility.

If the first point should strike us as an over-statement – albeit of a rather familiar sort, given the progress of this chapter so far – the second, I think, deserves to be taken seriously. The fact that there may be more than one way of understanding a thing doesn't, by itself, mean that these ways must rule one another out. In the case of painting, indeed, it may be that these ways, although distinguishable, are mutually sustaining. Certainly that is what Scruton suggests. He imagines someone claiming (Greenberg-like) that one can understand the composition of Raphael's *St George*, 'the balance of tensions between ascending and descending lines, the sequence of spatial planes, and so on', without paying any attention to the fact that the painting is representational. But this, says Scruton would be:

> wholly misguided. For it seems to suggest that these important aesthetic properties of the Raphael – composition, balance, spatial rhythm – are quite independent of the representation; whereas that is clearly not so. For example we perceive the balance between the upward thrust of the horse's hind legs and the downward pressure of the lance only because we see the two lines as filled with the forces of the things depicted – of the horse's muscles and the horseman's lance.[53]

Scruton is right about this, I think. And one of the things he can be taken to be saying is that, because the compositional properties and the representational properties of the painting cannot be (fully) prised apart and appreciated in isolation from one another, there is no sense to be made of the suggestion – which someone might be tempted to make – that Raphael's picture is understood as a representation when a 'match' is grasped between its compositional properties and properties of what it represents. (A view such as Greenberg's, for instance, cannot allow the relation between a painting and its 'subject' to be any less extrinsic, or more intimate, than this.) And, although Scruton certainly wouldn't agree, it seems to me that something similar can be said of *La Cathédrale Engloutie*. Consider, for instance, the weight of the musical timbre, of the sounds that the tolling piano chords produce (obviously an important aesthetic quality of the work). To my ears, that weight is increased, and made more material, as it were, when one hears Debussy's music *as* the tolling of cathedral bells (rather than as, say, a sound that 'matches' cathedral bells). Not heard like that, the sounds of course retain a certain timbre – just as Raphael's *St George* retains something of its 'sequence of spatial planes' when viewed as an abstract. But just as one's appreciation of Raphael's visual design is enhanced when one sees St George and his horse in it, so, I suggest, one's appreciation of Debussy's soundscape, and of the textural balances characteristic of it, is enhanced when one hears the bells.[54]

This strikes me as a modest enough proposal, at any rate, and I offer it for the reader-cum-listener's consideration. But even if it is rejected, and the judgement made that representational and 'purely' musical listening are orthogonal to one another here, it remains the case that a representational listening is possible, and is not ruled out by the mere possibility of 'purely' musical listening. And that, in the end, is all that Debussy's decision to put his title last requires for its sense. I'll be quite content with that. My purpose in this chapter has not, after all, been to prove that *La Cathédrale Engloutie* is a representational piece of music, although I think that it is one. It has been to show how autonomanic presuppositions so permeate a particular philosophical mind-set that certain questions, such as the question whether music is capable of representation, are hardly askable without being instantly begged. And that I think I have shown. Autonomania is a real philosophical phenomenon, or condition, and it is one that can be hard to shake off.

NOTES

1. Plato, *Republic*, 399.
2. Charles Batteux, *Les beaux-arts*, cited in Peter le Huray and James Day (eds), *Music and Aesthetics in the Eighteenth and Early-Nineteenth Centuries*, abridged edition (Cambridge: Cambridge University Press, 1988), p. 37.
3. – even if people did doubt whether music was a *fine* art, as opposed to a decorative one, say –
4. Eduard Hanslick, *On the Musically Beautiful*, trans. G. Payzant (Indianapolis, IN: Hackett, 1986), p. 12.
5. *Ibid.*, p. 20.
6. *Ibid.*, p. 14.
7. *Ibid.*, p. 15.
8. *Ibid.*, p. 83.
9. The claim that music is not representational is different, of course, from the claim that it is not expressive. One might agree with Hanslick that music is incapable of representing specific feelings, and yet still insist – as many have – that it is capable of expressing them. See the Background part of Chapter 3 for discussion.
10. Stephen Davies, *Musical Meaning and Expression* (Ithaca, NY: Cornell University Press, 1994), chapter 2. Davies's findings have not, so far as I am aware, been made redundant by any subsequent development in the area.
11. *Ibid.*, p. 53.
12. *Ibid.*, p. 58.
13. *Ibid.*, p. 77.
14. *Ibid.*, p. 88. Davies draws this condition from Roger Scruton's essay 'Representation in Music', in Scruton, *The Aesthetic Understanding* (London: Methuen, 1983) pp. 62–76.
15. Davies, p. 59 (see Note 10).
16. Scruton in fact specifies five necessary conditions for representation, including a version of condition 5, but I have followed Davies's more economical reformulation of them. I have not, however, followed either Davies or Scruton in my numbering of the various conditions at issue.
17. I shall, accordingly, have no more to say in this chapter about the comparative

strengths of the semantic and seeing-in accounts (although, for what it's worth, I'm inclined to prefer the latter). When discussing Scruton, I will simply accept that conditions 1–4 are what is at issue; when discussing Davies, I'll accept the priority of 1–3 and 5.

18. Peter Kivy, *Sound and Semblance* (Ithaca, NY: Cornell University Press, 1991).
19. Jenefer Robinson, 'Music as a Representational Art', in P. Alperson (ed.), *What is Music? An Introduction to the Philosophy of Music* (New York, NY: Haven, 1987), pp. 167–92. To the extent that I offer any sort of positive account of musical representation in this chapter, it is, I think, very close to Robinson's.
20. Strictly speaking, it therefore also fails to meet condition 1 (the 'intention' requirement), since one cannot intend – rather than wish, say – to achieve the impossible. I defer discussion of condition 5 to section IV, below. Scruton's reasons for doubting that music can meet it are much the same as those offered by Davies, whose views I discuss there.
21. Scruton, p. 62 (see Note 14).
22. *Ibid.*, p. 67. Scruton's source for this claim is P. F. Strawson, *Individuals* (London: Methuen, 1964).
23. *Ibid.*, p. 72.
24. *Ibid.*, p. 67.
25. Davies, pp. 91–2 (see Note 10).
26. *Ibid.*, p. 96.
27. Davies makes a related point when he notes that 'To aim to understand and appreciate' a piece of music is, among other things, 'to consider the effort and skill that goes into coaxing sounds from the instruments for which the composer wrote'; *ibid.*, p. 93.
28. Scruton, p. 63 (see Note 14).
29. Davies, p. 88 (see Note 10).
30. Kivy, p. 158 (see Note 18).
31. They strike Davies as sufficient to suggest that the 'thoughts' condition isn't a condition of representation (p. 89 (see Note 10)), a suggestion about which I shall remain agnostic.
32. Scruton, p. 66 (see Note 14).
33. *Ibid.*, p. 69.
34. *Ibid.*, p. 71.
35. Kivy also notes the tendency of Scruton's position to help itself to its conclusion, in *Sound and Semblance*, chapter 8 (see Note 18). For Scruton's response, uncompelling in my view, see his *The Aesthetics of Music* (Oxford: Oxford University Press, 1997), chapter 5. Davies, although he discusses Scruton at length, and is appreciative of Kivy's overall critique of Scruton, doesn't seem to pick up on this problem – perhaps, for reasons that I attempt to spell out in section IV, not altogether surprisingly.
36. Davies, p. 90 (see Note 10).
37. For Davies's 'reservations', and presumably also for the place where it is 'suggested' that music cannot allay them, see *ibid.*, p. 78.
38. Kivy, p. 147 (see Note 18).
39. Davies, pp. 100–1 (see Note 10).
40. In fact the reverse – obviously. You don't get clear-cut instances of impossibilities.
41. For a helpful discussion of the role of titles in aesthetic appreciation, see Jerrold Levinson, 'Titles', in his *Music, Art, and Metaphysics* (Ithaca, NY: Cornell University Press, 1990), pp.159–78.
42. An example also discussed by Kivy.
43. Davies, pp. 63, 100 (see Note 10).

44. *Ibid.*, p.108. It is an interesting question, which I do not propose to pursue here, whether – if titles can affect a work's properties in these ways – other factors might not be able to do so too, factors which – like titles – reveal artistic intentions that may not be manifest in the work taken cold. I have in mind things like diary-entries.
45. *Ibid.*, p. 109.
46. *Ibid.*, p. 110.
47. *Ibid.*, p. 112.
48. *Ibid.*, p. 113.
49. Actually, neither of them talks very much about condition 1, the 'intention' requirement, either. But that is because this condition is subsidiary, as I noted earlier. It is only if representation in a given medium is possible – that is, if the medium satisfies the other specified conditions – that anyone can *intend* to produce a representation in it.
50. See, for example, Scruton, 'Representation in Music', p. 68 (see Note 14); Davies, pp. 111-12 (see Note 10).
51. Clement Greenberg, 'Modernist Painting', in A. Neill and A. Ridley (eds), *The Philosophy of Art* (New York, NY: McGraw-Hill, 1995), p. 116.
52. *Ibid.*
53. Scruton, pp. 68–9 (see Note 14).
54. To deny this would, in effect, be to insist – as, indeed, Scruton and Davies do in their various ways insist – that the relation between a 'representational' piece of music and its 'subject' must, because it can amount to no more than a 'matching' relation, be entirely extrinsic. Which would, of course, be to deny that the music can be understood *as* a representation, since – as I argued in Chapter 1 – one must be able to understand something 'internally' if one is to understand it at all.

3

Expression

I went to hear the 'Illuminated Symphony' [by Holbrooke] ... [A]n entire failure ... [O]ne had to choose. Now for the poem & now for the music. The music was certainly not inspired by Trench's poem. Holbrooke might never have read the poem & I am not sure that he did – in any case he has not understood it ... the poem is infinitely better than the music. (Frederick Delius, letter to Granville Bantock, 1908)

PART 1. BACKGROUND

That there is a relation of some kind between music and emotion has always been acknowledged, even by those who doubt that much of aesthetic moment hangs on the fact. The problem, however, is to account for it. A satisfactory account would provide answers to at least three questions: How is the relation between music and emotion grounded? How is the emotional aspect of music experienced? What value, if any, does the experience of that aspect have, and why?

This way of posing the questions derives indirectly from Eduard Hanslick's *On the Musically Beautiful,* published in 1854, the book that first established the problem as a philosophically interesting one. Hanslick was not the first to write provocatively on music and emotion: as I mentioned in the previous chapter, the Greeks had attributed the relation between the two to the distinctive characters of the various modes or scales; eighteenth-century thinkers had conceived of music as exciting or imitating those 'animal spirits' in whose movements Descartes had located the origin of emotion; and Schopenhauer had attested more gloriously than anybody to the sheer depth that a passionate engagement with music can have. But it was Hanslick who sharpened the problem up and gave it the focus it still retains – by denying that the value of music has anything to do with emotion at all. 'Only on the basis of a number of ideas and judgments,' he argues, 'can our state of mind congeal into this or that specific feeling.' Feeling, so construed, 'can only be precisely set forth in concepts' (for instance, 'Love cannot be thought without the representation of a beloved person'), and these concepts 'lie beyond the scope of music'. Music is capable of 'reproducing' only 'the fluctuations of our inner activity' and these 'can be similar with different feelings'.[1] Therefore music cannot express or represent particular feelings; and this means that the relation of music to emotion cannot function as 'an aesthetic principle'.[2] The beauty and the value of music, Hanslick concludes, 'is a specifically musical kind of beauty', which 'consists simply and solely of tones and their artistic combination'.[3] Thus Hanslick inaugurates musical formalism (in theory, at least: in his criticism he is unexpectedly fond of describing music in emotional terms).

The formalist view that the value of music is rooted exclusively in 'tones and their artistic combination' encourages the claim that the relation between music and emotion, though real, is merely *causal*, and hence of little philosophical or aesthetic interest. This claim comes in two main forms. One involves the postulation of an innate or natural psychological mechanism, such that certain musical stimuli automatically produce an emotional response in the listener. A comparatively sophisticated version of this claim has been developed by Leonard Meyer, who suggests that patterns of musical tension and release, when perceived by the understanding listener, trigger emotions (probably more accurately, feelings) as a kind of side-effect.[4] But even this account renders the connection between music and emotion philosophically inert – in much the way that the connection between the smell of food and salivation is philosophically inert. The other form of the claim, of which no sophisticated version is even possible, involves the postulation of an associational mechanism, such that the listener feels an emotion in response to music because he or she associates that music with something else (a love affair, perhaps, or a period of deep gloom). This, too, removes all philosophical and aesthetic interest from the picture. Just as the bell that set Pavlov's dogs drooling might as well have been an air-raid siren, so music, on this account, might as well be wallpaper, so long as someone has come to associate it with something. Nothing of moment swings here on the relation between music, specifically, and emotion. Hence this account, like the previous one, leaves no room for the anti-formalist thought that music might be valuable at least partly in virtue of its relation to emotion.

It is, of course, perfectly possible that these causal accounts contain an element of truth – indeed they surely do. But neither (nor both together) can be exhaustive. For even if we are sometimes triggered into feeling something by an innate or associational mechanism, we can nonetheless *recognise* an emotional quality in a piece of music without ourselves feeling anything ('What a jolly tune!'). And this fact shows, first, that the power of music to *trigger* emotion is not the only link between music and emotion; and, second, that the philosophically interesting questions cannot be removed by the mere postulation of mechanism.

Observations of this kind have prompted a critical return to Hanslick, and a variety of efforts to avoid his conclusion that the relation between music and emotion cannot function as 'an aesthetic principle'. Opposite means to this end are well illustrated by two mid-twentieth century writers. Susanne Langer takes issue with Hanslick's claim that emotion 'can only be precisely set forth in concepts', and argues instead that emotion can be 'set forth' non-conceptually in 'presentational symbols' – such symbols being found in pieces of music.[5] Deryck Cooke, by contrast, appears to deny that the conceptual resources required to 'set forth' emotion 'lie beyond the scope of music': his claim is that music really functions as a 'language' of emotion, in which various musical phrases stand, like words, for various kinds of feeling.[6] Neither of these accounts, however, commands much support today. Among their many difficulties, Langer's 'presentational symbols' consistently defy explication, while Cooke's linguistic turn is both naive about language and mistaken about the degree to which any stable emotional connotation can be assigned to the same musical phrase in different musical contexts. Hanslick's doctrine of the 'specifically musical kind of beauty' can be expected to withstand criticism from either of these positions, however artfully refined.

In one sense, though, Langer's approach has proved the more durable. If no one now takes the idea of a 'presentational symbol' very seriously, it is nonetheless widely agreed that Langer was right to question the claim, central to Hanslick's formalism, that the conceptual inarticulateness of music necessarily debars it from 'setting forth' particular feelings. Indeed, scepticism about this claim is clearly discernible in the work of Donald Ferguson, whose book *Music as Metaphor* introduces a number of themes that have become central to the philosophy of music and emotion. Concepts are not everything, Ferguson suggests: for the movement of music 'may suggest distinctive characteristics of physical or nervous energy'; and these, in conjunction with 'the intrinsic motor impulses of consonant or dissonant harmony', may present 'an apparently corporeal musical mass whose weight and volume may be adjusted (as, for instance, no dancer's body could be adjusted) to the portrayal' of the 'vital impulse to motion activating a sentient being'.[7] In effect, Ferguson denies Hanslick's claim that 'the fluctuations of inner activity', which music *is* capable of 'reproducing', are always 'similar with different feelings'. Rather, in Ferguson's view, those motions (or 'fluctuations') may be distinctive, and so may allow music to 'set forth' particular emotions. Much of the remainder of Ferguson's book is devoted, appropriately, to the presentation of evidence in support of this claim, through close musical analyses which remain models of their kind.

Ferguson's position can be construed in either or both of two ways: as asserting a link of some kind between music and the outward manifestations of emotion, that is, expressive human behaviour; or as asserting a link of some kind between music and the inward dimension of the experience of emotion itself. These two constructions mark the limits within which most subsequent philosophical investigation has been conducted. Peter Kivy has inclined strongly to the former limit. In a series of books and articles he has revived and reinterpreted the eighteenth-century idea that the relation between music and emotion is grounded in the resemblance of the 'contours' of musical movement to the 'contours' of characteristic pieces of expressive behaviour, including speech – so that 'If the criteria of human expression are public, objective, immune from philosophical skepticism, so too are the criteria of expressiveness in music.'[8] In Kivy's view, to say of a piece of music that it has the property of 'sadness' may be to say something that is literally true, in just the way that it may be literally true to say that the piece has the property of being in E minor. Thus Kivy agrees with Hanslick that the beauty of music is a 'specifically musical kind of beauty'; but he does not accept that talk of the 'specifically musical' is confined 'simply and solely' to talk of 'tones and their artistic combination'. Rather, the expressiveness of a piece of music is every bit as much a musical feature of it as its tonality is.

This conclusion has won widespread acceptance, even if Kivy's warrant for drawing it is open to dispute. But perhaps the main problem with his account is that it cannot explain why someone might value a piece of music *because* of its expressive properties. To say that Mozart's *Requiem* would be a different piece of music without its terror-stricken quality is one thing; but to say that Mozart's work is valuable at least partly *in virtue* of its terror-stricken quality is quite another. Kivy's emphasis on the purely cognitive aspects of the listening experience – an experience in which the listener recognises resemblances between musical and behavioural 'contours' – renders him mute on this question. It is not surprising, then, that others have inclined to the alternative view that the crucial link is not so much between music and the outward manifestations of emotion as between music and the inward dimension of the experience of emotion itself. Malcolm Budd, for instance, impressed by Carroll Pratt's dictum that 'music *sounds* the way moods *feel*',[9] has argued that an imaginative engagement with music can enable 'the listener to experience imaginatively (or really) the inner nature of emotional states in a peculiarly vivid, satisfying and poignant form' – and in a form, moreover, whose value is inseparable from the value of the music so experienced.[10]

It may be, of course, that the truth lies somewhere between these views. For while Kivy's externalist position is hard-pressed to explain why it *matters* that music is expressive, the internalist position is equally at a loss to explain how the imaginative experience of music might be constrained in such a way as to allow the link between music and emotion to function as 'an aesthetic principle'. A hint here can be gained from Jerrold Levinson. He suggests that 'Recognizing emotion in music and experiencing emotion from music may not be as separable in principle as one might have liked.'[11] If this is correct, it is perhaps possible to answer the questions posed at the outset in the following way. How is the relation between music and emotion grounded? In the resemblance between various features of music and the outward (and maybe also the inward) features of emotion. How is the emotional aspect of music experienced? Imaginatively, so that the listener grasps the expressive quality of a piece of music in coming 'to experience imaginatively (or really)' the nature of the emotion expressed. What value does that experience have, and why? It has the value of granting the listener access to states of mind not otherwise available – for the experience described is conceivable *only* as a mode of experiencing particular pieces of music.[12]

These answers may fail to satisfy, of course. And if they do, that may be for either of two reasons: first, that Hanslick was right all along, and that the connection of music to emotion is not in the end aesthetically significant (a conclusion that few contemporary philosophers of music appear ready to accept); or, second, that these answers concede too much to Hanslick, and that the determination to work outward, as it were, from 'tones and their artistic combination' already represents a capitulation to autonomania, with all of the self-defeating consequences that that is liable to have (also a conclusion that few contemporary philosophers of music appear ready to accept). In the second part of this chapter, I explore some considerations that lend weight, even if only obliquely, to the latter of these possible reasons for dissatisfaction. Specifically, I consider one form of music – song – in which attempts to understand, and to do justice to, expressiveness by working outward from 'tones and their artistic combination' are at their most transparently (and therefore, I hope, instructively) futile.

PART 2. *CYNARA*

Frederick Delius (1862–1934) wrote most of *Cynara* in 1907, originally intending it as part of his song cycle, *Songs of Sunset*. In the event, however, *Cynara* was not included in the cycle, and it was not until the late 1920s that Delius returned to the song and completed it. It received its first performance in 1929. *Cynara*, like the other songs in *Songs of Sunset*, sets a poem by Ernest Dowson, who died in 1900, tubercular and dissolute, at the age of thirty-two:

> Last night, ah, yesternight, betwixt her lips and mine
> There fell thy shadow, Cynara! thy breath was shed
> Upon my soul between the kisses and the wine;
> And I was desolate and sick of an old passion,
> Yea, I was desolate and bowed my head:
> I have been faithful to thee, Cynara! in my fashion.
>
> All night upon mine heart I felt her warm heart beat,
> Night-long within mine arms in love and sleep she lay;
> Surely the kisses of her bought red mouth were sweet;
> But I was desolate and sick of an old passion,
> When I awoke and found the dawn was gray:
> I have been faithful to thee, Cynara! in my fashion.
>
> I have forgot much, Cynara! gone with the wind,
> Flung roses, roses riotously with the throng,
> Dancing, to put thy pale, lost lilies out of mind;
> But I was desolate and sick of an old passion,
> Yea, all the time, because the dance was long:
> I have been faithful to thee, Cynara! in my fashion.
>
> I cried for madder music and for stronger wine,
> But when the feast is finished and the lamps expire,
> Then falls thy shadow, Cynara! the night is thine;
> And I am desolate and sick of an old passion,

> Yea, hungry for the lips of my desire:
> I have been faithful to thee, Cynara! in my fashion.

Delius's setting exploits the forces for which he wrote some of his greatest music — baritone and orchestra — and if the results are not perhaps as searing as in his 1903 masterpiece, *Sea Drift* (which also includes a chorus), *Cynara* is still one of his most characteristic songs. Emerging, as so often with this composer, unassertively from silence, the initial hushed figures for strings prepare the way for the first appearance of a violin motif — Cynara herself, surely — which haunts the work throughout. And then, and again unassertively, the baritone enters, his line a sinuous and tender reverie which builds, in the final two verses, to a hollow parody of high spirits, before subsiding back into a silence occupied only by Cynara's motif. From beginning to end, the work is replete with Delius's unmistakable atmosphere, and in its orchestration and, above all, its final chord, clear reference is sounded to his symphonic poem of 1899, *Paris — the Song of a Great City*, prompting speculation that Delius may have had a Cynara of his own (he is said to have enjoyed Paris as a young man). All in all, it is hard to imagine a more appropriate setting of Dowson's poem; and it will be one concern of the present chapter to try to spell out what the 'appropriate' comes to in this context, especially with regard to expressiveness. As usual, however, quite a lot will need to be done first. Specifically, and this is perhaps the principal task for the following pages, it will be necessary to establish what sort of thing a song *is*, and what is involved in understanding and appreciating an object of that kind. For these questions, as will become clear, are both pivotal and surprisingly difficult to answer.

I. The Prejudice Against Song

One of the reasons that I have decided to build this chapter around Delius's *Cynara* is, quite simply, that it is a song. And to choose a song in this context is to offend against one fairly conspicuous tenet of the autonomanic position, namely, that if one wants to say anything useful about musical expressiveness, one must take as one's examples instances of purely instrumental music. The point of this view, evidently enough, is that if (expressive) music in its 'true' state is essentially autonomous, then purely instrumental music, in which the scope for the exercise of that alleged autonomy is at its most unfettered, must be taken as paradigmatic. I gave general reasons in the Introduction to be suspicious of this sort of move; and in what follows I want to do two things: I want to offer a case-study of what actually happens when the move is made, and I want to see what happens when one refuses to make it – when one doesn't, that is, just assume at the outset that the musical is the 'purely' musical and that the purely musical is music for instruments alone.

It goes without saying that songs are not examples of pure instrumental music. One philosopher, Stephen Davies, has even flirted with the suggestion that they are not examples of music, remarking darkly that 'It is significant' that artforms such as song and opera 'are not called 'music' (as one has orchestral music ... chamber music, and so on)', a point whose alleged significance is somewhat undermined when, elsewhere in the same passage, he acknowledges the existence of something called 'choral music'.[13] But if few have been keen to deny at least a certain musical status to song, there is a strong consensus that songs, although arguably musical, are, because not good examples of music in its pure state, not examples to which a philosopher interested in the nature and properties of music (properly so-called) should appeal. As Peter Kivy has trenchantly put it, songs 'are works with texts, and with regard to texted works all bets are off'.[14]

The intuition that the bets are off when there's a text about is very widely shared. It is also worth a closer look. Not altogether surprisingly, it receives its classic statement from Hanslick:

> whatever can be asserted of instrumental music holds good for all music as such. If some general definition of music be sought, something by which to characterise its essence and its nature, to establish its boundaries and purpose, we are entitled to confine ouselves to instrumental music. Of what *instrumental music* cannot do, it ought never be said that *music* can do it, because only instrumental music is music purely and absolutely. Whether, for its value and effects, one prefers vocal or instrumental music ... one will always have to grant that the concept 'music' does not apply strictly to a piece of music composed to a verbal text. In a piece of vocal music, the effectiveness of tones can never be so precisely separated from that of words, action, and ornamentation as to allow strict sorting of the musical from the poetical ... Union with poetry extends the power of music, but not its boundaries.[15]

The basic thought, clearly, is that words in some sense complicate and confuse the picture, introducing the temptation to treat verbal effects and phenomena as if they were musical ones. The claim here, then, is not so much that songs aren't music (although Hanslick, like Davies, can be seen to flirt with that idea), but that songs, if they are music, are a philosophically treacherous sort of music. The bald fashion in which, following Hanslick, I have set up this position allows us to see straight-away that at least one sort of defence of it won't do. It won't do, that is, to say that the bets are off on the grounds that the text, although part of the song, is not part of the song considered as a piece of music, since to say that would simply be to insist that music, properly so-called, is untexted stuff for instruments alone; and that is the very contention at issue. So how, without begging the question, might one try to defend the intuition that the bets are off when there's a text about?

One way, I suppose, would be to point to the different sorts of notation in play. The music, it might be said, is what's notated on staves with little dots, the text is what's written out in words. But this, while often true enough, doesn't tell us much, and certainly doesn't tell us why the text is irrelevant to the song considered as a piece of music. It can only do that if the further claim is made that *only* what can be notated on staves with little dots is properly to be considered musical, a claim whose overtly Goodmanian pedigree doesn't do much to disguise its real roots in the aesthetics of autonomy. This way of cutting the cake already presupposes the absolute priority of the 'purely' musical, and so can hardly be enlisted either to establish that priority or to cancel bets on the strength of it.

A second tack might be to insist on a conventional classificatory difference between words and music: words are one sort of thing, music is another, and we have no difficulty in ordinary contexts distinguishing the two. But this is hopeless. To be sure, I can tell the difference between hearing the news on the radio and hearing a string quartet on it. But then I can also tell the difference between vowels and consonants, without this fact making the word 'rhythm', say, an interestingly different sort of word from, say, the French 'oui', and without indicating anything treacherous or contra-standard in a word like 'metre', say, or indeed in a word like 'word'. That there is an obvious difference between instru-mental music and vocal music is not the issue. What I want to be told is why that difference is such as to make vocal music somehow less 'musical' than instrumental music, or is such as to disbar the texted aspect of vocal music from the philosophical casino.

A third answer to my question might be to point out that words and music are not only readily distinguishable, but that they do their respec-tive jobs differently, that they make a different sort of contribution to a song's overall effect. Again, I accept this, but don't think it shows any-thing. The brief storm movement from Haydn's string quartet, *Seven Last*

Words from the Cross, makes a very different sort of contribution to the overall effect of the work from that made by the previous eight movements, but this hardly disqualifies it as *part* of that work. Or, to vary the example, the metre of a poem makes a very different sort of contribution to the overall poetic effect from that made by the meanings of the words used, but this tells us nothing about what, in a poem, is to be regarded as truly 'poetic'. No, this response depends for whatever plausibility it has on the presence of another, suppressed, thought lurking beneath it – that the real difference in the way that words and music do their respective jobs is that words do their job in a specifically verbal way, while music does its job in a specifically musical way. And that, plainly enough, is simply to restate the autonomanic intuition, not to defend it. The bets are off, it seems, not because there is any independent and principled reason to think that songs are somehow less musical or more treacherous than sonatas, but because of the prejudice that 'real' music is 'pure' music, and that songs, in that sense at least, aren't pure.[16]

I should make clear at this point exactly what (modest) position I am defending. I am not denying that there are differences between music and words. Nor am I denying that there are differences between vocal music and instrumental music. I am, however, denying that there is any non-question-begging sense in which vocal music is to be thought of as less musical for not being purely instrumental. I can put that point in a more positive way. My view is that a song is every bit as much a piece of music as a piece of instrumental music is, and so, given that the words are part of what makes a song the song it is, that the words of a song are part of what makes a song the piece of music it is. Thus, I can see no reason at all to think that, from the perspective of the philosophy of music, the bets must be off when a text's about. This is not to say that there mightn't be a sub-division of the philosophy of music, say the philosophy of instrumental music, from the perspective of which song might be marginal, or even irrelevant (although that would be surprising). But it is to say that the absolute privileging of that sub-division is, in the end, arbitrary.

The position I am arguing against, however, is hugely well-entrenched. I can best bring out the depth of its entrenchment, I think, by looking at what contemporary philosophers of music have had to say about song when not simply dismissing it out of hand. On the whole, they are in accord with Jerrold Levinson's influential paper of 1984, 'Hybrid Art Forms'.[17] (One need only reflect on the title to detect the undeclared baggage.) Levinson argues that certain art forms, song and opera among them, are best seen as amalgams or hybrids of other art forms, and so are best assessed and understood in terms set, more or less independently, by those other art forms. Thus song, for instance, is a hybrid of poetry and music. Except for the odd mention of 'miscegenation', Levinson doesn't belabour the fact that the rhetoric of hybridity is ineluctably parasitic on the rhetoric of 'purity', but it is clear that he regards poetry and music as the 'pure' art forms whose purity and mutual autonomy is only half-disguised in their hybrid offspring. It goes without saying, I think, that this way of setting up the nature of song is unlikely to prove especially subversive of the autonomanic orthodoxy. But it is worth noting just how unsubversive, in Levinson's hands, it is, not least in the strange slippage exhibited between the chronological and the logical. Here's what he says:

> If works are artistic hybrids ... they must be understood in terms of and in light of their components ... If art form C has emerged as a combination of A and B, then we appropriately understand or gauge the A-aspect of a C-work ... against a background of norms, styles and concerns attaching to the preexisting practice of art A ... A thoroughbred art form [by contrast] is simply one that has *not* arisen from the interpenetration or interaction of previously existing art forms ... [So] to call a current artform nonhybrid will usefully be to say that with respect to its *recent* or *critically relevant* past it has been constituted as an art form in a fairly stable fashion, as opposed to having lately evolved from other activities in the artistic environment.[18]

At first blush, and whatever one makes of the details, this looks soberly chronological: if an art form has grown out of two or more pre-existing ones, then those ancestors are relevant to the understanding of the resultant hybrid. But on closer inspection it turns out that Levinson isn't quite saying that, since the identification of an art form as a thorough-bred swings not so much on the chronological question of its ancestry (which at one moment seems important, at the next not) as on the logical question of whether its ancestry is '*critically relevant*' to it; and that question, one can see, is not going to be settled by any merely historical enquiry. It is this slippage that allows Levinson simultaneously to maintain that opera is a hybrid (of the pre-existing art forms play and song), that song is a hybrid (of poetry and music), but that purely instrumental music, which arose in anything like its currently recognisable form much later than all but one of the above – that is, later than plays, songs or poems – is a thoroughbred. Here is Stephen Davies supporting Levinson on this point:

If composite artforms are always to be viewed in terms of the character and properties of their historical ancestors, is one to approach an artform that results from decomposition in a similar fashion? Pure instrumental music arose historically from practices that mixed music with words ... but we treat it as distinct from song ... in this case, the historical approach recommended for hybrids seems not to apply. It could be argued, however, that pure music has lost touch with its ancestors ... Pure music may have emerged by abstraction from song and dance, but the songs and dances from which it emerged are now lost to us, it might be said.[19]

Well yes, 'it might be said.' No doubt 'it could be argued'. But why say it? Where is the argument? The fact is that, for all its surface concern with history, the hybridity case is really only a way of *de*historicising certain favoured categories of art at the expense of others, so that purely instrumental music can be allowed to operate as a logical precondition of song at the same time as it is acknowledged that, from a merely chronological point of view, song both came first and made purely instrumental music possible. Only someone powerfully in the grip of a certain picture of music could rest content with this way of thinking.

Suppose, though, that one were to go along with Levinson and Davies, and accept the understanding of song that they recommend. What would it look like? Here is Levinson, in a paper written shortly after 'Hybrid Art Forms', explaining what sorts of things 'are relevant to appreciating and assessing a piece of vocal music': the first two questions to ask, he suggests, are: 'How good is the *music* of a song, considered as such?'; and 'How *integrated* are the purely musical materials, the accompaniment and vocal line, with one another?' These questions indicate pretty clearly which half of Levinson's hybrid wears the trousers, encouraging us, as they do, to treat song as consisting primarily in something called the music 'as such', and the song's quality as a function, primarily, of how well its 'purely musical materials' are integrated. His questions continue: 'How well does the music of a song, particularly the vocal line, *conform* to the 'natural music' of the words and phrases of the text?'; 'How well does the music *represent* or *depict* objects or events described in the text?'; 'How closely does the *expressiveness* of the music *match* the emotional tone or quality of the text?'; and 'How *suitable* expressively, is the music to the text, or the text to the music, that is, how *effective an expressive whole* is formed by the musical and verbal components in combination?'[20] None of Levinson's questions, it will be noted, enjoins a remotely similar level of attention to the text 'as such', or to the integration of a song's 'purely' textual materials. And this is both odd and revealing.[21] Nothing in the hybrid view of song, after all, implies the subordination of text to music, and one might have expected the two parents to receive separate and equal treatment before their mongrel progeny, in Levinson's last question, was allowed its moment in the sun. But no.

A clue as to why not can perhaps be gleaned from the frequently observed fact that great songs sometimes have rotten words, an observation customarily rounded out or off with a reference to Schubert. This observation is made often enough to be worth pausing over. What – exactly – is it meant to show? One can see how it fits with the hybrid model. Spelled out, the fit comes to this: viewed purely as a poem – that is, as a poem in its own right – the words to such and such a song are no good. The song itself, however, is felt to be first rate. Therefore the quality of the song must derive solely from its music 'as such', that is, from its music conceived as purely instrumental. Thus the observation both exploits the strictly bipartite picture encouraged by the hybrid model *and* offers a reason to suppose that the real point and value of a song – any song – must reside in its qualities as an autonomous musical artefact. To point out that Schubert's songs sometimes have rotten words, then, is, in this context, simultaneously to presuppose and to reinforce the thought that the genuinely musical is the purely musical.

It is no surprise, in light of this, that philosophers of music never point out the equally true and equally misleading fact that great songs often have lousy music. Here Schubert makes way for, for example, Bob Dylan: lousy music, badly sung, but great songs. What do 'lousy music' and 'badly sung' mean in this case? They mean 'would be lousy and bad if the music were to be judged by the standards appropriate to a piece of purely instrumental music' – standards relating to sophistication of structure, for instance, or to being in tune. The conclusion? By parity of reasoning, that the quality of a Dylan song must derive solely from its text 'as such', that is, from its text conceived as purely poetic, so that we now have an observation that both exploits the strictly bipartite character of the hybrid model *and* offers a reason to suppose that the real point and value of a song – any song – must reside in its qualities as an autonomous piece of poetry. And this, in effect, is simultaneously to presuppose and to reinforce the thought that the genuinely musical is the purely poetic.

Silly. But the Dylan and Schubert cases are mirror-images of one another, and both flow directly from the (mis)understanding of song as a hybrid art form, as a more or less unequal combination of poetry 'as such' and music 'as such'. I conclude accordingly: the hybrid model hopelessly misrepresents the nature of song, and fails to do anything but undermine confidence in the notion of 'pure' music 'as such'. Before moving on, however, I should again emphasise just how modest the position I am urging is. I am not denying that there is a difference between songs and purely instrumental music; I am not denying that purely instrumental music might be interesting, important or puzzling in a way that songs are not; I am not denying the right of philosophers of music to direct their attention to purely instrumental music if they choose to; I am not claiming that song is somehow more central to an understanding of the 'musical' than purely instrumental music is. All that I am claiming is, first, that the hybrid model does not represent a fruitful way of thinking about song; second, that the motivation for adopting the hybrid model stems from a misplaced emphasis on the unhelpful notion of purity; and third, and consequently, that there is no reason at all to conclude that song is in any interesting sense 'impure' or that the bets must be off when there's a text about. The prejudice against song really is just that – a prejudice.

II. Text and Music

I have spoken so far as if it were perfectly obvious what is meant by 'the text' (of a song) and 'the music' (of a song); and in a way it *is* obvious, or else the hybrid model would not even be intelligible. But one needs to be careful nonetheless. Indeed, if one does trouble to think about what is meant by 'text' and 'music' here, any residual attraction that the hybrid model might exert should evaporate entirely.

What is the text of *Cynara*? The obvious and tempting answer is 'Dowson's poem of the same name', that is, the poem printed at the beginning of this part of the present chapter. This answer, however, while not actually wrong, is in fact misleading, for reasons I'll come to in a moment. But even if one does accept the answer at face value, some noteworthy – if hardly very surprising – points emerge. First, the words of Dowson's poem have evidently been selected with some regard, not only to their meaning, but also to their *sound*. The most obvious examples are the rhymes pairing the first and third, the second and fifth, and the fourth and sixth lines of each stanza together; but one might also note the rather horrible alliterative effect of the third stanza's second line, or the somewhat heavy echo of the 'ah' in the poem's opening line upon the first mention of Cynara in the next. These devices, 'poetic' if anything is, are sound-effects, and in that much part of what makes (some) poetry 'musical'. Nor, so far as I can see, is there any reason to suspect this sense of 'musical' of being metaphorical or misleading. Indeed, it is precisely because of the sonically striking passion/fashion rhyme that the first stanza, again non-metaphorically, achieves 'cadence' (the other three achieve it that way too, but the effect is augmented by repetition). Also, Dowson's poem is metrical: the words are organised, not only with an eye to their sense, but with an ear to their rhythm. Indeed, Cynara (the woman) would not have been called 'Cynara!' but for this – imagine trying to handle 'Jolene!' in *Cynara's* general metrical scheme (or, to put the same point the other way round, the metrical scheme of *Cynara* is driven by Dowson's decision to call his woman Cynara). Again, and still without a trace of metaphor, this is part of what makes (some) poetry 'musical'. Finally, although I have to say that I don't detect much of this in Dowson's poem, some poetry occupies its own distinctive sound-world, in a way that goes beyond mere rhyme, alliteration or metre. What I have in mind here can be seen, or rather heard, in the famous opening verses of *Jabberwocky*:

> 'Twas brillig, and the slithy toves
> Did gyre and gimble in the wabe
> All mimsy were the borogroves,
> And the mome raths outgrabe.
>
> 'Beware the Jabberwock, my son!
> The jaws that bite, the claws that catch!
> Beware the Jubjub bird, and shun
> The frumious Bandersnatch!'

In these lines, Lewis Carroll marks out a highly specific sonic territory, one which might be characterised, self-referentially, as the sound of the English language as such (the invented words both trade off and reinforce the 'Englishness' of the sound). Or, to take an example that perhaps makes the point more directly, consider the third stanza of Edward Thomas's *Adlestrop*:

> And willows, willow-herb, and grass,
> And meadowsweet, and haycocks dry,
> No whit less still and lonely fair
> Than the high cloudlets in the sky.

Here, again, the poet has succeeded – to my ear, at least – in establishing a quite distinctive auditory terrain, one whose effect, viewed pragmatically, is to make quite impossible the inclusion within it of certain kinds of sound (sense aside, imagine replacing 'meadowsweet' with, for instance, 'xylophone' or, indeed, with 'Bandersnatch').

The point of the preceding paragraph is that a poem, considered, as it were, 'as such', may already be thoroughly imbued with musical qualities, and be imbued with them before anyone has got around to setting it to music. And this should certainly give one pause for thought before one decides, as the hybrid model enjoins one to decide, that the 'musical' aspect of a song can somehow be prised away from the textual aspect, and assessed in isolation. But this is only the beginning. For it is not really right to say that the text of *Cynara* is Dowson's poem, even if it is perfectly true that the text and the poem both consist of the same words in the same order.[22] The reason for this paradoxical-sounding claim is straightforward. Part of what makes *Cynara* – Dowson's poem – the poem it is, are its musical qualities, its metre, its rhyme and its alliteration; and these qualities are qualities of the poem *as read*. They are qualities that one apprehends as one reads the poem on the page, or as one listens to someone recite it. Nor are they incidental qualities: one could no more subtract them from the poem, and hope to leave the poem intact, than one could subtract from it its final stanza, or every third line. But it is precisely *these* qualities that are – always or often – modified, eliminated or transformed when a poem is set to music. Almost no trace of Dowson's original metre can be heard in Delius's *Cynara*: the composer has given to the words a far longer and more leisurely rhythm than they ever had in the poem. Nor are the great majority of Dowson's rhymes audible – the assonant words are, for the most part, too far separated in the song to be detectable as such. And even Dowson's nasty attack of alliteration is given point, and made bearable, in the desperate levity that Delius's setting imparts to it. The fact is that the musical qualities of the poem have been entirely altered in the setting of it: which is to say, the poem itself has been altered, in some ways out of recognition. The text of Delius's song, therefore, is *not* Dowson's poem, even if both do consist of the same words in the same order: the poem has one set of qualities, the text of the song has another.

What, then, is the text of Delius's song? The answer, simply, is that it is the words of Dowson's poem *as sung* in that song. And this means that the text of the song cannot be fully specified without reference to the singing of it, that is, without reference to the music of the song. Any attempt to strip the text away from the music yields, not the text, but – at best – a poem by Dowson.

The autonomaniac may not be too worried by this conclusion.

Perhaps, in abstracting the text, one does change it into something else. But what's left behind, surely, is the *music*, and that, as the hybrid model recommends, can now be assessed in isolation. Indeed, doesn't this make it more likely than ever that the value of a song really must be determined by the value of its music considered 'as such'? But this move is far too quick. For the abstraction of the text from a song not only denatures the text, it denatures the music. There are a number of ways of bringing out this point, but perhaps the most direct is to concentrate on the notion of timbre. It should not be controversial to note that part of what makes a piece of music the piece of music it is is the way that it sounds. Possibly some pieces of music are more amenable than others to a wide range of ways of sounding: it certainly seems to be possible to play a lot of Bach, for instance, on instruments that sound a good deal different from those originally envisaged. But for some music, including Delius's, the sound is crucial – the instrumental colour, the interplay of transparency and thickness, the separation of register, the balance of the percussive against the plangent, and so on. Timbre matters in Delius; and when he writes songs, the timbre of his leading instrument – the voice – matters. But the timbre of a voice isn't merely a matter of its being a voice. That is to say, the timbre of *Cynara* would not survive unaltered if – the text having been abstracted – the baritone were to sing his line as piece of vocalise, as a series of phrases sung to the syllable 'ah', say. For the timbre, colour and intonation of a voice change dramatically depending on what syllable is sung, and in which register. (Try singing a high note to the syllable 'ee' and then to 'oh': the sound is quite different.) And this is something that a composer who knows the instrument he is writing for takes into account. The sound of *Cynara*, then – part of what makes it *that* song – is a function not only of the notes that the baritone sings, but of his singing them to the syllables specified in the text: take these away, and you no longer have 'the music' of the song. Which means, I suggest, that 'the music' of a song cannot be fully specified without reference to its text, and so cannot be understood or assessed in isolation from it. Songs are not a hybrid of words and music. They are a *kind* of music – one that includes words.[23]

I foresee two main sorts of objection to what I have just argued. The first objection is this. To say, as I have said, that it matters to the sound of a song that the specified syllables are sung is all very well. But this, even if true, doesn't amount to much. After all, a string of syllables is just a string of sounds, and these, if it's the *sound* of a song that one is worried about, needn't be thought of as words. To be sure, when the baritone sings the syllables 'Cy', 'na' and 'ra' they do, as a matter of fact, add up to someone's name – but only from a linguistic point of view. *Musically*, they are just devices for producing certain sorts of timbre; and *musically* they should be heard and understood as such. This objection claims, in effect, that 'the music' can be abstracted from 'the text', even while the text – construed as a series of timbre-generating syllables – is left in place. My initial response to this objection is unashamedly *ad hominem*. For those who – like me – are principally impressed by songs in languages that they don't understand very well (German, French) the objection is seductive, in fact almost too good to be true. If it is right, after all, it means that we English-speaking monoglots are not only not missing anything through being unable to follow the words of songs by Brahms, say, or by Berlioz, we are actually in a better position than the Germans or the French.[24] What is easy for us – hearing the sung syllables as mere sounds – may be far harder, or plainly impossible, for them, and so it is we, and not they, who are best placed to understand what we hear. Mmm. My second response is to note that actual vocalise – that is, linguistically meaningless strings of sung sounds – has always been available to, and used by, composers, from the 'fa-la-la's of madrigal to the wordless twitterings of Berio's *A Ronne*: indeed, Delius himself employed it in his *Song of the High Hills*, which features a choir but not a text.[25] The most obvious explanation, surely, of why composers have not always written vocalise when they have wanted to write for voices is that they, at least, haven't thought of their song-texts as mere strings of timbre-generating syllables. They have thought of them as made up of words. And I don't think that one would have to be a paid-up Romantic intentionalist to conclude that this fact puts the ball back squarely into the autonomanic court. Why, exactly, should I believe that words that are in fact words, and which are set as such by composers who know that their primary audiences will hear them as the words that they are, are *really* to be understood as nothing more than phonemes to colour the voice? I await the argument with interest.[26]

The second objection is that I have played rather fast and loose with various identity conditions, some of which may be controversial. So, for example, I have simply asserted that part of what makes a poem the poem it is is its musical qualities; I have asserted that the text of a song, because it may lack these qualities, is not the same thing as the poem with which it shares all of its words in exactly the same order; I have asserted that the timbre of a piece of music may, in many cases, be part of what makes it the piece of music it is, and so that abstracting 'the music' of a song from its text cannot, in these cases, yield 'the music' *of* the song. None of these assertions has been argued for, and yet my case depends upon them. Therefore, the objection concludes, I have done nothing substantive to establish my own preferred, non-hybrid account of the nature of song.

My response to this objection is again in two parts. The first is that, to the extent that I am trading off anything grand enough to be called 'identity conditions', none that I have mentioned is of such a sort as to require pre-emptive defence. That the rhymes and metre of a poem, or the way that a piece of music sounds, are part of what makes individual poems and pieces of music the ones that they are is, as things stand, just banal. Neither is a metaphysical postulate; neither is a theoretical hypothesis; indeed neither is more than a statement of more or less pre-theoretical common sense, enlisted initially – it will be recalled – to indicate that the hybrid model is inadequate to the task of accounting for some fairly obvious facts about song. This suggests – to me, at least – that the onus is on my critic. I'll worry about the banalities I've mentioned only once I've been given some *independent reason* to think that they might be wrong or misleading. And the fact that they are inconvenient for the hybrid model doesn't amount to that. The second part of my response picks up on a reservation implicit in the first – namely, that I really don't think that I *am* making claims about anything worth calling 'identity conditions'.[27] It would be surprising if the metre of a poem had nothing to do with the poem's identity, to be sure. But what my banality was meant to highlight was that the metre of a poem *matters* to it, primarily in terms of appreciation and understanding: someone who recites Dowson's *Cynara* in a metrically garbled way gives good *prima facie* evidence that, in at least some respects, he has failed to understand the poem that he is reciting. Similarly, someone who sings Delius's *Cynara* with scant regard to the timbres invited by the syllables it contains has, in the absence of some interpretative argument to the contrary, got something wrong. Indeed, this point – and the whole of my response to the objections I've considered – can be encapsulated by asking what, in the relevant ways, an ideal performance of a song before an ideal audience would be like. My position commits me to the following less than earth-shaking thoughts.

1. The singer, unless in possession of intelligence to the effect that what he is singing was intended, against the appearances, as vocalise, should deliver the syllables of the text at least *as if* he understood them as constituents of the relevant words and phrases. (In practice, this thought would tend to favour native speakers.)
2. The audience, unless in possession of the same unusual intelligence,

should attempt to understand what it hears. (Again, this tends to favour native speakers.)

I am committed to no more than this. My opponent, on the other hand, is committed to the (surely uncomfortable) position that at least one, and presumably both, of these thoughts must be false. And that makes me think that autonomania comes at too high a price – or, and to put it no more strongly, it makes me impatient to see the missing arguments.

I have emphasised the modesty of my position throughout, and I should do so again. Am I claiming that there is some single, word-driven way of singing the syllables of a song? No. But I *am* claiming that their being word-driven is (at least often) relevant to understanding why a composer has asked for them to be sung in the way that he has, and so relevant to understanding how to sing them. And I would further claim that this fact makes intelligible, as the autonomanic alternative does not, how and why there might be legitimate – which is to say, reasonable – interpretative divergence: if it were all just 'fa-la-la's, disagreement of the sort that one actually finds simply couldn't arise. Am I claiming that someone who whistles *Cynara* isn't really whistling *it*? Well, in a way. But only in the sense that someone's whistling of *Cynara* doesn't offer the best opportunity to an audience to understand or appreciate Delius's song. It may be the case that the whistler succeeds in rendering the melodic line to perfection: but there is more to Delius's song than that, and that is all that I am saying. Am I claiming that only an English-speaking audience sung to by an English-speaking baritone can hope to understand *Cynara*? No. Am I claiming that *no* song is appropriately to be understood in the way recommended (for all songs) by my opponent? No. It may be the case, and indeed I rather think it is the case, that certain composers, impressed precisely by the autonomanic position whose universality I am denying, have written 'songs' which treat their texts purely as timbre-generating syllables, 'songs', that is, which are most appropriately to be understood as vocalise (I have a feeling that, for example, Webern's op. 18 songs for soprano, guitar and E-flat clarinet may need to be understood in this way). But this, even if true, shows only that vocalise-song-writing is among the alternatives available, for particular musical purposes, to composers wishing to write for the voice; it does *not* show that that alternative is in some way purer or more paradigmatic of the musical 'as such' than any of the others.

As far as I can see, then, I am claiming nothing that should offend any of the intuitions that the vast majority of us who listen to songs, and enjoy them, are at all likely to have – a point which receives support from some surprising quarters. For it is quite clear that the people that I have been arguing against actually, if only in their bones, agree with me. Earlier in this chapter I quoted a passage from Hanslick. Let me quote the end of it again, together with what follows immediately afterwards:

> In a piece of vocal music, the effectiveness of tones can never be so precisely separated from that of words ... as to allow strict sorting of the musical from the poetical ... In a vocal composition, we have an amalgam so perfectly fused that it would be impossible to assay any of its individual constituents.[28]

To which I can only say 'Hear, Hear!' And here is Jerrold Levinson talking about opera:

> My claim is that the standard of musical assessment appropriate to dramatic music is *neither* that appropriate to abstract music *nor* that appropriate to tone painting in the narrow sense. Rather, I suggest, there is a sort of mean between assessing music as strictly autonomous object and assessing it strictly as to representational accuracy and that, further, this is a mode of assessment that counts as an assessment of it *as music*. What I have in mind is the properly musical assessment of an operatic passage *in light of its dramatic function*, as opposed to the purely autonomous, and in such case inappropriate, assessment of the music with *no awareness* or else *total disregard* of its dramatic function.[29]

Again, one would want to second this, and to extend it, *mutatis mutandis*, to cover the sung relation between words and music – as, indeed, in a footnote, Levinson himself suggests that one should! And here, finally, is Peter Kivy:

> There is a temptation to think of vocal music, in the West, as a mixed-media art form. It is, after all, a combination of music and text. But it is both historically and, if I may say so, philosophically misleading to talk this way ... [W]e cannot look at a Renaissance motet, for example, and say: 'this is what the music does, and this is what the words do, and, by consequence, this is what the words and music do together.' That cannot be how the composers thought. Taking the text from the music and looking at them separately is like looking at a kidney in formaldehyde and expecting to see it perform its function.[30]

The fact is that many of the intuitions driving the position that I am defending are fully, if fitfully, acknowledged by precisely those who appear to be committed, when running the official, autonomanic line, to suppressing or falsifying them.

How is one to account for this? The first thing to be clear about is that there is nothing in the thought that music for instruments alone is in some sense 'pure' that entails the misrepresentation of song as a more or less unequal hybrid of words and music. One could, that is, be fully persuaded that instrumental music really is best to be understood as abstract, absolute, autonomous, and still say all of the right kinds of things about song. Indeed, the last three passages quoted show people doing just that. (Nor, as a corollary, is there anything in the position that I have been defending with respect to song to suggest that the absolute autonomy position is unsustainable with respect to purely instrumental music.) Things only go wrong when the character and force of the absolute autonomy position is overstated. Hanslick's overstatement of it is both seminal and typical: 'whatever can be asserted of instrumental music holds good for all music as such ... Of what *instrumental music* cannot do, it ought never be said that *music* can do it, because only instrumental music is music purely and absolutely.' With this step, signalled by the arrival on the scene of the notion of the 'purely' musical 'as such', we have moved from the absolute autonomy position to full-blown autonomania. But the step is quite unjustified. It no more follows from the fact (if it is one) that 'only instrumental music is music purely and absolutely' that if '*instrumental music*' cannot do something, '*music*' cannot do it, than it follows from the fact (if it is one) that only dead bodies are bodies 'purely and absolutely' that if dead bodies cannot do something, *bodies*, for instance living ones, can't do it either (or than it follows from the fact, if it is one, that only distilled water is water 'purely and absolutely' that if distilled water cannot do it, neither can, say, 'fire-water' or holy water). It is one thing, in other words, to claim that *whatever* 'can be asserted of instrumental music holds good for all music' (and for the moment I have no quarrel with that claim);[31] but it is quite another thing to claim that *only* what can be asserted of instrumental music can be asserted of any music at all. And it is this latter claim, for which an independent argument is required, although none is ever given, which is, first, constitutive of autonomania, and, second, responsible for the ways of thinking about song that I have objected to.

But why is the slip between the 'whatever' claim and the 'only' claim apparently so easy to make? The answer, I think, lies in a combination of two factors. First, with purely instrumental music one appears to have hit a kind of bed-rock, a form of music that has been pared down to its bare essentials. And it is a smallish-seeming step from this thought to the thought that one has run up against the *essence* of music ('as such'). Smallish-seeming, maybe – but still illicit; for it doesn't in the least follow from the fact that something has been stripped down to what might perfectly harmlessly be termed its 'bare essentials' that the thing in question even *has* an essence, let alone that these 'bare essentials' are what that essence is. The second factor is evaluative: the greatest pieces of purely instrumental music are widely felt to be (or at least to represent the majority of) the greatest pieces of music that there are. And this, by another small but illicit step, encourages the thought that the standards appropriate to understanding and assessing music 'as such' must be those appropriate to understanding and assessing these great works, music's finest moments. But it simply doesn't follow from the fact that such-and-such a standard is appropriate to the understanding and assessment of a sub-set of a class that the same standard is appropriate to under-standing and assessing the class as a whole.[32] Taken together, however, this pair of unwarranted thoughts – that instrumental music represents the essence of music as such and that the standards relevant to the understanding and assessment of instrumental music must be appropriate to the understanding and assessment of music as such – gets one across the gap separating the modest enough claim that *whatever* 'can be asserted of instrumental music holds good for all music' from the extra-vagant, autonomanic claim that *only* what can be asserted of instru-mental music can be asserted of any music at all. It goes without saying that I think that one should stay on the modest side of the gap.[33]

III. Appropriateness

Delius's *Cynara* is a piece of music that includes words. How, then, is it to be understood and appreciated? Here, as we've seen, the hybrid model of song has its own distinctively misleading kind of contribution to make, enjoining the understanding and appreciation of song as a combination of two mutually independent sorts of component, words and music. I hope that I have said enough in the previous sections to suggest that that picture is unsustainable, and why. It must be acknow-ledged, however, that even once one is committed to rejecting it, the hybrid model does continue to stalk the margins; and this is for the simple reason that the text and music of a song – although not, as I have argued, finally abstractable from one another – are nonetheless distin-guishable, at least in a crude and approximate way. And this creates the temptation to talk as if the hybrid model were adequate after all. Specifically, it creates the temptation to talk as if what were at issue in understanding and appreciating a given song is the *match* (or lack of it) between text and music – and this of course is to presuppose that the text and the music are two fully *separate* things. That this is how (intermittently conscious) supporters of the hybrid model speak is something that we have already seen. Recall the final two of Levinson's six questions: the fifth quite explicitly talks about the '*match*' between music and text, while the sixth, although mentioning what Levinson calls '*an expressive whole*', still construes that 'whole' as being 'formed by the musical and verbal components in combination'. Nor is Levinson alone. Peter Kivy, too, when he's not talking about kidneys in formaldehyde, thinks like this. He repeatedly refers to 'the match or mismatch of music to text',[34] and endorses the view that, in song, 'the *music* maintains whatever expressiveness it may (or may not) have had apart from the text.'[35] If we are to make any headway with the understanding and appreciation of song, then, we will have to be careful not to slip into this way of thinking.

One can see why it is, though, that the idea of a 'match' between the allegedly separate 'components' of song has been found so seductive. For it is unquestionably the case that some settings can be, and others can fail to be, *appropriate*, where appropriateness, other things being equal, is a virtue. And a naturally tempting way to think about the notion of appropriateness is to construe it as a kind of matching: the words and text of a song are appropriate to one another, it is tempting to say, if they match one another. For the reasons I've given, however, this temptation should be resisted – which leaves me with an obligation to provide an account of the (important) notion of 'appropriateness' that doesn't, explicitly or implicitly, boil down to talk of matching.

As a way into such an account, let me note a couple of cases in which talk of matching does make sense, although not of a sort that establishes that the relevant notion of appropriateness (as, other things being equal, a virtue) depends on it. Recall Levinson's third question: 'How well,' he asks, 'does the music of a song, particularly the vocal line, *conform* to the 'natural music' of the words and phrases of the text?' By 'natural music' Levinson means exactly the sorts of things that I described earlier as 'musical qualities' – metre, rhyme, alliteration and so forth. By 'conform to' Levinson clearly means 'match'. And by 'text' he evidently means 'poem', that is, the words as they were *before* they were set to music (otherwise his distinction between 'the music of a song, particularly [its] vocal line', and 'the text' is unintelligible). This last observation is the crucial one. I have no problem at all with the thought that the vocal line of a song might or might not be said to match the 'natural music' of the poem that it sets. But since, as I argued in the previous section, that poem is *not* the text of the song, the presence or absence of any such match is of no evident significance. It may be, as a matter of fact, that the musical qualities of a poem do survive its transformation into the text of some particular song largely intact: this is arguably the case in Schubert's setting of *Die Forelle*, for instance. But this, if so, really is just a matter of fact; and that it certainly carries with it no normative or virtuous implications is brought out forcefully by the ('musical') superiority of the text of Delius's *Cynara* over Dowson's poem of the same name.[36] The point here is that, while talk of matching (or mis-matching) in this context may be perfectly comprehensible, one of the parties to the putative match – the 'natural music' of the poem – bears only an extrinsic, contingent relation to the *song* being assessed, and so can make no direct contribution to that assessment. (And if one does concentrate on the song, of course, there is no longer anything to be said about matching: the words *as sung* have, quite simply, whatever musical qualities the singing *of* them has. There are not two things here.[37])

The second kind of matching I want to mention is less straight-forward. In this case the thought is that, in an appropriate setting, the expressive meaning of the song matches the expressive meaning of the poem that has been set. This could mean at least two things. First, it might mean that there is, in some sense, a direct correspondence between the two. But that, even if it were to be realised, would be of no more significance than any putative match between (the music of) a song and the 'natural music' of its (unset) words, and on just the same grounds. If the expressive meaning of a poem is a product partly of its 'natural music', as it surely is, then there can be no presumption at all, normative or otherwise, that that meaning should survive the poem's transformation into the text of a song, and so no reason to attach any particular significance to such matching as there is or might be between that meaning and the expressive meaning of the song. Or, second, it might mean that the music of the song takes up and exploits something of the atmosphere of the expressive meaning of the poem it sets. So, for example, one might feel it to be a noteworthy and commendable fact about Delius's *Cynara* that it exploits and augments the nostalgic yearning of Dowson's words, while also, in its passages for solo violin, giving us a more tangible hint of Cynara herself.

This point needs to be treated with some care. One way of taking it marks no advance over the previous suggestion. If the thought is that the expressive atmosphere of the poem, which the song in some way matches, is an atmosphere which that poem has *as read*, then we are back with precisely those musical qualities which may or may not survive the poem's transformation into a text; and this means that we have been given no reason to think that the song's matching of that atmosphere is in any way a significant (or meritorious) fact about it. The point only becomes potentially substantial, then, first, if the 'expressive meaning' of a poem is not, or is not primarily, a function of its 'natural music' (since the 'natural music' of a poem may be of no significance once the poem has become a song-text); and, second, if that meaning is distinguishable from the expressive meaning of the words of the poem *as sung* in the relevant song (otherwise there won't be two separable parties to the putative match).

Can these conditions be met? One suggestion certainly won't do. However superficially tempting, it certainly won't do to offer the sequence of words that the poem and text share as the bearer of the poem's expressive meaning – even if that would open up gaps of the right general sort between that meaning and the poem's 'natural music,' on the one hand, and between that meaning and the expressive meaning of those words as sung, on the other. It won't do, however, because a mere string of words, uninflected, whether by punctuation, intonation or period, is unlikely to have any settled meaning at all, let alone any expressive meaning. (Consider the loss of meaning sustained when, for example, the first three lines of *Cynara's* third verse are presented as a mere verbal string: 'I have forgot much cynara gone with the wind flung roses roses riotously with the throng dancing to put thy pale lost lilies out of mind'.) No. The only possible way of meeting the relevant conditions that I can see is to take the expressive meaning of the poem to be equivalent to whatever can be captured in a decent paraphrase of it. The thought here is that, since – as I argued in Chapter 1 – what goes missing in the paraphrase of a poem is precisely the *poetry* of it, which is to say, among other things, the 'natural music' of it, what is left is both distinguishable from the poem, but also, because whatever can be under-stood can be paraphrased, the same as the poem, in as much as that – at a relevantly coarse-grained level – the paraphrase and the poem share the same meaning. And because the paraphrase is clearly distinguishable, not only from the poem itself, but also from the poem as transformed into the text of a song, one can now, at least on the face of it, ask whether *this* meaning – the one captured in the paraphrase – is 'matched' by the meaning of the song. By these means, it would seem, we have arrived at a sense of appropriateness which first, and other things being equal, is a virtue (the presumption must be that a composer who sets a poem *as* a poem, rather than as a string of timbre-generating syllables, has at least some interest in what it means); and, second, is a form of 'matching'. A setting is appropriate, on this account, if the meaning of the song matches the meaning of the poem it sets, as captured in a decent paraphrase of it.[38]

There is, I think, something right about this suggestion – and also, importantly, quite a lot that is wrong. What is right about it is that it gives one a way of understanding why – to take a famous example – Gluck's *Che farò senza Euridice* strikes one as a hopelessly inappropriate setting of its words, while Delius's *Cynara* does not. Gluck's chirpily upbeat setting of Orfeo's 'I have lost her, I have lost her, I have lost my Euridice' – which in any minimally adequate paraphrase must surely come out on the unhappy side, to put it no higher – can hardly fail to jar, while Delius's nostalgic way with Dowson's poem – itself unparaphraseable, one would think, without at least *some* hint of nostalgia – seems, at this level anyway, entirely apt. And this (real) distinction has been made possible to draw, via the notion of paraphrase, without assuming that appropriateness (or the lack of it) resides in a match (or lack of it) between a song and the *poem* it sets. To this extent, the present suggestion does have something going for it.

But it is still inadequate. Specifically, it does not – cannot – show that appropriateness is, in the relevant sense, a matter of *matching*. The reason for this, crudely, is that while the notion of 'a decent paraphrase' is both intelligible and sufficiently normative to underwrite the rather coarse evaluative distinction between the Gluck and Delius songs drawn above, it is not, and cannot be made to be, fine-grained enough to do the real work demanded of it. Consider the following example. Suppose that, instead of the aching arch-shape that Delius has the baritone sing on the third appearance of the words 'I have been faithful to thee, Cynara! in my fashion', he had instead decided to set those words as he does on their final appearance, at the end of the last verse. It is just not plausible to think that comparison with a paraphrase, even a very decent one indeed, could possibly underwrite the judgement that every listener must surely arrive at, namely, that the choice that Delius in fact made was the more appropriate one. (Anyone sceptical about this should try imagining a smaller change to Delius's original.) The point here is not simply that the specificity of any (decent) paraphrase is more or less bound to be outstripped by the specificity of any (decent) setting, although that is true, and is enough by itself to disqualify the present suggestion as a remotely adequate account of appropriateness. No: the point is rather that the present suggestion just misidentifies the *kind* of judgement that a judgement of appropriateness is.

The truth of this last claim can be brought out by leaning for a moment on the notion of 'decent' as I have been attaching it to the notion of 'paraphrase'. What might 'decent' possibly mean here? The answer, surely, is that it must mean 'appropriate'. And what might make a paraphrase appropriate to the poem it paraphrases? The answer had better not be a 'match' of any sort; otherwise we are launched straight into a regress, where any judgement of appropriateness presupposes a prior judgement of matching which itself requires a judgement of appropriateness underwritten by a judgement of matching, and so on. What this suggests, clearly enough, is that the notion of appropriateness is *more basic* than the notion of matching, and so is not to be analysed in terms of it. And this is why, in the example offered above, the judgement that Delius's way of setting the final line of the third verse of *Cynara* is more appropriate than the suggested alternative was backed up only by appeal to what the *listener* must conclude, that is, by appeal to nothing *more* than, or outside of, the listener's experience of Delius's song. (The proof of the pudding, as one might put it, lies in the eating of it, not in any relation – for instance, a 'matching' relation – between the eating of it and something else.) The judgement that a setting is appropriate, then, is not to be vindicated (or refuted) by appeal to factors external to the setting itself.

So what *is* an 'appropriate' setting? The right answer, I think, is suggested if we return for a moment to the argument of Chapter 1. There, I showed how the notion of paraphrase, together with the notion of 'matching', is germane to one of the two senses of the word 'understanding', a sense that I called 'external'. And what we have just seen, in effect, is the inability of that sense (by itself) to capture what we mean when we commend a setting for its appropriateness. But, as I argued in the first chapter, one should not expect *either* sense of under-standing to operate alone. Both senses are required. And this indicates that the right answer to the question is that an appropriate setting is one that evinces an (internal) understanding of the poem set, by transform-ing it, in the setting, into *this* text rather than that. On this conception, then, the understanding in question just *is* the song's text – that is, is nothing more than, above or beyond the words of the poem *as sung* in that song. Which may seem rather a tame conclusion, given the amount of fuss that has led up to it. But if no one is now tempted to try to cash out the notion of 'an understanding' in terms of 'matching', the fuss was worth it. And, in my view, the tameness of what I have just said – that is, the ready, intuitive plausibility of it – not only speaks for its truth, but also represents the pay-off for my perhaps eccentric-seeming determination, until now, to keep a song and the poem that it sets at arm's length from one another. For now a connection of the right sort between the two has been established. In just the way that someone who recites a poem does so well, other things being equal, if he recites it with understanding – that is, if he recites it appropriately – so a composer who sets a poem well does so, other things being equal, if his setting shows that he understands it. And, because we have now put the unhelpful notion of 'matching' behind us, it should no longer come as any sort of surprise to find that the meaning or expressive point of Dowson's *Cynara* as appropriately recited may well be very different from that of Delius's eminently appropriate setting of the same poem.[39] The differences – and they may be significant differences – are due, simply, to the fact that a song, unlike a poem, is a piece of music.

IV. Song as Expressive Music

I conclude this chapter with a brief discussion of the consequences of what I have argued for thinking about the expressive character of song; and I take as my cue an account of that character offered by Peter Kivy.[40] Kivy's basic idea is this: in song, he suggests, 'the text' provides 'an intentionality which serves to particularize the expressiveness of the music'.[41] By 'an intentionality', he means, in effect, a context within which the expressiveness of a song acquires its specificity, and within which it has to be understood. Thus, for example, it is the 'intentionality' provided by Dowson's poem that makes the music of Delius's *Cynara* expressive of yearning *for a lost lover*, specifically, rather than expressive, merely, of some generalised sense of nostalgia. There is clearly *something* right about this suggestion; it does give one a reason to think, after all, what is surely intuitively correct, that songs can – sometimes, at any rate – be expressively more specific than (at least some) pieces of purely instrumental music, and that this fact has at least something to do with the inclusion in songs of words. On Kivy's account, this fact is to be explained by the 'particularising' effect on the music of what he calls 'the text'. But it is plain that Kivy's suggestion cannot be accepted, certainly not without major revision. For by 'the text', after all, he evidently means 'the poem', and by 'the music' of the song he clearly means the music of it construed as purely instrumental.[42] His account is rooted, that is, firmly within the picture of song encouraged by the hybrid model, and so, because the character of both text *and* music are misrepresented by that model, his account cannot hope to do justice to the facts, expressive and otherwise, about songs as properly understood.

So what should one say instead? The answer, baldly, is this. If, as I have argued, the text of a song cannot be specified without reference to the words it comprises *as sung*, and if the music of a song cannot be specified without reference to the singing *of* those words, then it is the words *as sung* that particularise – provide 'an intentionality' for – the singing *of* them. The upshot of this – still baldly – is that 'particularising' is a two-way street: the text and the music particularise one another, so that the 'intentionality' provided by the text is not in the end fully separable from that provided by the music, and vice versa. It is therefore quite wrong to attribute the particularising effect in song, as Kivy does, to 'the text' alone, that is, to the text *qua* poem (which is not of course to say that, without its words, a song would not lack the expressive particularity that it has – obviously it would. Without its words, after all, it would not be the song that it is). But this, as I say, is all rather bald.

A more informative indication of what I mean should emerge through an example. Take Delius's setting of the second line of the opening verse of *Cynara*. And let's first take it as Kivy would have us take it. The relevant line of Dowson's poem – 'There fell thy shadow, Cynara! thy breath was shed' – provides, on Kivy's account, 'an intentionality which serves to particularise the expressiveness of the music'. So, a 'musical line' which might, by itself, have had some sort of generalised connection with melancholy has been given, by the relevant line of Dowson's poem, a particular reference to Cynara's shadow, so that the feelings it expresses are now ('particularised') feelings of melancholy *as occasioned by* Cynara's shadow. This is fine as far as it goes. But it wholly overlooks the fact that the words – 'There fell thy shadow, Cynara! thy breath was shed' – *as sung* not only tell us that Cynara's shadow is what is at issue, but also that that shadow is pale, insubstantial, wraith-like, rather than brooding or dark, and so that the melancholy expressed is occasioned, not simply by Cynara's shadow, but by her shadow *as* pale, insubstantial and wraith-like. It is not, in other words, merely the case that the text particularises the expressiveness of the music, it is also the case that the music particularises the expressiveness of the text. The real expressive specificity of Delius's setting of Dowson's line, then, is indissolubly a function of its words and music taken together – a function, that is, of Delius's setting understood as *song*.

I might do well to leave it at that. But I can't resist pressing the point home by noting how much more explanatory power than Kivy's the account offered here has. Kivy encourages us to accept his account by asking us to agree that it is better able to explain the following four 'critical "facts" of life' than the alternatives (not a major hurdle, actually, given the self-refuting hopelessness of the alternatives that he considers). The first fact of life is this: 'Some musical settings are, by common critical consent, badly suited to the expressive character of their texts';[43] and Kivy's account offers to deal with this fact by claiming, as one would have guessed, that for a setting to be badly suited to its text is for there to be 'a mismatch of the expressive character of the music with the expressive character of the text, with the understanding that the expressive character of music alone is rough-hewn in comparison'.[44] This, however, for reasons that I have set out, can only hope to be convincing at a very coarse-grained level – for instance, with respect to a setting as inappropriate as Gluck's is of *Che farò* (the example that Kivy in fact uses). Anything more fine-grained and critically interesting requires treatment in terms, not of 'mismatching', but of misunderstanding: a setting is 'badly suited' to its text, that is, if it shows that the composer has in some way failed to understand the poem that he has set, where such misunderstandings might range from the very crude to the very, very subtle. Kivy's second critical fact of life is the converse of the first: 'Some musical settings,' he notes, 'are by common critical consent well suited to the 'expression' of their texts'[45] – a fact he accounts for by saying that 'the music roughly matches the text, and the text smooths out the fit.'[46] But this, for reasons already given in this section, simply misses out half the story. The music, just as much as the text, 'smooths out' (what one probably shouldn't call) 'the fit', to the kind of effect, sometimes, as that noted in Delius's setting of the line from *Cynara* discussed above.

The third consideration that Kivy addresses is in some ways more interesting, as well as being rather more revealing of the half-felt discomfort that he clearly experiences with his own position:

> Musicological research, particularly into the music of Bach and Handel, has revealed the re-use of music originally devised for one text, in setting another, with no loss of expressive appropriateness, even when the 'expression' of the texts is quite obviously different, as where Handel uses the music of an Italian secular chamber duet to set the words 'For unto us a son is born …' in *Messiah* (which accounts for the poor musical declamation).[47]

One is tempted to regard Kivy's concluding paranthetical remark as a throwing-in of the towel, as it surely should have been. But he doesn't see it that way. What he in fact offers in response to the case is this:

> My own … view is that music alone makes rough, but palpable expressive distinctions which texts and titles refine. [This view can

thus] accommodate the re-use of music in various expressive contexts, provided they are all similar enough; but [the view] is not so over-accommodating as to allow the music of Verdi's *Requiem* to be appropriate accompaniment for the libretto of *The Student Prince*.[48]

But surely this won't do. What the *Messiah* case really shows, as Kivy all but concedes in his remark about 'poor musical declamation', is that this particular piece of recycling didn't work, that is, that it did not add up to an appropriate setting – a fact which Kivy's coarse-grained thoughts about 'matching' cannot begin to acknowledge properly, let alone do justice to. On the account offered here, by contrast, the *Messiah* setting is simply and straightforwardly inappropriate, a conclusion not only implicitly endorsed by Kivy, but surely endorsable by any sensitive listener. And in (the rare) cases where different poems *are* appropriately set by the 'same' music,[49] the reason is not that the expressiveness of the poems is 'similar enough', although it may be true, in some particular case, that they are indeed similar, but that *each* of the resultant *songs* is convincing – that is, that each of the settings evinces an understanding of the poem set.

Kivy's final fact of critical life, which he accounts for in much the same way as the second (saying that one must 'give some positive role to music in the demarcation of expressive distinctions, while giving the text the role of "fine tuning"'),[50] is that 'There are instances in which the emotive descriptions that critics give of a piece of vocal music go far beyond, in detail, what anyone would accept as a description of "pure" instrumental music, and where the descriptions nevertheless seem appropriate in place.'[51] Whether or not Kivy is right about '"pure" instrumental music', he is certainly right about the detail of 'emotive' description appropriately possible in the context of song: and my account – which has music and words standing to one another in a relationship of mutual 'fine tuning' – is clearly far more able than his to explain and justify the levels of detail in question. Again, my approach – focused, as it is, on issues of (internal) understanding rather than matching – is just far more fine-grained in the dictinctions that it can be enlisted to underwrite.

On every count, it seems to me, the treatment offered here is more convincing, in terms both of explanatory power and intuitive rightness, than Kivy's. And this confirms me in my thought that the debilitating effects of the hybrid model really are quite far-reaching. We have seen in every section of this chapter how that model gets in the way of serious attempts by sensitive listeners to say the sorts of things one ought to want to say about song and its expressive possibilities. And I have suggested that the hybrid model owes its appeal, indeed its near stranglehold on the contemporary philosophical imagination, to a kind of systematic and fallacious over-estimation of the significance of the notion of 'purity', at least as that notion is linked to the phenomenon of music for instruments alone. It is an exaggerated determination to treat that sort of music as basic and fundamental that leads to the misrepresentation of song; and it is the corresponding determination to work outwards from 'tones and their artistic combination', as I put it in the first part of this chapter, that has rendered contemporary philosophy of music more or less incapable of saying anything convincing or consistent about one major variety of musical expression, namely, the variety that includes singing. If its capacity for expressiveness is one main source of music's value, as I believe that it is, then music has surely deserved better from its attendant philosophers than this. I hope that I have given some indication in this chapter of how it might start to receive it.

NOTES

1. Eduard Hanslick, *On the Musically Beautiful*, trans. G. Payzant (Indianapolis, IN: Hackett, 1986), pp. 9–10. It is worth noting that Hanslick's use of the term 'feeling' maps on to what, in contemporary philosophical parlance, would be called 'emotion'; in that vocabulary, the term 'feeling' would most usually be reserved for Hanslick's 'fluctuations of our inner activity'.
2. *Ibid.*, p. 21.
3. *Ibid.*, p. 28.
4. Leonard Meyer, *Emotion and Meaning in Music* (Chicago, IL: University of Chicago Press, 1956). For detailed and devastating criticism of Meyer's position, see Malcolm Budd, *Music and the Emotions* (London: Routledge and Kegan Paul, 1985), chapter 8.
5. Susanne K. Langer, *Feeling and Form* (London: Routledge and Kegan Paul, 1953).
6. Deryck Cooke, *The Language of Music* (Oxford: Oxford University Press, 1959). See Chapter 1 of the present book for further discussion.
7. Donald Ferguson, *Music as Metaphor* (Minneapolis, MN: University of Minnesota Press, 1960), p. 75.
8. Peter Kivy, *The Corded Shell: reflections on musical expression* (Princeton, NJ: Princeton University Press, 1980), p. 68.
9. Carroll Pratt, *The Meaning of Music* (New York, NY: McGraw-Hill, 1931), p. 203.
10. Malcolm Budd, *Values of Art* (London: Allen Lane, 1995), p. 154.
11. Jerrold Levinson, 'Music and Negative Emotion', *Pacific Philosophical Quarterly*, 1982, p. 335.
12. These are, in effect, the answers I gave in my book, *Music, Value and the Passions* (Ithaca, NY: Cornell University Press, 1995).
13. Stephen Davies, *Musical Meaning and Expression* (Ithaca, NY: Cornell University Press, 1994), p. 117.
14. Peter Kivy, *Philosophies of Art* (Cambridge: Cambridge University Press, 1997), p. 154.

15. Hanslick, pp. 14–15 (see Note 1). I return to this passage at greater length in section II, below.
16. This is an example of the sort of undue intimacy between theory and method discussed in the Introduction.
17. In Jerrold Levinson, *Music, Art, and Metaphysics* (Ithaca, NY: Cornell University Press, 1990), pp. 26–36.
18. *Ibid.*, pp. 28–30.
19. Stephen Davies, *Musical Meaning and Expression*, p. 114n (see Note 13).
20. Jerrold Levinson, 'Song and Music Drama', in his *The Pleasures of Aesthetics* (Ithaca, NY: Cornell University Press, 1996), pp. 48–9.
21. Or perhaps not. It might be suggested that the reason that Levinson pays less attention to the text 'as such' is that most songs, in the classical tradition at any rate, set pre-existing texts – texts whose virtues are (1) whatever they are independently of the role of those texts in the songs that set them, and so (2) unlikely to be of primary interest in the assessment of those *songs*. But this suggestion fails, I think, on two counts. First, the fact that a pre-existing text has whatever virtues it has considered independently of its appearance in a song does not show that those virtues are irrelevant to the assessment of the song itself; and, second, plenty of sung music in the classical tradition – for instance, most opera – does *not* set pre-existing texts. So it really is odd not to give as much consideration to the text as to the music.
22. I suppress Delius's repetition of the word 'Dancing' at the beginning of the third line of the third verse. So far as I can see, nothing swings on it.
23. Levinson does mention the possibility, in 'Hybrid Art Forms', of something that he calls a 'synthetic' hybrid, a case in which 'the individual components to some extent lose their original identities and are present in the hybrid in a form significantly different from that assumed in the pure state' (p. 31) (see Note 17). So I suppose he might – despite what he actually says about song – be able to agree with what I have just suggested. For the reasons given, however, the notion of 'hybridity' cannot offer a helpful route to that conclusion.
24. Levinson comes perilously close to flirting with just such a suggestion: 'Song and Music Drama', p. 48 (see Note 20).
25. It is interesting, although I don't know what it shows, that very few works by Delius with the word 'song' or 'songs' in the title are actually settings of texts. *Songs of Farewell* and *Songs of Sunset* are exceptions; but for the most part – *Paris – the Song of a Great City, Song of the High Hills, A Song before Sunrise, A Song of Summer*, and so on – the works are either for orchestra alone or for orchestra and wordless choir.
26. As, I suspect, would Delius have done. In a letter of 1908 to Ernest Newman, he wrote: 'When shall we have Opera in England? Do you think it will come whilst we are still alive? ... I must say I should like to hear my own musical dramatic works performed in the language they were written in before I disappear.' (At this time, most of Delius's texted works had been performed only on the Continent, and in German translation.)
27. For further discussion of 'identity conditions', and of the general pointlessness, in aesthetic contexts, of invoking them, see Chapter 4.
28. Hanslick, pp. 15–16 (see Note 1).
29. Levinson, 'Song and Music Drama', p. 55 (see Note 20).
30. Peter Kivy, 'Movements and "Movements"', in his *New Essays on Musical Understanding* (Oxford: Oxford University Press, 2001), p. 172.
31. Or rather, I have no quarrel with it so long as it is interpreted very modestly. To return to one of my parallel cases: to say that whatever can be asserted of dead

bodies can be asserted of bodies 'as such' is fine so long as the assertions in question are things like 'is an object', 'has a certain mass', 'occupies a certain location'; it is not fine if the assertions include, for example, 'is inanimate' or 'is fit for burial'. The legitimate assertions are confined to a certain neutral minimum – specifically, to claims which do not prejudge or foreclose the qualities and capacities of the various forms which bodies can, as a matter of fact, take.

32. – unless, of course, the sub-set in question is taken as paradigmatic of the class as such. But, for the reasons I have given, there are no non-arbitrary grounds for assigning that status to purely instrumental music.

33. With the reservations entered in the last footnote but one borne firmly in mind.

34. See, for example, *The Corded Shell* (see note 8, p. 75).

35. *Ibid.*, p. 108.

36. This is not to say that matching, where present, is never a virtue. It may be that, for particular purposes, a composer has set out to capture the 'natural music' of a poem in his setting of it; and if he succeeds, that is to his credit. It is only to say that the presence or absence of such matching is not necessarily, from the perspective of song *in general*, of the remotest evaluative significance.

37. I suspect that Levinson, at least, might agree with this: he speaks at one point of a kind of 'holistic suitability' that 'may not involve matching' – although he doesn't say quite what it might involve instead. See his 'Song and Music Drama', p. 52 (see Note 20).

38. For present purposes, I am going to ignore deliberate cases of (appropriate) mismatch adopted for, for example, ironic or parodic purposes. (See Levinson, 'Song and Music Drama', pp. 49–52, for examples (see Note 20).) It should be clear that what I am about to argue does, *mutatis mutandis*, cover these cases as well.

39. For discussion of interpretative and evaluative pluralism, see Aaron Ridley, 'Critical Conversions', in J. Bermudez and S. Gardner (eds), *Art and Morality* (London: Routledge, 2003), pp. 131–42.

40. And broadly endorsed, incidentally, by Levinson, 'Song and Music Drama', p. 49 (see Note 20).

41. Peter Kivy, *The Corded Shell*, pp. 103–4 (see Note 8).

42. Recall his endorsement, mentioned a moment ago, of the claim that 'the *music* maintains whatever expressiveness it may (or may not) have had apart from the text'.

43. *The Corded Shell*, p. 108 (see Note 8).

44. *Ibid.*, p. 109.

45. *Ibid.*, p. 108.

46. *Ibid.*, p. 109.

47. *Ibid.*, p. 108.

48. *Ibid.*, p. 110.

49. I do not consider in detail here the case of (rigidly) strophic songs, songs in which successive verses are all set identically. Two brief remarks are in order, however. First, since the words of each verse are (presumably) different, the 'music' of each verse is, to that extent, also different. And second, the effect of the 'same' music on its fourth appearance, say, is not the same as it is on its first. For these reasons, among others, I doubt that any counter-example to what I am claiming is likely to emerge from this direction.

50. *The Corded Shell*, p. 111 (see Note 8).

51. *Ibid.*, pp. 108–9.

4

Performance

Every notation is, in itself, the transcription of an abstract idea. The instant the pen seizes it, the idea loses its original form ... From this first transcription to a second the step is comparatively short and unimportant. And yet it is only the second, in general, of which any notice is taken ... Again, the performance of a work is also a transcription, and still, whatever liberties it may take, it can never annihilate the original. For the musical art-work exists, before its tones resound and after they die away, *complete and intact* ... both within and outside of time. (Feruccio Busoni, *Sketch of a New Aesthetic of Music*)

PART 1. BACKGROUND

Recent philosophical interest in issues surrounding musical performance has been fuelled, I think it is fair to say, by two main factors, one self-evidently philosophical, the other arising from a minor revolution in musical performance practice. The first factor was the publication of Nelson Goodman's *Languages of Art*,[1] a book which had some surprising and trenchant things to say about the conditions that a performance of a work needed to meet in order to count *as* a performance of it. The second factor was the emergence of the so-called 'authentic perform-ance movement', a movement of musicians devoted to creating performances of music from the past informed by the most up-to-date musicological and historical research. As I will try to show, these factors – although entirely independent of one another at source – have come together in the philosophical literature to produce a distinctive, if not actually hegemonic, way of thinking about musical performance in general. It is a style of thought that pushes ontological questions to the forefront.

Nelson Goodman argued as follows. A musical work, he held, is identical to the score in which it is notated. The score thus 'defines' the work.[2] It follows from this that 'complete compliance with the score is the only requirement for a genuine instance of a work' – or, to put it rather more strikingly, that even 'the most miserable performance without actual mistakes [counts] as such an instance, while the most brilliant performance with one wrong note does not'.[3] This, not surprisingly, has struck most readers as wildly implausible. If it were correct, after all, it would mean that some of the most venerated recorded 'performances' in existence – for instance, Arthur Schnabel's recordings of Beethoven's piano sonatas – couldn't be performances of the works they were supposed to be of at all. Schnabel's Beethoven recordings, to stick with the example, are notoriously technically wobbly, with fistfuls of wrong notes, if not on every page, then certainly in every sonata. And yet his readings have long been held to be among the most insightful and moving that there are. And can it really be right to think, for instance, that until the final chord of a given work has been played (and played correctly) it is an open question whether what one is hearing is a performance of *that* work at all? Surely not. But Goodman is of course aware that these will be the responses to his position. 'Could we not,' he asks, 'bring our theoretical vocabulary into better alignment with common practice and common sense by allowing some limited degree of deviation in performances admitted as instances of a work?' But the answer, he holds is, no, we couldn't. For:

> this is one of those cases where ordinary usage gets us quickly into trouble. The innocent-seeming principle that performances differing by just one note are instances of the same work risks the consequence – in view of the transitivity of identity – that all performances whatsoever are of the same work. If we allow the least deviation, all assurance of work-preservation ... is lost; for by a series of one–note errors of omission, addition, and modification, we can go all the way from Beethoven's *Fifth Symphony* to *Three Blind Mice*. Thus while a score may leave unspecified many features of a performance, and allow for considerable variation in others within prescribed limits, full compliance with the specifications given is categorically required.[4]

So Schnabel's Beethoven recordings, although doubtless to be regarded as 'performances' of the sonatas in 'ordinary usage', really cannot, in the strict sense required by theory, be regarded as 'instances' of those works at all.

No one, so far as I am aware, has thought that Goodman is right about this. The general feeling has been that any theory *this* seriously at odds with the intuitions shared by more or less everyone who has ever listened to or played a piece of music must be (and whatever 'the transitivity of identity' might suggest) mistaken. It must be noted, however, that Goodman is driven to conclude as he does by reasons that are, in the end, peculiar to his own highly distinctive theoretical priorities – in this case, most proximately, by a markedly rarefied and abstract conception of what it is for something to count as a 'notational system'.[5] It is his thinking about 'notational systems', that is, that both leads him to the views about performance that he espouses, and leaves him relaxed in the face of their extremely counter-intuitive character. This suggests two things. First, there can be no mileage, as some have thought there might be,[6] in construing Goodman's very stringent require-ment as a regulative, rather than a constitutive, ideal – as a recommenda-tion, in other words, about what one should be aiming at in giving a performance (getting all the notes right), rather than as a condition of one's performance counting *as* a performance of what it was meant to be of. It might very well be true that one should try to play all the right notes. But this fact, if it is one, is entirely extrinsic to the character of Goodman's concerns, and so cannot be enlisted to render the conclu-sions he actually draws more palatable. The second thing suggested by Goodman's motivations is that the natural move, if one disagrees with him, must be to declare oneself motivated by different priorities – by musical ones, say – and pass by on the other side. I think that this is in fact the right move to make. There is no need, it seems to me, to be drawn into argument here.

That is not, however, how things have gone. What the literature shows instead is a quite remarkable willingness to take Goodman as having thrown down the gauntlet. What, it is asked, if one disagrees with Goodman's conclusions, *is* a musical work identical to (if not the score in which it is notated)? What *is* it for a performance to be of the work it purports to be of (if not getting all the notes right)? Thinking about musical performance has been assimilated, that is, to asking what might constitute the essence of a musical work, and what identity conditions anything that is taken as an 'instance' of a given work, for example a performance of it, must satisfy. Ontological questions, in other words, have been placed firmly in the front line.

So, for instance, and to tease out just one strand in the post-Goodman literature, a number of broadly Platonist positions have been advanced, in conscious opposition to Goodman's own nominalism. Peter Kivy, for example, has argued for a fairly full-blooded, if forgivably broad-brush, version of Platonism, suggesting that 'works are universals, or types, or kinds, performances related to them as particulars, tokens, or instances';[7] that a 'sound structure' (considered as a universal, type, or kind) is 'a concrete identity criterion' for a work's being the work that it is;[8] and that such sound structures are notated in scores, where a score, 'in a loose sense of "uniquely"':

> uniquely determines a correct performance, under a given set of implicit conventions for interpreting the score − conventions which may be quite different in different historical contexts − and a performance uniquely determines a score under a similar set of historically bound conventions.[9]

Kivy's Platonism, then, identifies a musical work with an (abstract) 'sound structure' and regards as 'correct' any performance that allows that structure − or something 'loosely' like it − to be heard. He also expressly embraces the consequence of his Platonism, namely, that if 'works are universals, or types, or kinds' they can neither come into nor go out of existence, and hence that the 'composing' of works, so construed, must be a matter of discovery rather than creation.[10] It is partly out of a reluctance to accept this sort of conclusion that Jerrold Levinson has proposed a different kind of Platonism.[11] According to this, a work is to be regarded, not merely as a 'sound structure', that is, as 'a sequence of sounds qualitatively defined', but as 'a compound … of a sound structure and a performing-means structure', where the latter is 'a parallel sequence of performing means specified for realising the sounds at each point'. Levinson suggests that we call the resultant compound 'an 'S/PM' structure, for short'.[12] 'S/PM structures', described by Levinson as 'implicit types', include every logically possible combination of sounds in every logically possible combination with every logically possible combination of performing means. Such types are Platonic through and through; they can neither come into nor go out of existence. But not all 'S/PM structures' are works; the overwhelming majority of the possibilities that they represent never have been, and never will be, realised. What distinguishes works from other 'S/PM structures' is that they are what Levinson calls '*initiated* types', that is, types that 'begin to exist only when they are initiated by an intentional human act'. Works, then, as 'initiated types', can be said to be brought into being, created rather than discovered, by the intentional act of composing.[13] A performance of a given work is then specified as 'a sound event that is *intended* to instantiate' the work, that 'represents an attempt to exemplify' the work's

'S/PM structure in accordance with' the composer's 'initiation' of it – 'and which *succeeds to a reasonable degree*.'[14]

These examples should give some indication of the sorts of effort that have been made to address the ontological questions I mentioned a moment ago, while also attempting to avoid some of the counter-intuitive consequences of Goodman's position. There is, so far as I am aware, no consensus – nor even a hint of it – in these matters, except perhaps for a growing feeling that the sheer diversity of things that might, in various times and places, be thought of as music or as performance makes it unlikely that any monolithic account, however tolerant of deviation, will suffice. A more catholic approach to ontology has emerged accordingly[15] – an approach perhaps most comprehensively evinced by Stephen Davies's *Musical Works and Performances*, in which distinctions are drawn between six sorts of thing a work can *be* and between a correspondingly large number of ways in which something might be said to be a performance of it.[16] This does, as I say, represent a development. But it doesn't represent any kind of departure: ontological questions still dominate.

The second factor informing recent philosophical reflection upon musical performance was, as I said at the outset, the rise – from, roughly, the late 1960s to the early 1980s – of the so-called 'authentic performance movement'. Its advocates argued that (then) contemporary performance practices seriously misrepresented music from the past by, among other things, playing it on the wrong instruments, and by playing it with scant regard to any of the stylistic expectations that its composers might plausibly have had. So, for example, the habit of playing Bach's keyboard music on the modern grand piano, an instrument not in existence until more than a century after Bach's death, and sounding completely different in almost every respect from the harpsichords, organs and so forth which Bach might actually have heard, was held radically to misrepresent the character of his music. So was the (then) contemporary habit of playing and singing Bach's larger orchestral and choral works as if they had been written by a rather backward-looking composer in about 1890: music-historical research had shown that early eighteenth-century performance style wasn't like that at all. And – as a corrective – advocates of 'authentic performance' began to play and record music from the past on the 'right' instruments, or reproductions of them, and in the 'right' style. It is difficult, now, to imagine the sheer heat of the controversy that followed their performances, for two reasons. The first is that, for better or worse, they won the stylistic argument, at least to a very large extent. It wasn't long before players of even the 'wrong' instruments were paying lip-service to the findings of music-historical research, and not a lot longer after that before a more or less 'authentic' approach to performance style (if not, always, to choice of instrument) had become the norm. The other reason is that people have, since those early performances, had time to learn how to play their instruments properly. The truly horrible sounds that pioneeringly 'authentic' performances made – astringent strings, plinkety keyboards and plainly laughable brass and winds, all played by less than first-rate musicians – are no longer to be heard.[17] At the time, these noises provided opponents of 'authentic performance' with their most compelling argument: no one, they rightly thought, could possibly want to listen to *this* while decent, cultured playing of the same music was available elsewhere. And also at the same time, of course, advocates of 'authentic performance' had to pretend to find – or, still worse, actually did find – the sonic horrors on offer 'thrilling', 'revelatory' and full of 'fresh insights'. Now, however, a quarter of a century or so later, it has turned out that the astringency, plinketiness and laughableness were all largely avoidable. First-rate musicians have found out how to play the relevant instruments well (and instrument makers to make better reproductions of them), and, although there are still undeniable differences in timbre between those instruments and their modern successors, to play them in ways that are least acceptable to devotees of the latter. So if the 'authentic performance movement' triumphed, to a large extent, in matters of style, its own increasing competence ensured that it also reached some sort of accommodation with (i.e. measured up to the standards of) those who initially opposed it. Nowadays, as a result, there's no longer much of a fuss.

It is easy to see how this debate both fuelled and fitted into the prevailing habits of philosophical thought. If it were true, after all, that anachronistic performance practices really did radically misrepresent works from the past, mightn't that mean that certain aspects of historically appropriate practice are in fact integral to a work's identity? Or – from the other side – if it were true that 'authentic' performing practices really did yield results such as those to be heard in the (then) pioneering efforts at reproducing them, mightn't that mean – in light of the altogether more musical results to be achieved through allegedly anachronistic performance practices – that the real essence of a given work transcends any way of performing it at all? Battle was joined; and much was and still is said about, for example, whether or not, or to what extent, a composer's intentions are constitutive of his compositions; whether or not, or to what extent, instrumentation is essential to a work's identity;

whether or not, or to what extent, historically appropriate listening habits contribute to the determination of a work's essential properties; whether or not, or to what extent, a work can survive transcription or arrangement; and so on. And, to pick up on my protagonists of a moment ago, those who, like Kivy (or, in a different way, Goodman), thought or think that preserving work identity in performance is a matter, essentially, of producing the right sequence of pitches (whether 'loosely' or absolutely) have tended to be relatively hostile to the ideals represented by 'authentic performance'.[18] While those who, like Levinson, think that the preservation of work identity involves, for instance, the production of the right sequence of pitches via the originally specified 'performing means', have tended to be relatively hospitable.[19] On either side, though, the issues raised, and the positions invited, have been taken to be overwhelmingly ontological in character.

I think that this is a mistake. Indeed, I think that the whole move to ontology in thinking about musical performance is a mistake, and I shall have some stern things to say about it in the second part of this chapter. Before proceeding, though, I should make clear how I will be taking the term 'performance' from now on – which is to say, very broadly. By 'performance' I will mean not only the playing of a work by an individual or group before an audience, but also recordings, transcriptions, arrangements, versions and, in general, renditions of every kind. I take my lead in this from Peter Kivy, who argues, first, that a performance is 'an arrangement or version of the musical work that has been performed, and, as such, a subject of the kind of evaluation and aesthetic satisfaction that artworks support and provide', and, second, that the 'performer is an artist, somewhat akin to a composer or, better, "arranger" of musical works.'[20] The relatively capacious conception of performance that results will allow me, I hope, to make the argument I want to make in a reasonably direct manner, without getting bogged down in (or indeed, for that matter, traducing) such finer-grained details as might or might not be at issue.

PART 2. *CHACONNE*

Feruccio Busoni (1866–1924) was a virtuoso pianist and a composer of large ambition, an ambition which, in his longer works, tended some-times to outstrip his achievement. He was also a devotee of the practice of transcription, of arranging or recomposing for one instrument music originally written for another. At this he was a master. His primary subject of transcription was, boldly enough, J. S. Bach, almost certainly the most revered musician of his or any other age. And the best of Busoni's Bach-transcriptions are, quite simply, breathtaking. Busoni made piano transcriptions of organ works by Bach, of sacred cantatas, of orchestral works, and, perhaps most famously of all, of the *Chaconne* movement from Bach's Partita No. 2 for solo violin. This movement is widely held to be Bach's single most sustained and concentrated musical utterance – a veritable pinnacle of the art, in other words. There are other transcriptions of it. Versions have been done for lute, for guitar, for clarinet and for orchestra, for instance, and, in typically self-abnegating mood, by Brahms for piano, to be played with the left hand alone. There is something to be said for the Brahms transcription. In restricting himself to what can be done at the piano with just one hand, he captured something of the technical stretch and difficulty of Bach's original, which often – and to great effect – has the violin operating close to the limits of its capabilities. As a result, the Brahms, like the original Bach, conveys a real sense of technical embattlement. Unlike the Bach original, however, Brahms's version of embattlement has a rather dour and dogged air about it, and it is hard, in the end, not to feel that his transcription has somehow diminished Bach's music. Busoni's transcription is a salutary contrast. Incomparably less faithful to the letter of Bach's music, he nevertheless succeeds in capturing the sheer scale of the piece in a way that Brahms doesn't come close to, and in showing how its ferociously intellectual processes can be reimagined for keyboard without sounding merely reverent or dutiful. I say 'keyboard' rather than 'piano', moreover; and this points to another striking aspect of Busoni's transcription. The piano didn't exist when Bach was composing, and Busoni clearly felt that the keyboard for which Bach's chaconne would most naturally be transcribed was Bach's own instrument, the organ – or certainly his transcription suggests that he felt this. It is as if he had first imagined Bach's violin original as it might sound transcribed for organ, and had then transcribed that – the (imaginary) organ version – for piano. The piano sonorities he gives us are organ-like throughout, and in the octave-doublings, register-shifts and handling of the bass line one finds precisely the techniques that Busoni used when transcribing works that were, actually, organ works first. This, then, is a transcription that is really, or at any rate sounds as if it is really, a double-transcription. And all this before any issues of performance arise – before anyone has got around, that is, to giving us a played rendition of a piece for piano that is a rendition of a non-existent piece for organ that is a rendition of the piece for violin that Bach originally wrote. It is, at least on the face of it, exactly the sort of case that ought to respond maximally to a good account of performance, or rendition; and it is, of course, just such an account that I hope, in the remainder of this chapter, to begin to sketch in. In the first section, I say some of the stern things I promised to say about the move to ontology, and show, I think, that such a move has no place in the philosophy of music. In section II I say the remainder of those stern things. And in the final section I try to suggest what, once ontology is out of the way, one might want to say about the Bach–Busoni *Chaconne*.

I. Against Ontology

When was the last time you came away from a performance of a piece of music – live or recorded – seriously wondering whether the performance had been of *it*? My guess is, never. Even if you were to hear the Bach–Busoni *Chaconne* as played by me, or by some comparably giftless pianist,[21] it still would not occur to you to doubt that the victim of the musical murder you had witnessed was, indeed, the *Chaconne*. In fact, if it were played any worse, in such a way that the victim was actually unidentifiable, there would be no reason to think that you had witnessed any sort of performance at all – no reason to think, that is, that you had witnessed a performance *of* anything. Indeed, it is precisely because doubts of the relevant sort have next to no tendency to arise that muzak'd versions of, say, the *Ode to Joy* theme have the power to enrage and depress that they do. One would not suffer as one does in elevators and supermarkets if the doubts were real. One would not be reduced to misanthropic cursings, to mutterings of 'How *could* they? How *dare* they?', if it really did strike one as a serious possibility that the miserable, denatured pap oozing from the speakers was not the Beethoven after all. It clearly *is* the Beethoven, and that is why it makes one feel so low and vicious. In cases like these, then, one's doubts are not about what a rendition is *of* – far from it – but about whether any penalty could feasibly reflect the gravity of the offence. These thoughts, admittedly much understated, suggest two conclusions. The first is that, in our ordinary – indeed in our actual – aesthetic encounters with renderings of pieces of music, our primary concern, or at the very least one of our most prominent concerns, is whether a given rendition is any good; or, if it isn't, whether it is so bad as to merit further action. As listeners, that is, we are chiefly alert and sensitive to issues about the value of what we are hearing. The second conclusion is that, since these sensitivities are operative, and even virulent, against the background of an apparently rather robust sense of work–identity, issues concerning work-identity can hardly be very urgent if what we are chiefly interested in is our aesthetic experience of renditions of pieces of music. If we are doing aesthetics, that is, ontological questions deserve a place in the back row, at best.

I think that both of these conclusions are correct. Neither, however, commands evidently overwhelming support from contemporary philosophers of music, as a moment's reflection on the material covered in the Background part of this chapter will confirm. What we find there is, essentially, a range of views about the room for manoeuvre that a performance has before it ceases to be a performance of what it was supposed to be of, backed up by a range of views about what constitutes a work's essence or identity. From this sort of starting point, it is hardly surprising that the closest we get to evaluative questions are confined questions of legitimacy – to asking whether this or that performance of a given work is faithful enough to whatever happen to be the favoured set of identity conditions to count as acceptable, legitimate instances of performances *of* it. The question whether this or that performance, or style of performance, is actually any good, or is minimally worth listening to, is scarcely raised.[22]

If one is serious about the philosophy of music, this last fact should strike one as scandalous. Not as inexplicable, perhaps: philosophers are drawn to metaphysics, and the chance to go on about identity conditions, and related ontological matters, has possibly been found too good to pass up. But one really ought to be shocked, even so. The most direct way to bring out why, perhaps, is to note that an indifference to genuinely evaluative issues – to issues that animate the experience of actual listeners when they listen to actual pieces of music – presupposes a sharp distinction between what it is to take a philosophical interest in music and what it is to take a critical interest in it. It is true that such a distinction can be drawn. It is true, that is, that the philosophy of music is not identical to music criticism. But the distinction is not, and cannot be made to be, a sharp one, for unless one's philosophical engagement with music is driven by, and is of a sort that might pay dividends for, one's musical experience – including one's evaluative experience – there is no obvious sense in which one is engaged in philosophical *aesthetics* at all. At best, and instead, one might be engaged in the metaphysics of music, and that is a very different activity.

I can imagine two kinds of response to what I have just said. The first is simply to grant that what is being done is indeed musical metaphysics rather than musical aesthetics. If one has made no attempt to do aesthetics, after all, how much of a scandal can it be that one's results are aesthetically inert?[23] I propose, for the moment, to accept this response – although I'll be coming back to it. It is the second response, however, that most self-avowed philosophers of music are likely to reach for. According to this, one cannot hope to do justice to the kinds of evaluative concern that I have mentioned unless one has got one's metaphysics – one's ontology – into good shape first. There is no point, that is, in asking whether a performance of such-and-such is of any value until one has determined that that performance is, indeed, *of* such-and-such; and this means that one must first work out what it *is* to be such-and-such, that is, determine the relevant identity conditions, and then satisfy oneself that the putative performance meets them. Only after that has been done, the response concludes, can one ask whether the performance is, aesthetically, any good. First things first.

This way of thinking strikes me as quite profoundly mistaken; and the examples I've already given, the muzak example especially, show why. Imagine yourself seized with a furious sadness at some particularly vile, beat-enhanced, edges-smoothed-over version of the *Ode to Joy* theme. And now imagine yourself thinking as the second response invites you to. On the face of it, things could go in either of two ways, depending on whether one takes one's ontology prescriptively or descriptively. Taken prescriptively, one might decide that what one was hearing did not meet one's own rather stringent conditions for work-identity, that is, that the muzak wasn't really, and despite appearances, a rendition of Beethoven's theme at all. But in which case, why the rage? Or – and still prescriptively – one might decide that the muzak did meet one's conditions, in which case it is hard to see how that decision, given one's enraged response, has left one any the wiser. And taken descriptively the result is the same: one's enraged response shows either that one's identity conditions are wrong (if the muzak doesn't satisfy them) or that they are superfluous (if it does) – superfluous in the sense that their deployment is not any sort of precondition of pointfully raising questions of aesthetic value. This way of thinking is surely a matter of putting misleading or redundant things first, not first things.

It will be objected, no doubt, that I have stacked the deck in my favour by stipulating that what one hears fills one with rage and depression. It is only this stipulation, after all, that makes pre-emptive ontological beavering look either misleading or redundant. But this objection has force, clearly enough, only if ontological considerations, in musical contexts, are allowed to trump one's experience of what one actually hears. And the single case in which that possibility has any potential bite is the first one I considered – where one decides, on prescriptive work-identity grounds, that what one is hearing isn't the *Ode to Joy* theme at all, and therefore, presumably, that one shouldn't (necessarily) mind it. But here, I have to say, I begin to lose touch with what might be being said. In the sort of example I'm imagining – which is to say, a case where the *Ode to Joy* theme is clearly being murdered – one could only, surely, decide that it wasn't that theme after all if it had first occurred to one that it might be, if it sounded enough like it to be worth giving it the ontological once-over for that possibility, specifically. But now it looks as if the decision to deny the title *Ode to Joy* to what one is hearing (assuming that that is the decision one arrives at) can't be anything more than an elliptical and rather unhelpful way of expressing one's disapproval at what has been done to Beethoven's original. The idea of wondering, perfectly seriously, and from scratch, as it were, whether the prevailing ontological conditions are such as to warrant one's disapproval is either impossible to understand, it seems to me, or else a symptom of something close to aesthetic autism.

But perhaps I'm tilting at straw men here. Perhaps the position I should be considering is not, as I've been assuming, that one must always, in every case, get one's ontology straight before evaluative questions can pointfully be raised, but rather that evaluative questions will, in general, be more perspicuously framed if raised against the backdrop of a convincing ontology. It is possible, I think, to discern the outlines of such a thought in the following passage from Peter Kivy, who is wondering whether it is desirable that a performer should attempt to realise a composer's intentions. It 'all comes down,' Kivy concludes, to having 'an adequate analysis of the musical work.' But, he continues:

> I have no such analysis of the nature of the musical work to offer or endorse that would either enfranchise or disenfranchise ... intentions ... as part of the musical work. In lieu of such an analysis, since [such an analysis] must constitute the heart of the best argument I can think of for the view that realising the composer's ... intentions is, for performance, an end in itself, I shall conclude, at least for the purposes of this book ... [that the realisation of] the composer's ... intentions must be evaluated ... in terms of its [aesthetic] payoff.[24]

Kivy's line of thought, that is, appears to be that while one would, in the best of all possible worlds, have a decently worked out ontology in place first, one can, if one lacks such an ontology, still attempt to raise evaluative questions, even if one is hardly ideally placed to do so. The implication, clearly enough, is that while one can, as it were, make the best of a bad job of framing of one's evaluative questions in the absence of a convincing ontology, one would be altogether better off if such an ontology were in place. And if this is right, it might be thought, metaphysically inclined philosophers of music need neither be flummoxed in the face of their muzak-inspired paroxysms, supposing they have them, nor fearful for their status as aestheticians.

On the face of it, there is no doubt that this modified and more modest position is an improvement on its predecessor. But it is still deeply unpersuasive. How, exactly, is a convincing ontological backdrop supposed to lend perspicuity to evaluative questions? No one, so far as I am aware, has actually asked this. Certainly no one has given any sort of explicit answer. But we can begin to see how such an answer might go from something that Stephen Davies says:

> To be of a work, a performance must satisfy three conditions. There must be a suitable degree of matching between the performance and the work's contents, the performers must intend to follow most of the instructions specifying the work in question ... and there must be a robust causal chain from the performance to the work's creation, so that the matching achieved is systematically responsive to the composer's work-determinative decisions.[25]

Davies is here addressing the metaphysical-cum-evaluative question – what conditions must a performance of a work satisfy if it is to count as a legitimate performance *of* it? And his answer – that the performance must 'match' the contents of the work, where those contents are determined by the composer's decisions as embodied in the instructions (as found, for instance, in the score) which mark out the work as the work that it is – gives us what I have been calling the 'ontological backdrop'. According to this, then, a performance is legitimate if it 'matches' the work's contents. How might one attempt to understand this backdrop as lending perspicuity to the framing of genuinely evaluative questions? What, in other words, if this is the backdrop, does it suggest that a question about the value of some particular performance ought to look like? The only possible answer is this: how *well*, how *closely* does the performance 'match' the contents of the work? – with the presumption that the better it 'matches' the better it is. One can see how someone might offer this sort of formulation in an effort to capture what we mean when we commend a performance for its faithfulness to the work performed; and indeed, one can see how someone might think that, in order to make or to understand such a commendation, something appropriately ontological must be going on in the background. But the discussion of the previous chapter should already have made one highly sceptical whether the notion of 'matching' is capable of doing any such work. And a moment's reflection now should be sufficient to confirm that it isn't.

The problem, of course, is that to make the value of a performance a function of how well it 'matches' the contents of the work performed, we would have to be able to specify, quite independently of this or that performance, what, precisely, those contents were – what exactly, in other words, the performance was supposed to 'match'. We would have to be able, that is, to give an exhaustive prescription for the production of a performance that was, not merely legitimate, but excellent, first-rate, admirable. And that is of course quite impossible, in just the same way and for just the same reasons as it is impossible to give an exhaustive prescription for the production of a great work of art.[26] However apt Davies's talk of 'matching' might be in the context of *legitimacy*, then, it certainly fails to carry over into genuinely evaluative contexts. His ontological reflections, that is, do nothing – as backdrop – to assist in the perspicuous framing of evaluative questions. Indeed, quite the reverse: they actively encourage the framing of those questions in a misleading way. Nor is this a problem peculiar to Davies. I have chosen to discuss Davies explicitly only because he, explicitly, refers to 'matching'. But the point is quite general: to the extent that one's ontological reflections are geared to the specification of work-identity conditions – that is, to conditions that might be satisfied by a *range* of different performances – one is necessarily committed to the specification of conditions that are, in the operative sense, *not* specific to any performance in particular – that is, to the specification of conditions of precisely the sort that 'matching'-talk is most obviously suited to. And this means, clearly enough, that the kinds of discrimination that one is able to make within the relevant range will not include discriminations between good performances and merely legitimate ones – a point brought out forcefully by Peter Strawson:

> objects primarily of aesthetic assessment [for instance, perform-
> ances] have plenty of shareable properties: there are plenty of ways
> in which we find resemblances between them. But in naming
> these, we do not name, in non-evaluative terms, those features
> directly on account of which we make aesthetic judgments of the
> individual bearers of those properties; for either these names of
> shareable general properties are themselves evaluative, or, if they are
> not, then, in applying them, we leave our listeners in the dark as to

what evaluations to make of the individual [performances] to which they are applied.[27]

The thought that a well-ordered ontology is any sort of precondition of perspicuously framed evaluative questions founders, and founders decisively, on this point.

But things get even worse for the purveyor of identity conditions, as we can see if we ask what *is* meant by a performance's being 'faithful' to a work – the genuinely evaluative notion, as I've just suggested, that no talk of 'matching' can hope to capture. The answer, I believe, is exactly the same as the answer to the corresponding question that I gave in the previous chapter. Just as the musical setting of a poem is 'appropriate' if it evinces an (internal) understanding of the poem set,[28] so a performance of a work is 'faithful' to it if it evinces an (internal) understanding of it. A performance is then to be valued in proportion to the richness, depth, insight, subtlety and so on of the understanding it evinces.[29] But if this is right, evidently enough, much of the 'content' of a given work is only revealed *in* the understandings that faithful performances of it evince. And that means that any attempt to specify that content – the content to which a good performance is faithful – *in advance* of evaluative judgements about particular performances of it, or independently of such judgements, must be futile and self-defeating. The fact is, in other words, that since faithfulness is a matter of understanding, and since understanding is not a matter of bringing off a 'match' of any sort with some independently specifiable content, nothing *at all* can be said in advance of any particular faithful performance about what 'faithfulness', in its case, will amount to. This is why some performances, in evincing an original or especially penetrating understanding of the work performed, and so in bringing to light aspects or dimensions of its content that other performances have not, are described as 'revelatory'.

But why is this bad news for the ontologist? Or why, rather, is it *more* bad news, rather than just a gloating restatement of the bad news already announced, namely, that the specification of identity conditions cannot hope to do any evaluative work? Here's why. Until just now, it might have seemed that the evaluative impotence of identity conditions at least left in place their claim to *be* identity conditions – that is, their claim to be the arbiters of legitimacy, even if not of quality. It might have seemed, in other words, as if aspects of a work's content not revealed exclusively through performance might be specified independently, and taken, if a performance 'matches' them, to show that the performance is indeed a legitimate performance *of* the work. But even this toe-hold is now denied. For if, as I've argued, a revelatory performance is one that is faithful to a work in a way that necessarily defies specification in advance, then, first, as a performance that is faithful to the work it is, trivially, *of* it, and second, amongst its unforeseeable qualities may well be the disregard of any, or even of all, of the independently specifiable bits of 'content' that it was supposed, as a legitimate performance, to have to match. This is not to deny that such bits of 'content' may indeed be specifiable independently. But it is to deny that their being so specifiable accords to them any special authority. It is just as futile, in other words, to hope that one's 'identity conditions' will trump the evidence of one's ears in this case, where the performance strikes one as masterly, as tremendous, as it is in the case discussed earlier, where the performance strikes one as an infuriating, depressing travesty.[30] And this means that one's 'identity conditions', whichever ones they happen to be, cannot be *identity* conditions, or even conditions. If an exemplary performance can violate them, then they are, at best, an expression of some more or less reasonable set of expectations, or, as one might rather more grandly put it, a set of defeasible criteria. And this means, in turn, that they lose any claim to report the fundamental ontology of the matter: if some – or perhaps even all – of a work's allegedly identity-confirming properties can fail to be reflected in a faithful performance *of* it, then those properties can have nothing to do with the work's being what, essentially, it is. Rather, if what I've been arguing is right, one finds out what a work is, what properties it has, by experiencing performances of it, or by giving performances of it, and that is a process of discovery that may well have no determinate end.

The upshot of all this is twofold. First, it means that neither of the possible ways of cashing out the second response to the charge of 'scandal' – the response that a well-worked out ontology is a precondition of pointful evaluative enquiry – is able to deliver. And, second, it means that retreat to the first response – to the claim that what ontologically inclined philosophers of music are doing is musical metaphysics, not musical aesthetics – is doomed to failure too. For what the foregoing shows is that ontological questions about pieces of music are only perspicuously to be framed, if they are to be framed at all, against an aesthetic backdrop of *already-answered* questions about the value of performances *of* them. Strawson is again helpful here:

> To use a fashionable phrase, the *criterion of identity* of a work of art is the totality of features which are relevant to its aesthetic appraisal ... Perhaps I could also express the point in this way: the only

method of describing a work of art which is both … adequate for the purpose of aesthetic appraisal, and does not use evaluative language, is to say 'It goes like this' – and then reproduce it. And, of course, this is not a method of *describing* at all.[31]

If the second response to the charge of 'scandal' put the ontological cart before the evaluative horse, and so forfeited its claim to be engaged in either ontology or aesthetics, although not its claim to be engaged with music, albeit in a thin way, this first response, in attempting to put the horse and cart in different fields entirely, forfeits any claim to be concerned with *music*, with a 'method of *describing*' music, at all. Its proponents must cut themselves off from what Davies calls a work's 'content' – that is, from what can be understood and appreciated in it. And in doing so they confine themselves, at best, to the metaphysics of sounds that might, conceivably, be heard as music, or maybe to the metaphysics of scores. Musical metaphysics is predicated on musical aesthetics; and in musical aesthetics, ontology comes last (at the end of time, perhaps).

II. Some Objections

One might wonder, if the argument of the previous section is right, why it is that the temptation to begin thinking about performance in terms of ontology and identity conditions should have been felt at all. In part, and I'm convinced of this, it does have to do with the lure of metaphysics: metaphysics is grown-up philosophy, and insecure aestheticians may reach for it too readily. It also has to do with the unwittingly baneful influence of Nelson Goodman, as I suggested in the Background part of this chapter. But I can also think of two less *ad-* or *ab-hominem* sorts of reason, both superficially understandable, but neither, when one looks at all closely, compelling. The first concerns 'hard cases'; the second, first performances. I'll take them in turn.

'Hard cases': the examples I've used have tended to suppress the possibility of genuine borderline cases, cases in which it really isn't clear whether a given 'performance' is of a given work. It's all very well to concentrate on obvious outbreaks of musical murder, but sometimes, at least, things aren't so straightforward. What is one to make, for instance, of a case in which one is genuinely puzzled by what one is hearing – not enraged or bilious, just puzzled? It is *possible*, one thinks, that one is hearing a performance of such-and-such. But, then again, one might not be. Surely, it will be said, this sort of case, a genuine borderline case, shows precisely why one needs to have some ontological views to draw upon, some identity conditions that will, at least in principle, allow one either to settle the question, or else to characterise the borderline on which the case sits in a perspicuous way. And surely neither result would be aesthetically worthless: ontology cannot, then, be written off so quickly.

I am perfectly happy to agree, at least for the sake of argument, that there might be genuine borderline cases. I am ready to agree that it might not always be clear, or may be simply undecidable, whether a particular 'performance' is, indeed, of a given work. But this fact, if it is one, doesn't have any of the redemptive consequences for ontology envisaged. For one thing, and in light of the argument of the previous section, it would be a bit odd, to put it no higher, if ontology suddenly turned out to be splendid for borderline cases while being irrelevant or misleading for uncontentious ones. But be that as it may, the problem with the present suggestion is that it simply *ignores* the argument I've offered. Suppose that one were able to decide, in some particular border-line case, that a performance was, in fact, of such-and-such a work. This would indeed be because one had decided that it satisfied certain conditions – conditions relating, presumably, to the 'content' of the work in question. But since, as I have argued, and I think shown, that content is crucially revealed by the understandings evinced in faithful perform-ances of the work, one's capacity to decide in favour, as it were, of some particular putative performance represents a triumph, not for ontology, but for aesthetics. And the same goes if what is sought is a perspicuous characterisation of the borderline that a 'performance' occupies. That is going to be yielded, not, say, by a list of the identity conditions that the 'performance' matches or fails to match, but by evaluatively driven critical enquiry. As far as I can see, then, 'hard cases' offer no comfort at all to those who would like to see ontology done first. At most, it needs to be done last.

First performances: according to me, much of the 'content' of a given work is revealed through the understandings evinced of it by faithful performances. But what if there have *been* no performances, faithful or otherwise? What if *this* performance is the first one? There is now no 'aesthetic backdrop', as I put it a moment ago, against which ontological questions might be raised. And yet there is surely an answer to the question: is this (first) performance a performance of the work it purports to be of? And if there *is* an answer to that question, that surely shows that one can determine the identity of a work on independently specifiable grounds – on the grounds, that is, of precisely the sorts of ontological consideration that I have been so busy maligning. So again, the suggestion goes, ontology is not to be seen off so quickly.

My response to this point begins with what is, essentially, an expression of puzzlement. What, exactly, is the difficulty supposed to be here? One shows up at a concert hall expecting to hear, as the programme promises, the first performance of such-and-such by so-and-so; the orchestra have their scores open in front of them, the conductor does the usual conductorly things, and they play a piece one has never heard before. How, precisely, is the question whether this (first) performance is a performance of the work it purports to be of meant to arise? To what dark suspicions would one have to be prey for this to strike one, genuinely, as a pressing or pointful question? What I'm trying to suggest, in other words, is that if all of the surrounding circumstances are exactly as one would expect, if everything is outwardly consistent with the performance's being what it purports to be, namely, the first performance of such-and-such, the question whether it *is* of what it purports to be of simply doesn't come up. The context doesn't invite the question, and the motivation for asking it is, as things stand, wholly inscrutable. Any appearance of intelligibility the question might have, I think, it owes to the resistible temptations of abstraction – to the thought that, because we can understand what, in ordinary contexts, it *is* for something to be a first performance of a musical work, we can abstract the ideas of 'first performance' and 'musical work' from ordinary contexts entirely, and expect them, and the question they appear to be being used to ask, to remain meaningful. But of course neither they, nor the so-called 'question', means anything at all when so abstracted. (Imagine a Martian suddenly beaming down into a concert hall where the first performance of such-and-such is taking place. He knows nothing whatever of music, musical works or performances, or of the contexts within which those things can be understood. There is, clearly enough, nothing that the Martian could *mean* in asking 'Is this (first) performance a performance of what it purports to be of?' Without the context, he hasn't the concepts; and without the concepts, he hasn't a question.) Scepticism for its own sake is as difficult to make sense of here, in other words, as it is anywhere else. For the question to be worth asking it must, first, be raised in acknowledgement of ordinary contextual considerations and, second, be motivated by factors that might, given those considerations, be intelligible grounds for doubt. So there really do have to be some dark suspicions in play – some genuine reasons to wonder whether what one is hearing really is what it was said to be – before the question 'Is the performance *of* the work' is so much as askable. Let's imagine some cases.

First, imagine that one is familiar with all of the composer's previous works, and that what one is hearing sounds as if it couldn't possibly have come from the same hand. This might well be perplexing, and it might well make one wonder what was going on. Possible explanations? Perhaps one is not as good as one had thought at making judgements about composers' styles. Or perhaps the composer's style has changed, or he has simply written something uncharacteristically good or bad. Or perhaps the programme has been altered at the last minute. Or perhaps the performance is a hoax, and not of a work by the advertised composer at all. The question we are concerned with can be answered or dealt with in each case. In the first two, and in the absence of further complicating details, the answer is yes, the performance is indeed *of* such-and-such. In the third case, where the programme has been changed, the state of affairs originally purported has ceased, in the relevant way, to *be* purported, and so the question doesn't arise. And in the final case, the answer is no, the performance is a hoax – it is not what it presents itself as being. How have these answers been arrived at? Certainly not through the specification of identity conditions. All that is required for any of them is the wholly uncontentious observation that composers standardly compose their own works – an observation that is consistent with any minimally plausible ontology, and so presupposes none.

Second, imagine that one has had a sneak-preview of the score, and that what the orchestra are playing seems to have nothing whatever to do with it. Again, one would wonder what was going on. And, again, there might be several explanations. It might be that one is very bad at reading scores. Or it might be that the score one saw was a forgery. Or it might be that the programme has been changed at the last minute. Or it might be that the performance is a hoax. The answers to the question whether the performance is of what it purports to be of are exactly the same as in the previous case: yes, yes, not an issue, and no. And this time, all that is required to arrive at them is the humdrum truth that works are standardly notated *in* and performed *from* scores, again not a thought that either presupposes or suggests any particular set of ontological commitments rather than any other.

Finally, and even less interestingly, suppose that one has seen the score in advance, and that one creates for oneself a vividly imagined performance in one's head. And then suppose that the performance one hears in the concert hall isn't like that at all. But this is hopeless. First, if the performance one hears isn't like that *at all*, this example collapses into the previous one. But if it *is* enough like it to make one concerned about the divergence, then a dilemma presents itself. If, on the one hand, it is granted that the imaginary rendition is equivalent to a genuine performance, then (1) the performance one hears in the concert hall isn't, in the relevant sense, a *first* performance, and so cannot prompt the question we're supposed to be worrying about; and (2) the most, anyway, that the divergence at issue could indicate is that the actual performance is either significantly better or significantly worse than the imagined one (and not, that is, that the actual performance wasn't of what it was meant to be of). Whereas if, on the other hand, the imaginary rendition is denied the status of 'performance', its divergence from the actual performance can indicate only (1) that actual performances are different from non-performances; and (2) that that difference is sufficient to entail the collapse of this example into the previous one, as before. Neither alternative can give the example even the appearance of bite. However one looks at it, it seems to me, first performances pose no threat whatever to my contention that musical ontology is, at best, superfluous if what one is interested in is musical aesthetics.

But have I not, it might be asked (in what I would hope was a suitably last-gasp spirit), committed myself to a whole set of ontological claims throughout the course of my own argument? Have I not claimed, in effect, that works are identical to faithful performances *of* them? And have I not nailed my colours to a firmly realist view of the properties of works that faithful performances reveal? And haven't I just helped myself – a bit conveniently – to thoughts about the relations between composers and works and between works and scores that look, for all the world, like covertly specified identity conditions? Have I not, in short, shot myself repeatedly in the foot?

The answer, it will come as no surprise to learn that I think, is no, I haven't. I have nowhere, in effect or otherwise, claimed or assumed that works are identical to (some? all?) faithful performances of them, and nor can I see why anyone would want to. All that I have argued is that performances can show us things about works; and that requires nothing more than the thought that (some) performances are interpretations *of* works – not, I surmise, a proposition likely to provoke a storm of protest, and certainly not one that involves or presupposes (or should prompt) the slightest flicker of ontological reflection. With respect to the second charge, it is true that I have cast a number of my sentences in undeniably realist terms. It is true, that is, that I have spoken of aspects of a work's content as being *revealed* by faithful performances of it, rather than as being brought into existence by them, say. But I've put it like that largely as a matter of convenience, and also out of deference to the convention that, unless there is some good reason not to, one should assume that what one is talking about is, in a straightforward and common-sensical way, real. I don't insist upon this, though. If someone feels more comfortable with the thought that performances 'create' content rather than 'discover' it, that's fine by me. Nothing in what I've said or want to say depends on the distinction. And finally, to the suggestion that I've really just helped myself covertly to a raft of identity conditions, I simply deny that I have. At most, I've helped myself to some perfectly neutral, pre-theoretical thoughts. And these are, first, of a sort that no one, whatever their ontological views, could possibly object to; and second, of a sort which, if they were (by someone else) misconstrued as quasi-theoretical items, would not thereby become identity conditions, but – as I have already argued – expressions, merely, of some more or less reasonable sets of expectations. My position, it seems to me, is steadfastly devoid of ontological commitments; and it is, for the reasons I've given, in much the better shape for that. If it is the philosophy of music that one is interested in doing, then ontology is an idle distraction, or worse, and I propose to have nothing further to do with it.

III. 'Authenticity'

The main objection that has tended to be raised against Busoni's transcription of Bach's *Chaconne* is that it is profoundly inauthentic. It is arranged for an instrument – the piano – that is not only different from the one that Bach composed it for, but is one that he could never even have heard; and it is arranged for it in a way that seems actively intent on concealing its origins as a work for violin. The Brahms transcription is also, admittedly, for piano. But at least his version, in confining itself to what can be done with the left hand alone, retains the spread chords characteristic of violin playing, and conveys something of the sense of technical challenge to be heard in the original. Busoni's transcription, by contrast, yields a grand, late-Romantic and not very conspicuously difficult piece for piano. The objection, then, is that Busoni's transcription represents an inauthentic rendition because it is, in some sense, unfaithful to the work by Bach that it transcribes.

I have already reviewed, in the Background part of this chapter, the sorts of argument that philosophers inclined to make, or to rebut, charges of inauthenticity are given to reaching for. And those arguments, it will be recalled, are ontological ones: people who think 'authenticity' important tend to want to specify work-identity conditions that tie the work, essentially, to one or another set of historical factors concerning its inception, or at any rate its early career; while those who have no

objection to what might be considered anachronistic styles of performance, although also wanting to specify work-identity conditions, tend to
offer ones which exclude historical factors from the list, sometimes to
the extent, at the autonomanic extreme, of insisting that works are,
essentially, abstract structures of sound. It will be clear from the progress
of this chapter so far that I do not think that either of these approaches is
worth a hill of beans. For the reasons I've given, the specification of
identity conditions is a non-starter, not only aesthetically, but ontologically;[32] and, as I've also given reasons to conclude, nothing that is at
bottom an aesthetic dispute, such as the present one about authenticity,
has the least chance of being addressed, let alone resolved, by turning
one's hand to a bit of metaphysics. Does this mean, then, that the dispute
is just empty, a red herring – that the 'charge' raised against Busoni fails
actually to allege anything?

No, it doesn't mean that. It means only that a genuine disagreement
has become occluded by irrelevant and misleading pontificating, born of
bad philosophical habits. Indeed, the present case is really, and merely, a
very good illustration of the way in which, as I argued in section I,
evaluative questions get skewed if one insists on doing one's ontology
first. There *is* a disagreement here, and it seems fairly obvious how, once
one has weaned oneself off ontology, it ought to be framed. Does
Busoni's transcription evince an understanding of Bach's work, or does
it travesty it? Is it, that is, *faithful* to the Bach (rather than offering, say, a
good match of it)? These – evidently and appropriately – are *critical*
questions, not metaphysical ones. And one can see at once, as soon as the
questions are properly posed, how the various 'identity conditions' offered
by the parties to the dispute immediately resolve themselves into reasons
of a sort that might, potentially, be regarded as critically relevant reasons,
and not as ontologically motivated pontificating at all. So, for example,
the reasons that someone who opposes Busoni's transcription might
offer for disparaging it include, in no particular order, the following
(with the 'identity conditions' they might wrongly have been stated as in
brackets afterwards). The Busoni wholly fails to capture the violinistic
quality of the original (being for violin is an essential property of the
Chaconne).[33] The Busoni fails to convey the sense of technical embattlement so striking when the piece is played on the violin (it is a condition
of the *Chaconne*'s identity that it be, or sound, technically embattled).
Bach cannot possibly have intended his work to have anything like the
big, late-Romantic feel that Busoni has imparted to it (Bach's intentions
are partly constitutive of what it is for the *Chaconne* to be the *Chaconne*).
No audience made up of Bach's contemporaries would recognise in

Busoni's transcription a faithful rendition of Bach's original (historically appropriate listening habits contribute to the determination of the *Chaconne's* essential properties). And so on. From the other side, by contrast, those who are impressed by Busoni's transcription might offer as reasons in its favour, again in no particular order, these (and again with the 'identity conditions' they might have been mis-stated as in brackets). Busoni brings out the sheer scale of Bach's invention marvellously (its 'scale' is an essential property of the *Chaconne*). Busoni illuminates the progression of Bach's musical argument in a particularly telling way (the *Chaconne* is, essentially, an intellectually articulated structure of sound). Busoni highlights facets of Bach's work that could not have been appreciated in the original version (the essential properties of the *Chaconne* are not identical to or exhausted by the properties revealed in 'historically appropriate' renditions of it). Busoni creates Bach's work anew (a rendition of a work can, in effect, determine new conditions of what it is to *be* that work). And so on. In each case, and on either side of the disagreement, the unbracketed remarks represent, with varying degrees of persuasiveness, the kinds of reasons that might feature in a genuinely pointful critical debate. The remarks in brackets, on the other hand, are decent examples of the sorts of thing that reliably stifle any such debate at source.

For the record, I'm on the pro-Busoni side of the argument, even if I do agree that there are aspects of his transcription that are less than faithful to Bach's original. It is true that, in listening to the Busoni, one must forego the undeniable thrill of hearing a violin operating close to its limits. But in exchange one gets, not only a terrific sense of scale and an altogether undiminished sense of musical inevitability, but the strangely stimulating experience of hearing the work as not quite played on the organ – an experience whose stimulating aspects include, but are not confined to, the provision of a non-standard context in which to listen to and think about Bach's piece, namely, his keyboard music. None of this is to say that Busoni's transcription is superior to the original, of course.[34] But it is to say that, in evincing a rich and far-reaching understanding of that original – as well as, arguably, of the non-existent organ work it sounds most like a version of – Busoni's transcription represents a thoroughly valuable rendition of it. Or so, at least, it seems to me.

The primary point here, though, is the one that I've been labouring – that a philosophical interest in music and its performance is best satisfied when pursued independently of ontological considerations. And this point has not, I can now reveal, and despite my Lone Ranger-ish posturings, gone altogether ungrasped – even by those who have seemed most ardently committed to the specification of identity conditions and the rest.[35] I have already referred elsewhere in this chapter to Peter Kivy's Platonising moments, to Jerrold Levinson's bold invention of a completely new ontological category (the 'initiated type') and to Stephen Davies's unhelpful invocation of 'matching'. But Davies, for instance, also has this to say: 'If ontology is to be other than a philosopher's game, it must reflect the "what"s and "why"s informing the esteem that draws us to art works. Musical ontology should be responsive to the ways we engage with and discuss music and its works'[36] – an overly modest claim, in my view, but one that at least points in the right direction. And Levinson's remark, that 'A piece of music … is an irreducibly perceptual affair. What this means is that no conceptual condensation of its core content is really possible [or] central to its appreciation',[37] is surely just right, refreshingly so. And Kivy, in insisting that 'There is no a priori road to the best performance – only the genius of the performer tested by the listener's ear',[38] shows as clearly as one could wish a sense of the priorities proper to the issue. The fact is, and as one should expect it would be, that each of these philosophers of music – sensitive listeners as they all are – knows full well, in his heart if not always his head, that evaluative questions are what matter and are what come first, and that ontological speculation is, at bottom, nothing more than irrelevant philosophising.[39]

NOTES

1. Nelson Goodman, *Languages of Art* (Indianapolis, IN: Hackett, 1976). Goodman was certainly not the first to think about the relation between musical works and performances. But his conclusions undeniably stimulated more intensive discussion of the issue than had been evident before.
2. *Ibid.*, p. 178.
3. *Ibid.*, p. 186.
4. *Ibid.*, pp. 186–7.
5. *Ibid.*, pp. 148–57.
6. See, for discussion, Lydia Goehr, *The Imaginary Museum of Musical Works* (Oxford: Oxford University Press, 1992), pp. 98–101,
7. Peter Kivy, 'Orchestrating Platonism', in his *The Fine Art of Repetition* (Cambridge: Cambridge University Press, 1993), p. 75. For a harder-nosed sort of Platonism, see Nicholas Wolterstorff, *Works and Worlds of Art* (Oxford: Clarendon Press, 1980).
8. Kivy, 'Platonism in Music: Another Kind of Defense', in *The Fine Art of Repetition*, p. 63 (see Note 7).
9. Kivy, 'Platonism in Music: A Kind of Defense', in *The Fine Art of Repetition*, p. 56 (see Note 7). Kivy's sense of 'uniquely', by the way, has to be a 'loose' one, otherwise his characterisation of the relation between score and performance would be identical

to Goodman's characterisation of the relation between a score, understood as 'a character in a notational system', and its 'compliance-class', a class which includes performances. (See Goodman, pp. 177–8 (see Note 1).) Kivy needs to keep his distance from Goodman, not only because he rejects Goodman's nominalism, but because he wants his own conclusions to be intuitively plausible.

10. Kivy, *ibid.*, pp. 38–47.
11. Or, more strictly, had already proposed a different kind. Levinson's work on the topic pre-dates Kivy's by several years.
12. Jerrold Levinson, 'What a Musical Work Is', in his *Music, Art, and Metaphysics* (Ithaca, NY: Cornell University Press, 1990), p. 78.
13. *Ibid.*, pp. 80–1.
14. *Ibid.*, p. 86.
15. Such an approach is evident in, for example, Stan Godlovitch, *Musical Performance* (London: Routledge, 1998).
16. Stephen Davies, *Musical Works and Performances: A Philosophical Exploration* (Oxford: Oxford University Press, 2001).
17. Except, of course, to the extent that bad performances can always be found somewhere. A shame, arguably: some of my most treasured LPs from the late 1970s still afford terrific opportunities for malicious entertainment.
18. See, for example, Peter Kivy, 'On the Concept of the "Historically Authentic" Performance', in his *The Fine Art of Repetition*, pp. 117–33 (see Note 7).
19. See, for example, Jerrold Levinson, 'Authentic Performance and Performance Means', in his *Music, Art, and Metaphysics*, pp. 393–408 (see Note 12).
20. Peter Kivy, *Authenticities: Philosophical Reflections on Musical Performance* (Ithaca, NY: Cornell University Press, 1995), p. 261. I will remain agnostic with respect to Kivy's further contention that performances are to be regarded as works of art in their own right.
21. And they must exist, they must exist …
22. There are exceptions, of course – the most honourable recent one, in my view, being the raising of just that question by Peter Kivy in his generally splendid *Authenticities: Philosophical Reflections on Musical Performance* (see Note 20). I am also attracted to the sort of answer that Kivy gives, namely, that what makes a performance of a work a good one is that it makes the most of the work's virtues and minimises, to whatever extent possible, its vices (pp. 155–61) – provided, for reasons that will soon become clear, that Kivy doesn't think that those virtues and vices must always be specifiable in advance of the performance itself. I am not wholly certain whether Kivy does think this.
23. This might be Goodman's response, given his evident indifference to evaluative matters.
24. Kivy, *Authenticities*, pp. 150–1 (see Note 22). Kivy appears to have rescinded, or at least suspended, the Platonist ontology he used to espouse (see the Background part of this chapter); and he comes very close to saying that *Authenticities* presupposes no ontology at all (pp. 261–2). The passage just quoted, however, shows clearly that ontological hankerings still beset him.
25. Stephen Davies, *Musical Works and Performances*, p. 5 (see Note 16).
26. For a parallel, if rather more provisional, line of thought, see Kivy, *Authenticities*, pp. 272–3 (see Note 22).
27. P. F. Strawson, 'Aesthetic Appraisal and Works of Art', in his *Freedom and Resentment* (London: Methuen, 1974), p. 188.
28. 'Internal' in the sense set out in Chapter 1.

29. Imagine thinking of rich, deep, insightful or subtle cases of 'matching' …

30. To vary the 'travesty' example: one would have thought it a non-negotiable condition of something's counting as an instance of Dave Brubeck's *Take Five* that it be grouped, metrically, into fives. Yet the version I hear most often, on pub juke boxes, groups it into sixes – and it's still obviously *it*.

31. Strawson, p. 185 (see Note 27). I take it that Strawson's 'totality' of relevant features is exactly the sort of thing that the process of discovery referred to above would, at some notional end-point, have brought to light.

32. – here, moreover, a non-starter that represents a peculiarly transparent attempt to legislate one's likes or dislikes into the very fabric of things.

33. It is interesting to wonder, by the way, whether it might not be precisely the strongly violinistic quality of the *Chaconne* that makes it respond so well to transcription. For, as Adorno has pointed out, 'The more specifically an instrumental work is written with an eye to the potential of the instruments which are to be deployed, the easier it is to transpose it into a completely different instrumental sound, to 'arrange' it.' And this for the reason that '[o]nly when the instrumental tone has been precisely imagined and realised can it be rethought through. The transposing imagination is given a clear lead …' Theodor Adorno, *Quasi una Fantasia*, trans. R. Livingstone (London: Verso, 1994), pp. 19–20.

34. Although there may well be instances where the transcription *is* better: Ravel's orchestral version of Moussorgsky's piano work, *Pictures from an Exhibition*, is, or certainly once was, widely held to be better than the work it transcribes, for instance, and my Dad insists that the (a?) piano trio version of Schoenberg's *Verklärte Nacht* is better than either the string sextet original or the composer's own transcription of it for string orchestra. I find this very hard to believe, but, as ever, the proof is in the listening, and I haven't yet managed to track down a performance or recording of it.

35. Much of Lydia Goehr's argument in *The Imaginary Museum of Musical Works*, for instance, might be regarded as an extended and richer way of making much the same sort of point – although she starts from somewhere different and also ends up, I think, somewhere rather different (see Note 6).

36. *Musical Works and Performances*, p. 9 (see Note 16). Whether or not Davies actually follows his own precept is another matter.

37. *Music in the Moment* (Ithaca, NY: Cornell University Press, 1997), p. 171.

38. *Authenticities*, p. xiii (see Note 22).

39. With this borne in mind, I can do no better than recommend, to readers eager for something perhaps less thin than I have been able to offer here, two books: Jerrold Levinson's *Music in the Moment* (see Note 16), a provocative and wholly ontology-free account of what the experience of music in performance might actually amount to; and Peter Kivy's *Authenticities* (see Note 22), an impressively even-handed and insightful exploration of the philosophical issues raised by 'authentic' performance practices. I take my contribution to what they have written to be the modest but useful one of showing why, whatever Levinson and Kivy might say or think in their more metaphysical moods, their respective books are, in fact, worth reading. They are genuine exercises in musical aesthetics, and not (merely) botched bits of ontology.

5

Profundity

The older I grow the more difficult I find it to say anything about the art [of music]. Superficial tittle-tattle about music seems to me just as if someone amid all the row and crowd of a *palais de danse* were to ask his partner: 'Do you believe in the existence of God?' (Jean Sibelius, cited in Goss (ed.), *The Sibelius Companion*)

PART 1. BACKGROUND

There is a tradition, stretching back at least as far as the late eighteenth century, of describing certain pieces of music as 'profound', of attributing to them the capacity to express, to embody or in some other way to convey deep and important insights into the world, or perhaps into the human condition. What it is for a work of art – any work of art – to be profound, however, is a question that has received surprisingly little discussion, despite the fact that to describe a work so is to mobilise one of the least ambiguously positive terms in the language of criticism. It is relatively easy, perhaps, to see, at least in a crude and general way, what an attribution of profundity might amount to in the cases of the (straightforwardly) representational arts: a novel, say, or a play, might be held to be profound in virtue of its subject matter, and of what it shows or suggests about that subject matter. But in the case of music the issue is much less clear, even at a crude or general level. A song, no doubt, might be thought profound at least partly in virtue of its text.[1] An opera might be thought profound because of the characters and situations it contains. And perhaps an orchestral work based upon *Faust*, for instance, might be held to have inherited some of the profundity of Goethe's poetic masterpiece. But music all by itself? Purely instrumental music? How could a string quartet or a fugue or a symphony be profound?[2]

One answer – the autonomanic answer – is that they couldn't be. Here, the suggestion is that purely instrumental music is simply too abstract, too free of content, to qualify as (even potentially) profound. When one understands a piece of music, on this view, there is nothing that one understands beyond the music itself; thus, there is nothing that the music can be understood as being profound *about*, and so no sense in which the music is, in any meaningful way, to be described *as* profound. But if this is the case, it is puzzling that so many people have believed that certain pieces of purely instrumental music are, indeed, appropriately so to be described. It might be suggested, perhaps, that by 'profound' such people have really meant something like 'great'; and if this is right, then the autonomaniac has no reason to demur, except, as it might be, on grounds of terminological exactitude. But the existence of a tradition of describing music, or at least certain pieces of music, as profound suggests that there might be something rather more going on here than simple error or hyperbole.

The tradition in question finds one of its most memorable expressions in the philosophy of Schopenhauer, who embedded his thoughts about the arts in a grand and ambitious metaphysical system. In Schopenhauer's view, the essence of reality is 'the Will'; and music, uniquely, stands to the Will as a 'copy', as the sole mode of access to reality as, in its ultimate nature, it really is. Thus Schopenhauer assigned to music a deeply metaphysical quality, and went on to talk about it in terms that exerted a real influence over the ways in which many nineteenth-century musicians – such as Richard Wagner – came to conceive of and to describe their art. As Schopenhauer put it:

> I recognize in the deepest tones of harmony, in the ground-bass, the lowest grades of the will's objectification, inorganic nature, the mass of the planet ... Those that are higher represent to me the plant and animal worlds ... Finally, in the melody, in the high, singing, principal voice, leading the whole and progressing with unrestrained freedom ... I recognize the highest grade of the will's objectification, the intellectual life and endeavour of man ... [There is an] immediate knowledge of the inner nature of the world unknown to [the] faculty of reason ... [Music's] imitative reference to the world must be very profound, infinitely true, and really striking, since it is instantly understood by everyone ... Yet the point of comparison between music and the world, the regard in which it stands to the world in the relation of a copy, or a repetition, is very obscure.[3]

Schopenhauer's glorification of music is a good deal more evocative than it is clear, and altogether more baffling than illuminating: few philosophers nowadays would accept his claims about music as they stand, nor would many accept the metaphysical views upon which those claims rest. But his claim that music is capable of being 'very profound' has stuck. And implicit in what Schopenhauer says are answers to three pertinent questions, which can be stated as follows: (1) What kind of property is profundity – what do we mean when we call something profound? (2) What do we understand when we understand a piece of music? (3) Is what we understand when we understand a piece of music capable of having the property of profundity? Schopenhauer's answers to these questions run, in effect, as follows: (1) profundity is a property of metaphysical knowledge; (2) in understanding music we understand the innermost nature of the world. Music, that is, may be a source of metaphysical knowledge; and therefore (3) yes, what we understand when we understand a piece of music can be profound.

This way of setting up Schopenhauer's position has the advantage of highlighting a lacuna in it. For even if his answers to the three questions that I have mentioned were to be accepted, they would not establish that a piece of music, itself, might properly be considered profound. They establish only that music may have profound subject matter.[4] It is possible, perhaps, that Schopenhauer could appeal to the uniqueness of music's access to that subject matter as a way of getting the profundity to attach itself to the music, specifically. But the argument would need to be made; and it isn't at all obvious, to me at any rate, how it might go, not least in light of Schopenhauer's own admission that 'the point of comparison between music and the world, the regard in which it stands to the world in the relation of a copy, or a repetition, is very obscure.'

Interest in questions relating to musical profundity has been rekindled recently by the publication of Peter Kivy's book, *Music Alone*, which devotes a chapter to the issue. Kivy has little time for approaches such as Schopenhauer's, and argues instead for a version of what he calls musical 'purism',[5] the view that music 'is a quasi-syntactical structure of sound understandable solely in musical terms and having no semantic or representational content, no meaning, and making no reference to anything beyond itself'.[6] Here, we can already see an answer to question (2), above: what we understand when we understand a piece of music, according to Kivy, is something purely musical, something that has no reference to anything outside the music itself. And he gives an answer to question (1) as well. In order for a work of art to be profound, he says, 'it must be able to be 'about' (that is, it must possess the possibility of subject matter); it must be about something profound (which is to say, something of abiding interest or importance to human beings); [and] it must treat its profound subject matter in some exemplary way or other adequate to that subject matter.'[7] This view of course makes the problem of profound music extremely puzzling for Kivy. For if music refers to nothing beyond itself, as he says in answering question (2), then there can be nothing profound for music to be about. But if, as he says in answer to question (1), a profound work of art must be *about* something profound, then it would seem to follow directly that no piece of music can possibly *be* profound. Kivy is reluctant to accept this conclusion, however. His intuitions suggest to him that the right answer to question (3) is 'Yes' – that what we understand when we understand a piece of music can, indeed, be appropriately described as profound. But since, on his view, this means that music must be about something, he is left with only one option: to suggest that, although music cannot have reference to any- thing beyond itself, it may yet have reference to itself – that is, that music may be about music. And since music is a subject of abiding interest or importance, he concludes – albeit in a somewhat sceptical spirit – that music itself might be the profound subject matter which certain musical works are about. Such musical works, then, as treat that subject matter in a way that is 'adequate' to it have a claim, on this model, to be regarded as profound.

Kivy's rather minimalist account of musical profundity has attracted a certain amount of discussion, primarily from those who agree with him that some pieces of music can indeed be described as profound, but who are nonetheless reluctant to settle for an account which restricts the kind of profundity that music can have to the self-referential. Indeed, there may be reasons to worry, not merely about the minimalism of Kivy's account, but about its coherence. For if, as Kivy suggests, certain pieces of music are profound in virtue of being 'adequate' to their subject matter, where that subject matter – music – is itself profound (in the sense of being 'of abiding interest or importance to human beings'), one might well want to ask how it is that this primary sort of profundity, the profundity of music *as subject matter*, is supposed to be explained. One might well want to know, in other words, what it is about music as subject matter that makes it worthy of being regarded as abidingly interesting or important. Kivy has nothing to say about this. And while one can imagine how the outline of an answer might go – perhaps referring to the place and function of music in our lives – it is difficult to resist the suspicion that, fully spelt out, that answer must, in the end, attribute to music a capacity to make 'reference to [something] beyond itself'. If music, as subject matter, is restricted *entirely* to self-reference, after all, there is no route by which profundity could, as it were, have got into the loop in the first place. And if that's right, Kivy's insistence that *individual pieces of music* can only be profound in virtue of self-reference begins to look merely and self-defeatingly stipulative.

But this is not the only reason to doubt the coherence of Kivy's account, and, specifically, to wonder about its reliance on the notion of 'adequacy'. The idea, clearly enough, is that the 'adequacy' condition is supposed to supply the lack in Schopenhauer's treatment of the issue, as noted above. The idea, in other words, is that in being 'adequate' to its profound subject matter, music *itself*, and not merely that subject matter, gains the right to be considered profound. But the appeal to 'adequacy' in this context is unhelpful in at least two ways. First, it invites a regress: the profundity of one thing (for instance, of a piece of music) is made conditional upon its adequacy to something else (the profundity of its subject matter); in which case the profundity of that subject matter ought itself to be conditional upon its adequacy to the profundity of some third thing; and so on. (Unless, of course, there is some further factor that is supposed to halt the regress. But if there is such a factor, it would be good, first, to have been told what it is, and difficult, second, to see how it would not entail a rather radical change in the character of the whole account.) This suggests that it may be a mistake, or at any rate rather harder than Kivy assumes, to make the profundity of one thing dependent on the profundity of something else. And second, the idea of one thing's being 'adequate' to another invites the thought that the first thing, if it is to be considered profound, must *measure up* in some way to the profundity of the second, a thought that should be found resistible by anyone who has got this far in the present book. For talk of 'measuring up', here, is clearly in danger of reducing to talk of 'matching', and it should be plain by now that talk of 'matching' is quite peculiarly ill-suited, in aesthetic contexts at any rate, to shed much light.

Kivy doesn't tell us enough about his notion of 'adequacy' to decide whether it does in fact boil down to a matter of 'measuring up' or 'matching'. Sometimes it looks as if it must. His chief illustrations of putative musical profundity are pieces of contrapuntal music which are said to be adequately 'about' the profound 'possibilities of musical sound itself',[8] that is, pieces which are 'adequate' to the profundity of those possibilities. But in order for this to mean anything at all, those possibilities – and their profundity – would have to be independently specifiable (and independently measurable). One would have to be able to say: '*These* are the possibilities of musical sound itself, and this piece of

music measures up to them.' I take it that the hopelessness of trying to
say any such thing is manifest: it is, after all, precisely, and indeed only, in
the greatest music – that is, in music that has the strongest claim to be
considered profound – that one *discovers* what the possibilities inherent
in music *are*. That a piece measured up to some independently specifiable set of musical possibilities would be good evidence that it was, not
profound, but hack-work, run-of-the-mill – a student piece, perhaps. So
one must hope that Kivy does not intend his notion of 'adequacy' to be
construed in this way. How *else* he might intend it to be construed,
however, must remain a matter for conjecture, since nothing in what he
says, so far as I can see, suggests an alternative way of taking the notion.

Kivy's answer to question (1), then – that a piece of music may be
profound if it is about, and adequately about, something profound – is
incomplete at best. As it stands, it does rather little to inform us about
the sort of property that profundity is, and it does nothing to plug the
gap that Schopenhauer left between the alleged profundity of music and
the profundity of its alleged subject matter.

This has not, however, been the principal worry that commentators
have felt with Kivy's position. The principal worry has been that his
account is just too minimalist to do justice to (at least some of) the
intuitions (often) expressed when someone says that some particular
piece of music is, not merely phenomenally musically accomplished, or
the product of a phenomenally profound musicianship, but, itself,
profound.[9] Jerrold Levinson expresses the worry as follows: Kivy's account
must be inadequate, he says, because – in its insistence on treating musical
profundity as a variety of profundity that is, as it were, hermetically
sealed within the realm of the purely musical – it cannot begin to capture
the sense in which 'the experiencer of a profound piece of music
centrally has the impression of having been *shown or revealed* something
particular about how life is, or goes, or might be, something previously
undisclosed to him.'[10] And Levinson links this deficiency to Kivy's over-
hasty rejection of the thought that music may be 'about' certain non-
musical items, namely emotions:

> If musical works have expressive properties, if composers generally
> intend them to have such, if listeners generally expect them to
> have such, and if it is widely acknowledged that a considerable ...
> part of the interest in much music resides there, I don't see why we
> should be barred from saying that one of the things that music as a
> whole is *about*, i.e. is concerned with, is emotional expression, and
> so by extension the realm of emotions expressed, nor from saying

that some particular piece of music is partly *about*, i.e. concerned with, the emotions it reaches out to through its structure ... In addition, if we consider that when music is expressive of emotional states, listeners who grasp that are often led to reflect, if obscurely, on such states – possibly through inhabiting them temporarily in imagination – and that this result must often be envisaged by the creators and transmitters of music, then it is hard to see what can be so wrong in allowing that some music is about emotional states and their expression.[11]

If we accept that certain musical works can indeed be 'about' certain psychological states, Levinson suggests, then the way is clear to construe the profundity of at least some pieces of music as a function of their exploring 'the emotional or psychic realm in a more insightful or eye-opening way than most music' – the 'emotional or psychic realm' being itself, uncontroversially, a matter of abiding interest and importance to human beings.[12] And this, he concludes, promises a link of the right general sort between music and the impression that someone might have of being '*shown or revealed* something' by a piece of music 'about how life is, or goes, or might be, something previously undisclosed to him'.[13] It offers, in other words, the beginnings of a far more intuitively satisfying account of musical profundity than one which insists that profound music can only ever be music that is profound about itself.

Levinson, then, appears to accept Kivy's incomplete answer to question (1), above – that something is profound if it treats adequately of some profound subject matter. But he disagrees with Kivy's answer to the second question, suggesting that what one understands when one understands a piece of music may not be restricted, as Kivy holds, to the purely musical, but may extend beyond the musical into 'the emotional or psychic realm'. And so, while he endorses Kivy's affirmative answer to the final question (Can what one understands when one understands a piece of music be profound?), the profound subject matter that he holds some pieces of music to be adequately 'about' is not music itself, as Kivy would have it, but life, human existence. Levinson's account is, as he himself emphasises, no more than an outline, a series of what he calls 'promissory notes';[14] and certainly, as it stands, it does no more than suggest that his own preferred answers to the relevant questions may have an immediate intuitive plausibility about them that Kivy's more autonomanic answers lack. But Levinson's hunches deserve a run for their money, it seems to me; and in the second part of this chapter, I attempt to develop a fuller version of the sort of account toward which he might be thought to be gesturing (although not, I hasten to add, a version that Levinson himself would be likely to, or should be taken to, endorse).[15] It is a version, moreover, that is careful to avoid the construal of profundity as consisting in any kind of 'matching' relation.

PART 2. *TAPIOLA*

Jean Sibelius (1865–1957) completed his last significant work, the symphonic poem *Tapiola*, in 1926. In its formal concentration it recalls his final symphony, the seventh, and in its atmosphere his fourth and sixth symphonies. Yet despite these echoes, and despite its immediately and unmistakably Sibelian tone, *Tapiola* is a one-off, a *sui generis* master-piece that many regard as the composer's finest achievement. Tapio, in Finnish mythology, is the god of the forest, of the immense cold northern expanses of Sibelius's native land; and for his symphonic poem (at his publisher's request) he provided the following, perhaps mildly ill-advised, gloss:

> Widespread they stand, the Northland's dusky forests,
> Ancient, mysterious, brooding savage dreams;
> Within them dwells the Forest's mighty god,
> And wood-sprites in the gloom weave magic secrets.

The fairy-tale, almost pixie-ish effect of the final line is about as far as it is possible to get from the spirit of Sibelius's music, which would surely freeze a mere wood-sprite at thirty paces. Indeed, in *Tapiola* Sibelius has written what is probably the chilliest and bleakest piece of music in existence. The remarkable effect of this work is achieved through several means, chief among which are an utterly original style of orchestration, allowing Sibelius to tease out from a fairly standard symphony orchestra an altogether unprecedented iciness of sound, and a tremendous thematic frugality – the whole work, and it lasts for the better part of twenty minutes, is built up out of the slender materials presented in the opening few bars. Add to these a quite phenomenally slow rate of underlying movement and a condition of near tonal stasis (the work never really gets away from the key of B minor) and you have a musical edifice that can only be described as glacial. At just one point, to my ear, is the sunless chill of *Tapiola*'s soundscape intruded onto by something like ordinary human feeling, and that is towards the very end, when the strings give voice to an almost unbearable sense of yearning loneliness; otherwise, Sibelius's world seems unpeopled, untouched. That this is an altogether exceptional and astonishing piece of music is beyond doubt –

there is nothing else remotely like it. But is it a profound piece of music? Does it convey any deep or important insights into the world, or into the human condition? That is the question that the remainder of this chapter will attempt to address. In the first three sections I develop a sketch of an account of musical profundity. In the fourth section I consider some objections to that account and attempt in my responses to them to fill out the original sketch in greater and more convincing detail. Finally, in the fifth section, I turn explicitly to Sibelius and to the question of the profundity of *Tapiola* – a question, I might add, whose proper answer is, as I write this, wholly obscure to me. But that is why I have chosen the piece: it struck me as likely to offer a particularly unforgiving challenge to the account that I mean to propose.

I. *The Concept of Profundity*

Let's begin with a distinction. Something may be described as profound because it reveals or shows or suggests something significant about a matter of real importance to us – about the world, say, or about the human condition. In this sense, we might describe *King Lear* as profound, or Darwin's theory of natural selection, or Bellini's *Pietà*, or Copernicus's heliocentrism, or Kant's 'Copernican revolution' in philosophy. Each of these has the capacity, at least, to affect at a fundamental level, and perhaps to transform, the ways in which we think about ourselves, the world, and our place in the world. And this, I take it, is the primary sense of the profound, the sense that is likely to come to mind first. Call profundity of this kind 'epistemic profundity'. But there is another sense of the profound – related, to be sure, but worth keeping distinct. This second sense has to do with the structuring role that something plays within a system of which it is a part. Thus, a profound economic indicator is one that sits at or near the centre of a web of economic variables; a profound alteration in an ecosystem is one that determines the subsequent nature and development of the ecosystem in all its aspects; a profound innovation in chess is one that decisively revises the tactical or strategic options open to a player who grasps it; and so on. In each case, the thing described as profound is picked out, not merely for being deeply embedded in a system of some kind, but for being a key to understanding the system as a whole – a role it might play in a variety of ways. So, to take a parallel, the final piece in a jigsaw might, once properly placed, resolve a meaningless jumble into a recognisable picture; or, alternatively, it might resolve what seemed to be a picture of one thing into a picture of something else; or, conceivably, it might transform the jigsaw itself, previously thought of as no more than a harmless diversion, into something having a quite different significance – into a devotional object, for instance. To grasp something as profound in this sense, then, is to see how it might be decisive for one's understanding of or one's ways of thinking about the whole system in which it is embedded (where 'decisive', incidentally, needn't mean 'transformative'. One's understanding might be decisively affected in the relevant sense simply by being made to settle more firmly, as it were, into a pattern that it already exhibited). Call this second kind of profundity 'structural profundity'.[16]

I have said that these two senses of profundity are distinct but related. The most obvious way in which they are related, I take it, is that something is plausibly to be thought of as epistemically profound only if it reveals, shows or suggests something that may be structurally profound for our understanding of a matter of real importance for us. So, for instance, the epistemic profundity of Darwin's theory of natural selection lies in the fact that it reveals a feature of the natural world – namely, the absence of design in it – which, once grasped and thought through, may be structurally profound for, and so fundamentally affect, the ways in which we think about ourselves and our place in nature. Similarly, Bellini's *Pietà* is plausibly to be thought of as epistemically profound because it brings to light a feature of living – namely, the possibility of grace – which again, once fully appreciated, may be structurally profound for, and so decisively affect, our apprehension of the human condition. The distinctive value of things that are epistemically profound, then, lies in the kinds of understanding they make possible; and they make these kinds of understanding possible by bringing to light features of the world or the human condition that may be structurally profound for our grasp of them. This relation is not reversible. It is not the case, in other words, that, whenever a structurally profound feature of something is shown or revealed, epistemic profundity attaches to the showing or revealing of it. And the reason for that, straightforwardly enough, is that not every system that is capable of being understood in terms of its structurally profound features is one that is, or that deserves to be taken as being, of real interest or importance to us. So, for example, my discovery that the profitability of roulette for a particular casino is due to a slightly enlarged '0' slot in the wheel, though doubtless the discovery of something structurally profound for an understanding of that system, is not an epistemically profound discovery, since roulette simply doesn't matter that much.[17]

The account of profundity that I've just sketched in succeeds, it seems to me, in capturing the intuitively central features of the concept, explicitly or implicitly. These features are, I suggest, the connection to depth, the connection to insight, the connection to significance, and the connection to value. With respect to depth, the present account relates profundity to structure, and does so in two ways. First, it explicates the depth proper to profundity in terms of the structuring role that something plays in a system of which it is part: the more deeply embedded in a system something is – which is to say, the more far-reaching the consequences are of grasping its significance for an understanding of the system as a whole – the profounder it is (relative to that system). So, for example, one's understanding of Nietzsche's philosophy goes deeper once one has grasped its essential Kantianism than it does if one reads it through the prism of Hegel: Kantianism is more deeply embedded in Nietzsche's thought, and so is a structurally profounder feature of it, than Hegelianism is. Second, the account implicitly connects the profundity of something to the depth of its embeddedness in the structure of the mental life of a person who grasps it as profound: the more significant the system in which it is embedded is taken by that person as being, the deeper, psychologically, will be the ramifications of his grasping it – which is to say, the more structurally profound for an understanding of that person it will be. So, for example, if I appreciate the structural profundity of Kant's thought for an understanding of the ethical, and if the ethical is, for me, of the greatest significance, the effect on me (construed, if you like, as a structured system) will be far-reaching: a certain Kantianism will be deeply embedded in my subsequent thinking, and so will be structurally profound for an understanding of the sort of person I am, or have become. Depth, then, on the present account, is to be explicated in terms of structure.

The second feature of profundity that I take to be intuitively central to it is its connection to the notion of insight. To say that a view, or a theory, or a work of art is profound, but that it offers no insight, would be puzzling at best, and more likely oxymoronic. I suggest, then, that the capacity to offer insight is necessary to anything plausibly to be considered (epistemically) profound. The converse, however, does not hold. It is not the case that anything offering insight is *thereby* epistemically profound: my discovery that the '0' slot in the roulette wheel is slightly enlarged certainly offers insight into the pattern of results that the wheel produces; but, since roulette doesn't matter that much, my discovery isn't (can't be) an epistemically profound one, even if it does reveal something structurally profound for an understanding of what, with the roulette, is going on. On the present account, then, something counts as an insight

– rather than as a mildly interesting observation, say – if what it says about its object is structurally important for an understanding of the system of which it is a part (which, given the argument of the previous paragraph, gives us the connection between 'insight' and 'depth' that we would expect to find). And, if that system is of real interest or importance to us, the relevant insight, or the offering of it, counts as epistemically profound. Thus, there can be genuine insights into things that don't much matter; and profound ones, into things that do. This strikes me as entirely consonant both with ordinary usage and with pre-theoretical intuition.

The third feature of profundity that I have picked out is its connection to 'significance', and here it might be felt that the present account is on stickier ground. So far, after all, I've just helped myself to the notion, and have simply stipulated that life, the world, nature, the human condition and so on are of real interest or importance, while roulette, for instance, isn't. I've also talked about certain things – for example, 'the ethical' – as being 'taken by someone' to be significant. And together, these aspects of the present account might seem to reduce it to the merest relativism: the stipulation that the human condition, say, is of more 'real' significance than roulette, say, appears to be no more than a short-hand way of saying that I think that it is, that is, that it is 'taken by me' as being so. And if that is right, the notion of *epistemic* profundity loses its bite. The bringing to light of any feature that might be structurally profound for an understanding of the system of which it is part would seem to count as epistemically profound on this conception, so long as someone does or could regard that system as significant; which, given the variety of human enthusiasms, means more or less any system at all. But, intuitively at least, it seems that profundity must be connected to a properly normative sense of 'significance', to the *really* significant, in other words, and not merely to whatever might be thought to be so by just anyone – by a very shallow person, for instance, or by a lunatic, a child or a narrow-minded bore. So it may appear as if the present account has run into trouble.

I think it has not, however. It is true that profundity must be connected to a properly normative sense of 'significance', and it is true that I have been prepared to relativise 'significance', at least here and there, to what certain people do, as a matter of fact, take to be significant. But there is no incompatibility here. Or – rather – there is no incompatibility *unless* one thinks that a properly normative sense of 'significance' must be one that is somehow divorced from and independent of any actual (or potential) human concerns. And I can see no reason to think that it must be, or indeed intelligibly to suppose that it could be. This is not to deny that something not previously regarded as significant might come to be recognised as being so – it is not to deny, that is, that something can be genuinely significant even if no one currently thinks that it is. So, for example, the subject matter of electromagnetics was of just as much significance for human beings before the existence of such a subject matter was so much as suspected as it is now, when it governs large swathes of our lives.[18] Nor is it to deny that we can arrive at a better grasp of why something is – and always was – significant than we previously had. So, for example, the system comprising the relations between hygiene and health may always have been, and have been taken to be, significant, but it was only with the advent of the germ theory of disease that that significance, and the reasons for it, could be properly appreciated. Neither of these points, however, requires that the notion of 'significance' be detached from actual (or potential) human concerns. Indeed quite the reverse: electromagnetism and the relations of hygiene to health are important to us precisely because we are the kinds of creatures we are, with the kinds of concerns that such creatures have; and we come to recognise or appreciate their importance as we come to recognise or appreciate the bearing that they have on matters that are of concern to us. At the minimum, then, any plausible conception of 'significance' must be relativised at least to this extent – that nothing can be understood as 'significant' unless for some (concerned) creature or other; and, since what we are currently interested in is the significance that things can have for *us*, the creatures that any plausible conception of 'significance' must be relativised to is human beings, together with their actual (or potential) concerns.

The relevant conception of 'significance', then, is one that is relative to human concerns, which may themselves be variable and relative to circumstance. And this conception gets its normativity from the same source, in the sense that anything genuinely or properly to be considered significant is to be considered so in virtue of the bearing it has on some matter of genuine, rather than merely passing or casual, human concern. This is why my list of significant things included life, the world, nature, the human condition and so on, but excluded, for instance, roulette. The former subjects bear (or should bear) on the deeper concerns of any human being whatsoever, while the last, roulette, does not, and arguably should not – however all-absorbing for some particular person it might, as a matter of fact, be.[19] And between these extremes lie any number of intermediate cases, about whose ultimate significance there is very little of a general sort to be said. Some will plausibly be thought to bear on concerns held, by at least some people in some times and places, to have the relevant kind of universality; others won't. And which are which, or which are most deservingly to be regarded as which, must remain a matter of debate for those people in those times and places. I make no apology for any remaining hint of relativism that this might leave: it is ineliminable, and not regrettably so. On the present account, then, something is epistemically profound if it brings to light a feature that may be structurally profound for our understanding of a matter that is of genuine significance for us, which is to say, a matter that bears on concerns that might plausibly be held to be more than merely passing or local, and which may indeed be held – perhaps, in the event, wrongly, but again with plausibility, that is, with good reason – to be universal.

The final feature of profundity that I mentioned was its connection to value, an issue about which rather little should now need to be said. If something is epistemically profound then, given the arguments of the previous paragraphs, it offers (deep) insight into something that really matters; and that is why it is of value. Beyond which, I take it, nothing further is required. The present account thus succeeds, it seems to me, in capturing the central features of the concept it is concerned with. It connects profundity to its most intuitively important relata – namely, depth, insight, significance and value – and shows how, in the case of epistemic profundity, those relata come together to form a tightly-knit package, indeed to constitute an analysis of what it is for something to *be* (epistemically) profound. This conception of profundity will be assumed in, and will underpin, the remaining sections of this chapter.

II. Expressive Profundity

So far I have said nothing about music, and it is time that I started to rectify that. In this section I concentrate on the notion of structural profundity as it features in musical cases, especially – and in accordance with the suggestion canvassed at the outset of the present chapter – in cases where a musical work is felt to be *expressively* profound. But before turning to expressiveness specifically, let me just note that we already have the resources to hand to account perfectly plausibly for one kind of musical profundity. Peter Kivy, it will be recalled, suggests that certain pieces of contrapuntal music might be regarded as profound because they are in some sense about (and adequately about) the possibilities inherent in music, which are themselves profound. I have already given reasons, in the Background part of this chapter, to doubt that Kivy's analysis is successful. But I think we can now see what one ought to want to say about the sorts of cases that interest him, namely, that the music is *profoundly contrapuntal* – that every aspect of the music is informed, controlled, and given shape by the counterpoint that lies at its heart. The contrapuntal, on this conception, is thus a structurally profound feature of the music in question, and so one that offers a key to understanding the system that that music comprises. It seems to me that this captures, and captures economically, everything that Kivy might originally have meant. (It is also, of course, open to someone who thinks – as I suspect Kivy does, and as I do – that some pieces of contrapuntal music are of genuine, as opposed to merely passing, significance, to argue that epistemic profundity attaches to the demonstration that counterpoint is indeed structurally profound for an understanding of those pieces of music.) So here is one way in which the notion of structural profundity bears directly on musical cases.

But what about music that has profound expressive properties? Here, if we are to get the emphasis right, we shall have to tread carefully. It might, for example, appear tempting to claim that a piece of music will be, say, profoundly cheerful – in the sense that cheerfulness is a structurally profound property of it – if it is frequently or exclusively expressive of cheerfulness.[20] But there is a difference between being profoundly cheerful and being merely regularly or relentlessly cheerful. Consider Natasha: suppose that she leads an immensely agreeable life, surrounded on all sides by engaging companions and diversions, with never a cloud in her sky. She is almost always cheerful. This would be quite insufficient to establish that her cheerfulness was (structurally) profound. We would want to see how she responded to misfortune, for example, or how she would be if she were surrounded by drudges, pedants and bores. If her responses seemed *still* to be unchanged, or to be suffused by a kind of underlying cheerfulness, which gave form to each of her passing feelings, then – and only then – would we be warranted in concluding that her cheerfulness was (structurally) profound. For cheerfulness would now be a *key* to understanding Natasha's character, rather than merely a superficial effect of her circumstances. We could attempt to understand and to interpret Natasha as a personality structured by her profoundly cheerful nature, rather than as merely happening to be having a reasonably agreeable time of things. Or suppose instead that that Natasha is astonishingly gullible, and that she is capable of being persuaded of just about anything; that most of her actions are determined by beliefs far less critically acquired than they might have been; that she is continually surprised to learn that what she has just taken for gospel is really baloney; that her whole life is structured, at every level, by her tendency too willingly to believe whatever she is told. Again, and (I take it) uncontroversially, Natasha is to be regarded as profoundly gullible, in the sense that gullibility is a structurally profound feature of her personality. What this means for the musical case is that we shall have to be careful not to confound the mere preponderance of some expressive (or psychological) quality with the kind of quality that underlies, and breathes life into, the various expressive episodes which the music contains. It is only the second kind of quality that will have any claim to be described as structurally profound. Consider two examples.

Beethoven's Fifth Symphony is rather famously associated with defiance. But on the surface (as one might say) it is only intermittently expressive of defiance in a direct way: the expressive character of its surface is – variously – turbulent, rumbustious, jolly, laconic, triumphant, anguished, benign – and, from time to time, defiant. Yet the defiance of the piece seems to permeate its other expressive qualities, so that underlying the various episodes of laconic good humour, for instance, is always a sense that the latter quality is maintained either against the odds, or only as a respite from the chief business of outfacing the world. The quality of defiance, in other words, appears to structure the expressive content of the symphony as a whole – to be the interpretative key to understanding the affective terrain which the work, in all its various aspects, inhabits. Which of course means that, in my view, Beethoven's Fifth Symphony is profoundly defiant – that the expressive quality of defiance is a structurally profound quality of the work. But compare this with the prevailing expressive quality of, for instance, Scarlatti's B-flat major Sonata K.529. Its principal thematic idea, which is light-hearted and cheerful, alternates with a section of very slightly darker music, whose modest shadow looms briefly, before being deftly dispelled. Its musicianship aside, nothing in this sonata invites description as profound. Its cheeriness lies on the surface only; for although that quality is almost constantly in evidence, it does not relate to any other qualities which – taken collectively – could, without strain, be regarded as a *system* of any kind. Scarlatti's sonata simply *has* no underlying expressive quality, for there is nothing that such a quality might be heard to underlie or to structure. Thus its cheeriness cannot be regarded as a structurally profound property of it.[21] These examples ought to indicate somewhat more clearly the kind of distinction I mean to draw between music whose expressiveness is structurally profound, and music which is – merely – frequently or exclusively expressive of some particular feeling.

At a purely structural level, then, certain expressive qualities of certain pieces of music can properly be regarded as profound, in the sense that they provide a key to understanding the expressive systems which those works constitute. It is important at this point, however, to be clear just how much, or perhaps how little, this claim amounts to. Specifically, it is important to recall that the attribution of structural profundity to some particular feature of a given system does not, by itself, entail the attribution of *epistemic* profundity to anything whatever, and so does not entail the kinds of normative and evaluative considerations that an attribution of epistemic profundity would bring in its train. In the example just given, for instance, the bare attribution of structural profundity to the defiance expressed in Beethoven's Fifth Symphony, and the corresponding description of that work as profoundly defiant, carries with it no evaluative implications at all: the work is neither better nor worse for being so describable, since defiance is not, in itself, a good-making or a bad-making quality of pieces of music.[22] In other cases, by contrast, the bare attribution of structural profundity to a given feature does have – or can have – evaluative implications. So, for example, the description of Natasha as profoundly gullible almost certainly constitutes a criticism of her, since gullibility is a trait that a person would generally be better without. And Ernst Bloch is clearly not intending to compliment Strauss's *Elektra* when he remarks that 'A soul is lacking, however lyrical-erotic the prevalent mood ... In its deepest passages Strauss' music wears at the best the melancholy expression of a brilliant hollowness.'[23] The 'brilliant hollowness' that Bloch detects is taken by him – and plausibly, I think – to be a structurally profound quality of *Elektra*, to be a key to understanding the expressive world of that work. But to describe *Elektra* as profoundly, if brilliantly, hollow is of course at the same time to condemn it. In these cases, then, the bare attribution of structural profundity to a feature of a given system certainly does carry evaluative implications – but *not* in virtue of any considerations having to do with epistemic profundity. The moral here, then, is that the description of a system as profoundly X, where that description constitutes the attribution to X of structural profundity, has evaluative force *only* to the extent that being X is a strength or a weakness in systems of that kind; it does not derive its evaluative force – if it has any – from the mere presence in the description of the word 'profoundly'.[24]

A couple of related points may also be worth noting. The first is that, whatever evaluative implications a particular attribution of structural profundity may have, the attribution itself, if it is plausible, will standardly be valuable. So, for example, if I'm genuinely interested in *Elektra*, and really do want to understand it, or what's off-putting about it, then I may well be glad to recognize, with Bloch's help, just how profoundly hollow it is: appreciating its 'brilliant hollowness' might unlock for me the (soulless!) heart of the music's expressive world. The value of recognising the structural profundity of this feature of Strauss's work, then, is a function of the understanding that it yields. Or, to put the point another way, Bloch's remark is a valuable one precisely because it expresses an *insight*; and this is the only reliable connection there is between an attribution of structural profundity and any issue of value. The second thing to note is that, just as the value of Bloch's insight doesn't somehow accrue to its object, *Elektra*, so, if an insight happens to be a profound one – which is to say an epistemically profound one, that is, an insight into something of genuine significance – still nothing follows about the value of its object. Even if *Elektra* were plausibly to be regarded as something of genuine significance, in other words, its fundamental hollowness would remain a defect in it, no matter how profoundly valuable the insight required to bring that defect to light.[25] The basic point here, then, as in the previous paragraph, is that the mere use of the concept of profundity in describing, or in expressing an insight into, some structural feature of a given system has no evaluative implications for that system at all. A system can be as profoundly thus-and-so as you like, and I can very valuably point out that this is true of it, and still the system can be quite worthless. To the extent that the discussion of this section has been restricted to the structural profundity of certain expressive properties of certain pieces of music, therefore, it has had nothing whatever to say about the profundity or value of those pieces themselves. That is the issue to be addressed in the next section.

III. Attitudes and Outlooks

Suppose that Natasha is profoundly defiant, in a way analogous to that in which Beethoven's Fifth is defiant: defiance underlies and gives structure to her personality as a whole. We could simply describe her as profoundly defiant, and leave it at that. Or we could, if we wished, say more. For although her defiance is not about anything in particular, it certainly does presuppose an attitude *towards* things in general. No one would be likely, in any specific case, to respond defiantly to an event that they regarded as amenable or devoid of threat; or to an event that they thought threatening but altogether impossible to outface. There is, in other words, a description – perhaps 'the threatening but outfaceable'[26] – which one has to perceive an event as fitting if one is to respond to it defiantly. This is so for particular episodes of defiance. But Natasha's defiance is structurally profound. There is nothing in particular that she perceives as threatening but outfaceable – rather, she has a disposition to regard things in general as fitting that description. She has, one might say, a distinctive attitude towards life or the world that is intimated through the profoundly defiant quality of her character.[27] Thus, in describing Natasha as profoundly defiant, we at the same time impute to her a distinctive outlook, or, more grandly, a *Weltanschauung* (which she herself may be only imperfectly aware of having). I think that this is true, *mutatis mutandis*, whenever a profound characteristic of a psychological kind is attributed to someone. And something similar is also the case, I would claim, when such a characteristic is attributed to a piece of music. I am not suggesting, of course, that the music literally *has* an outlook of some kind, or that it has some particular way of viewing life or the world. But I am suggesting that, in experiencing certain pieces of music intently, and responsively, and so coming to grasp their profoundly expressive qualities, we at the same time gain an intimation of the outlook implicit *in* those qualities: so that, for example, in grasping the profoundly defiant character of Beethoven's Fifth Symphony we gain an intimation of what it would be to have a defiant outlook on the world, of what it would be to view the world as threatening but outfaceable.[28]

If this is right, then, because the object of an attitude or an outlook is the world, say, or life (that is, something of a sort plausibly to be regarded as genuinely significant), it is possible to ask of a given attitude or outlook whether or not it is epistemically profound. And to ask this is, in effect, to ask whether it offers insight into its object, whether it highlights or privileges features of life or the world that are, or that might come to be, structurally profound for our understanding of them. And if the answer to that is yes, I suggest, then the attitude or outlook is, indeed, to be regarded as epistemically profound.

As it stands, of course, this suggestion is compressed and telegraphic. But we can begin to get a more perspicuous idea of what it amounts to, I think, if we turn to a recent discussion of emotional profundity offered by David Pugmire. Pugmire argues, in a substantial and subtle essay, that, in order for the attribution of profundity to an emotion to be warranted, it is not sufficient that it merely play a structuring role in some system of the relevant sort; it is not enough, as he puts it, that it be fully 'embedded' in a person's character or concerns, for example. It must also, he holds, have an 'alethic' quality.[29] Pugmire imagines someone who 'views his every performance as a judgement on him, each effort as a failure or success that reflects on him absolutely'. He then imagines this person making a mess of some footling task, and experiencing his failure as calamity. In his emotion, Pugmire says, he 'gives his poor showing a significance it lacks. The portentousness is of emotion only, not of fact. Here the subjective embedding of the event for the person is just what makes his emotion shallow. What the world feels like to the person is not what it is like.'[30] And the requirement that a response be commensurate with the world as it is, can, when unmet, mean that the response amounts not only to hysterical over-reaction, say, or to frivolous emotional indulgence, but to a kind of emotional hollowness that constitutes what Pugmire calls 'betrayal':

> The valuational function of an emotion involves not only having valuational thoughts (which may range from images to propositional value judgements), but also recasting the values as experiences in the shape of feelings. Thus, my guilt projects itself in the chastising pangs of it that I feel; in adoration, the loveliness of something reappears in the warmth of my delight in the contemplation of it. Thus, when an emotion is false to the values resident in its object, it is not just untrue to them in the way that a mistaken judgement is but also in the way that a travesty or caricature is. In the feelings that register the object, there is injury and diminishment, a failure to mark and pay tribute to its actual qualities.[31]

Genuine depth of emotion, Pugmire concludes, resides not merely in the relation between some particular emotion and other facts about the person whose emotion it is, but in the relation between that emotion and the facts, full stop.[32] The world has to be a certain way, that is, in order for certain emotions about it to be (even potentially) profound.

Pugmire's reflections, which strike me as compelling, are devoted to depth of emotion, specifically. But it is clear that his remarks apply, *mutatis mutandis*, to attitudes or outlooks as well. It is clear, in other words, that, if Pugmire is right, it is necessary that any attitude or outlook that is (even potentially) to be considered epistemically profound must have an 'alethic' quality – that it must answer to the way the world is, or at least to a way that the world might plausibly or pointfully be taken as being. And this constraint, I take it, will disqualify certain outlooks or attitudes, however fully 'embedded' in a person's psychological life, from counting as profound. So, for example, the outlook of a paranoiac, for whom the world falls under the description 'has it in for me' or 'is out to get me', is unlikely to qualify, as is that of the sentimentalist, who suppresses or distorts certain aspects of the world or of his experience of it so as to secure, in Oscar Wilde's words, 'the luxury of an emotion without paying for it'.[33] Nor is Natasha's gullibility likely to qualify: the world is not, as her attitude towards it would suggest, everything that it seems to be, certainly not *simpliciter*. When I suggest, then, that the content of someone's view of life or the world might be considered epistemically profound in virtue of its capacity to reveal a structurally profound feature of a system of concerns that is, to us, of great interest and importance, its capacity to play that role must be understood to depend, at least in part, on its not constituting a 'betrayal', 'travesty or caricature' of the relevant facts. In order to be (even potentially) profound, that is, an attitude or outlook must answer to the way things are, or might truthfully be thought to be.[34]

This, it seems to me, is the way to capture the thought that Peter Kivy may have been reaching for when construing profundity in terms of one thing's being 'adequately' about another. But whereas Kivy's construal appeared to depend, as I suggested in the Background part of this chapter, on the unsustainable notion of 'matching', Pugmire's certainly does not. The simplest way to bring this out is to focus for a moment on his invocation of 'caricature'. A caricature is recognisable as such precisely because its subject can be recognised in it – precisely, that is, because it *does* capture some possible feature or aspect of the subject it caricatures. The paranoiac's attitude, for example, does at least constitute a caricature of the world. It is not, cannot be, a profound attitude. But because it does capture a possibility about the world, the question whether it is profound can at least intelligibly be raised, even if only to be answered in the negative. The idea of an attitude towards the world that failed even to caricature it, by contrast, is unintelligible: one could know neither that the world was its object, nor, indeed, that it was an attitude. The point, then, is that the sort of failure of depth that Pugmire highlights is only possible once one is *already within* the ambit marked out by appeal to 'matching', and so cannot be cashed out in terms of a failure of it. One sees a caricature for the caricature that it is, not because it fails to match its subject (it does match it), but because it sells its subject short, because the understanding it evinces doesn't go as far as it might, or – if what is at issue really matters to us – as far as it should. No amount of 'matching'-talk can hope to capture this. Pugmire's 'alethic' requirement, then, passes muster. So an attitude is epistemically profound, on the present account, if the understanding of the world or the human condition that it evinces caricatures neither. It is profound, that is, if it offers a perspective which gives perspicuous structure to our thoughts about matters that are of real significance to us.

So let's return to music. The defiance that I argued earlier was a profound quality of Beethoven's Fifth Symphony, for example, is a structurally profound property of it. But the attitude towards the world that I claimed was implicit in that quality – an attitude for which the world falls under the description 'threatening but outfaceable' – is of course a candidate for having epistemic profundity attributed to it as well, even if, for its candidacy to be plausible, more will have to be said. Specifically, the unique *shade* of the attitude evinced will have to be taken into account – a uniqueness that is a function of the fact that, since the structural profundity of a given property, and hence the character of that property itself, cannot be appreciated *except* through the work that it structures in the way that it does, the character of the attitude it evinces is, likewise, tied indissolubly to, and is uniquely revealed by, the character of the work. So what, more concretely, might one want to say about the (unique) attitude evinced by the Fifth? Something like this, perhaps. If defiance goes to the brink, shows a willingness to give everything in the struggle, and shows, in that, the value of what it is prepared to give up, then defiance may be tantamount to the most supreme and exhilarating sense of life: certainly the symphony conveys that, not least in its repeated burstings through, as it were, to new and ever vaster horizons. And in *this* defiance, there is a largeness, the possibility of magnanimity, of generosity. It is the opposite of the embittered railing of some mean little spirit intent on claiming its rights; and the opposite, in another way, of a braggart's belligerence, of a call to arms from the soap-box. There is, here, a graciousness, a lightness of heart, even, that is quite incompatible with either resentment or tub-thumping, or with vindictiveness, and which speaks instead from a standpoint shot to the core with affirmation. And I could go on; but anyone with ears will be able to do better for themselves just by listening to Beethoven's music. It is *this* attitude, then – which is to say, the attitude intimated through the unique shade of defiance with which Beethoven's symphony is suffused[35] – that might plausibly be regarded as one that highlights or privileges features of life or the world that are, or that might come to be, structurally profound for our understanding of them.

So, with the foregoing borne in mind, one might put the matter like this. The attitude evinced by Beethoven's Fifth contains one possible answer to the metaphysical question, What is the world really like? (threatening), and one possible answer to the ethical question, How ought one to regard such a world? (as something to be outfaced), answers whose 'alethic' quality, to follow Pugmire, is open to, and indeed requires, assessment. It seems quite feasible to me that the attitude evinced by Beethoven's symphony is, indeed, an epistemically profound one – and certainly it is an attitude more likely to qualify than, say, the attitude evinced by Strauss's *Elektra*: the world construed as a world of glitzy surface has caricature written all over it. Perhaps the attitude implicit in Beethoven's Fifth could only be regarded as profound by a listener whose perplexities and character were of a particular kind. But the essential point is that music which has an expressive quality that is structurally profound may also, in virtue of that, be epistemically profound, in as much as that the attitude it evinces is, or might plausibly be thought to be, structurally profound for our understanding of life or of the world. And where the attitude evinced *is* of that sort, the music itself is, quite properly, to be considered profound,[36] and is valuable in virtue of that, in just the way that Darwin's theory of natural selection, say, or Bellini's *Pietà*, are to be considered profound and, therefore, valuable. And that, in effect, completes the explication that I want to give of musical profundity.

IV. Two Clarifications

Peter Kivy has objected at some length to the account that I have been developing.[37] He is wholly unconvinced by my attribution to music of the capacity to offer answers to the kind of ethical and metaphysical questions that I have mentioned, and invites us, in corrective mood, to consider the following alleged parallel:

> Now if my Uncle Harry put his arm around my shoulder and, with great earnestness, imparted the intelligence that the world is threatening and one should try to outface it, I would think him a Polonius for enunciating such a platitude. Yet Ridley would have us believe that this banality is the profound content of one of the most profound of musical utterances (if profound musical utterances there be), what E. M. Forster called 'the most sublime noise that has ever penetrated the ear of man.' I cannot credit it. If *this* is what the mighty Fifth tells us, then, indeed, *parturient montes, nascetur ridiculus mus.*[38]

Kivy's objection fails, it seems to me, to cut very deep. If his Uncle Harry were to inform him that pride goes before a fall, say, or that reflection can get in the way of action, the fact that his remarks are platitudinous counts not a whit against the suggestion, for instance, that the going of pride before a fall is part of the profound content of Shakespeare's *Coriolanus*, or that the obstruction of action by reflection is part of the profound content of *Hamlet*. Kivy appears to have made the error, in other words, of supposing that the value of an artistic utterance is equivalent to the value of a paraphrase or gloss of it; and that, for reasons that I have emphasised repeatedly, is simply to miss the point of paraphrase, and of what a paraphrase can sensibly be expected to do. When I suggest that Beethoven's Fifth evinces a particular attitude towards the world, namely, that the world is threatening but outfaceable, the words 'the world is threatening but outfaceable' are intended as a gloss of the attitude evinced, as an entirely adequate indication of the sort of attitude that it is. They are not intended as, and could not sensibly be intended as, a substitute for or an equivalent of that attitude as it is evinced by Beethoven's Fifth Symphony (or as a substitute for or an equivalent of that attitude as it is imaginatively inhabited by the responsive listener). The fact, therefore, that 'the intelligence that the world is threatening and one should try to outface it' is, as Kivy puts it, a 'banality' is entirely consistent with the thought that, as I would have it, that very same 'banality' indicates part of the profound content of Beethoven's symphony, and one of the principal sources of that symphony's value. Indeed, and to labour the point, another symphony – Tchaikovsky's Fourth seems a good enough example – might plausibly be held to evince an attitude glossable in much the same terms as the attitude evinced by Beethoven's Fifth. But this fact, if it is one, no more shows that the two works are equally epistemically profound, or of equal value, than the fact that *The Bonfire of the Vanities* might be thought to concern the going of pride before a fall shows that Wolfe's novel is as deep or as valuable as *Coriolanus*. The value of what is said in a paraphrase is one thing; the value of what is said in the thing paraphrased is quite another.

That is the first clarification. The second, which is perhaps rather more necessary, is prompted by Kivy's parting shot at my account. He complains that:

> Ridley, throughout his discussion, does not talk about any of the things that I would adduce to support the belief that Beethoven's Fifth Symphony is musically profound. He has not talked about the incredible thematic economy and concentration with which the master has constructed the sonata movement, the wonderful fugato passages of the scherzo's trio, the miraculous harmonic bridge between the scherzo and the finale. In a word, he hasn't talked about the *music*. If there is profundity in Beethoven's Fifth Symphony, *there* is where to look for it. If not there, then the game is lost.[39]

Kivy is right that I have not talked in the quasi-technical terms that he mentions, although wrong in thinking that this means that I have not 'talked about the *music*.' In my view – as, indeed, in his[40] – the expressive properties of a piece of music are properties of it *as* a piece of music. In my view, therefore, to talk about those properties, as I have done for the last two sections, is, very directly, to talk 'about the *music*'.

To put it slightly more fully, my view – in the relevant respects – is this. Music can be described in the technical vocabulary of musical analysis. Music can also be described in expressive terms. The features in which musical expressiveness resides – for instance, melody, harmony and rhythm – are, as a matter of fact, the very same features as those addressed by musical analysis. The difference between analytic and expressive description – and it is not a sharp difference; the two can merge with and reinforce one another – is a difference, therefore, in the ways in which those features are picked out, and in the ways in which they are subsequently enlisted to articulate understandings of the piece of music heard. Except perhaps in some (minimally) aspectival sense, then, the difference between them is not a difference of subject matter: both are about the music. One might offer a structural description of a piece of music in analytic terms. One might equally offer such a description in expressive terms. The two descriptions may, but need not, map on to one another. There may be divergences of emphasis, or even, occasionally, incompatibilities. But what one should expect to find, if both are good and helpful examples of their respective sorts, is a coming together. And this is no coincidence. For it is very often the case that the prominence accorded to a musical feature in an analytic description is *explained* by its expressive prominence, and, equally, that the prominence accorded to a musical feature in an expressive description is *explained* by its analytic prominence.[41] In the standard case, that is, good, helpful examples of the two kinds of description are mutually sustaining.

So, for example, when I suggest that the defiance expressed by Beethoven's Fifth Symphony is structurally profound – and mean by that, as I hope I have made clear, that the work's defiance is a structuring property of it, that is, a key to understanding the unity of its apparently diverse expressive episodes – that suggestion is entirely consistent with Kivy's claim that one ought to be attending, for example, to 'the incredible thematic economy and concentration' of the symphony's first movement. For it may very well be the case, indeed it would be surprising in this instance if it were not the case, that to point to the structural profundity of the symphony's defiance and to point to the economy and concentration of its thematic material is to point to exactly the same features of the work under two different, mutually sustaining descriptions.[42] And it is for just this sort of reason that one should hesitate before attributing to Tchaikovsky's Fourth Symphony the same degree of epistemic profundity that one might attribute to Beethoven's Fifth. Both, to be sure, can reasonably be said to evince an attitude towards the world that is describable as defiant. But since the defiance of the Tchaikovsky is undeniably more episodic, and less expressively structural, than that of the Beethoven – a fact non-coincidentally shadowed, I would suggest, by Tchaikovsky's relative thematic largesse and lack of concentration – the defiance of the Tchaikovsky is less structurally profound. Tchaikovsky's defiance is implicated less deeply than Beethoven's in the symphony's expressive narrative; it informs the work's expressive surface less systematically. As a corollary, it acquires far less focus and nuance than Beethoven's, and, as a consequence, strikes one as evincing an attitude altogether cruder and more general-purpose than Beethoven's (and hence altogether more vulnerable to charges of 'betrayal' or 'caricature'). Tchaikovsky's defiance, that is, has a far weaker claim to be appreciated (even potentially) as epistemically profound. This, I hope, makes it clear exactly why, and in what sense, I have insisted that the putative epistemic profundity of an attitude evinced by a piece of music is conditional upon the actual structural profundity, for an understanding of that piece of music, of the expressive quality in which the attitude is intimated.

Given the extent of our agreement about the relation between the analytic and the expressive, it is surprising that Kivy shouldn't have foreseen this kind of response, or at least have seen in some general way that my talk of Beethoven's defiance and his talk of, for instance, 'incredible thematic economy' might be complements to one another in an explication of musical profundity, rather than rivals. It would then, of course, require a further step for Kivy to acknowledge the transition, central to my account, from the structural profundity of a given expressive quality to the (potential) epistemic profundity of an attitude – a step which, given his commitment to the autonomanic view that music has 'no reference to anything beyond itself', he is unlikely to want to take. But his reluctance in this case is founded precisely *on* that commitment (i.e. is not backed up by any independent argumentation), and so cannot be taken as an indication that the transition I'm insisting on is either unintelligible or, if intelligible, without instances. For the reasons given, then, I cannot see that Kivy's strictures really, in the end, offer any very serious challenge to the account that I have been developing, and I set them aside accordingly.

V. Sibelius's Profundity

In terms of the questions set out in the Background part of the present chapter, then, my account comes to this. (1) What kind of property is profundity? Profundity can be understood either in structural terms or in epistemic terms. A property of a piece of music is structurally profound if it gives structure to the other properties of that piece of music, if it provides a key to understanding the system constituting the work as a whole. Some structurally profound properties, such as the properties that Kivy concentrates on, may be picked out in, as it were, 'purely' musical terms. Others, such as the defiance of Beethoven's Fifth, may be picked out in expressive terms. A property that is structurally profound in the expressive sense may also be a candidate, when construed as an attitude towards life or the world, to be considered epistemically profound. Such an attitude is epistemically profound if it highlights or reveals features of life or the world that are, or that might plausibly be taken to be, structurally profound for our understanding of them – if, in other words, it can be understood as giving structure to metaphysical, existential or other concerns that are, to us, of real moment, and if, in imparting that structure, the attitude travesties none of the relevant facts (Pugmire's 'alethic' requirement). (2) What do we understand when we understand a piece of music? We understand, among other things, its 'purely' musical properties and its expressive properties. We therefore understand, among other things, whatever structurally profound properties the music might have, and, where such properties are expressive properties, and the appropriate conditions are met, may come to understand the attitudes implicit in those properties as epistemically profound. (3) Is what we understand when we understand a piece of music capable of having the property of profundity? Yes – in either of two ways. What we understand may be structurally profound; or what we understand may be structurally profound *and* epistemically profound. Much of the most valuable music we have, I would contend, is music that can be understood as profound in the second of these ways.

It is now time to see what sort of sense this account is capable of making of *Tapiola*. I do not propose to devote much space to one sort of thought, namely, that *Tapiola* has 'purely' musical properties that are structurally profound. First, such a thought is hardly controversial: the profound musicianship of this work is more or less universally acknowledged, and the capacity of the present account to capture its musicianly qualities would hardly set it apart from any other. Second, I am principally interested, as will have become clear, in the potential of music to be epistemically profound, and that potential, on the account that I have offered, is grounded on structurally profound properties of an expressive rather than a 'purely' musical sort. And third, I simply do not have the kind of expertise necessary to demonstrate in an insightful or original way that such and such a feature of Sibelius's music, for instance its extreme thematic frugality, is indeed a structurally profound property of it. From this point of view, I can do no better than appeal to Robert Layton, whose authority in the relevant respect vastly exceeds mine:

> It is indeed arguable that *Tapiola* is [Sibelius's] greatest achievement ... [In it, he] exhibits the most subtle and complete mastery of symphonic procedure, in the sense that he achieves a continuity of thought paralleled only in the symphonies. *Tapiola* is unique even in Sibelius's output: its world is new and unexplored, a world of strange new sounds ... [showing] the most profound originality in its handling of the orchestra ... A large amount of Sibelius's music ... is so completely identified with the orchestral source of sound that it is impossible to conceive of [it] in other terms. Of no work is this more true than *Tapiola*. It is this score, too, that exhibits the most thorough-going and imaginative use of the pedal point in all Sibelius ... In its homogeneity, concentration of utterance and intensity of vision it is a masterpiece of the first order.[43]

Layton concludes that *Tapiola*'s 'greatness lies in its impact in terms of pure music',[44] and it is certainly true that its greatness derives largely from that. But is it great – or profound – in any other way?

The account that I have offered suggests that we should now ask whether *Tapiola* has any expressive properties that might, potentially, be considered structurally profound. And at once we run up against a problem. For the 'homogeneity' of the work is such that, with the exception of the outbreak of yearning loneliness towards the end, it is tempting to describe its expressive quality as, simply, very very chilly throughout. It is tempting, that is, to regard *Tapiola* as a work that continuously exhibits just one expressive quality, and so as a work that comprises no expressive system that any putatively structurally profound property could be heard to underlie. If this is true, *Tapiola* cannot be understood, even potentially, as epistemically profound. I'm not sure that this is right, however. Listen to *Tapiola* again. One hears, once its rather icy and faceless thematic material has first been announced, much that is certainly merely chilly. Yet one might also feel tempted to say that one hears moments of relative levity, and perhaps also of awe, ardour, and, arguably, sheer terror. These episodes are, to be sure, suffused with chilliness – as, indeed, is the yearningly lonely passage I mentioned a moment ago. But the fact that each of these surface effects is shot to the core with chill may suggest that chilliness is not only a feature of the music's surface, although it certainly is that, but is the principle about which *Tapiola's* entire expressive world is structured. If so, the quality of chilliness may have a claim to be considered structurally profound.

Suppose that one accepts this. What, if chilliness is a structurally profound property of it, does the attitude or outlook evinced by *Tapiola* amount to? The answer, presumably, is that it amounts to an attitude in which the world presents itself as bleak, indifferent to human concerns, inimical to the flourishing of any kind of warmth – as hostile, in short, to life. And is this an attitude that might, even potentially, be considered epistemically profound? I have to say that the suggestion makes me queasy. For one thing, the attitude seems too general-purpose. A lot of facts about the way the world really is would have to be otherwise in order for *this* to be a truthful or appropriate take on it; as a *Weltanschauung*, that is, this one has the air of travesty or caricature about it. And for another thing, I'm simply not convinced that chilliness – understood as an attitude that someone might take towards the world – is what *Tapiola* evinces. I'm sceptical about this for several reasons, but the chief one is that the passages of 'levity', 'awe', 'ardour' and 'terror' that I invoked a moment ago do not, in the event, seem to me to be best described in that way, as episodes of expressed emotion. Rather, they strike me as offering *occasions* for awe, ardour, terror and so forth. They do not, that is, seem to me to constitute the elements of an expressive system that chilliness might be heard as underlying or giving structure to. So I doubt that its chilliness can be either a structurally or an epistemically profound property of *Tapiola*.

One might conclude from this that *Tapiola* is musically profound, *simpliciter*, and leave it at that. But I think there may be more to be said. First, and drawing on the argument of Chapter 2, *Tapiola* has a title, and its title tells us that it is to be heard, or that it legitimately can be heard, as having to do with the forests and icy wastes of northern Finland. Nature, then, rather than the world as such, is the context within which any claim this work has to epistemic profundity may require to be understood. Second, the one undeniable moment of musical expressiveness is not of awe or terror or any of those, but is the passage immediately before the end, the yearningly lonely one. And the more I listen to the work, the more this passage strikes me as pivotal, as the moment to which everything else has been, as it were, a prelude or build-up.[45] It strikes me, in fact, as the moment at which the work's *real* underlying expressive quality is, finally, declared and made explicit. These considerations suggest two possible, and possibly complementary, lines of thought; and I'll come to them in a moment. But first, and perhaps as no more than a sort of scene-setter, although I suspect it might be more than that, consider the following wonderful passage from Schopenhauer:

> Now if in the depth of winter, when the whole of nature is frozen and stiff, we see the rays of the setting sun reflected by masses of stone, where they illuminate without warming, and are thus favourable only to the purest kind of knowledge, not to the will, then contemplation of the beautiful effect of light on these masses moves us into the state of pure knowing, as all beauty does. Yet here, through the faint recollection of the lack of warmth from those rays, in other words, of the absence of the principle of life, a certain transcending of the interest of the will is required ... [and so] we have a transition from the feeling of the beautiful to that of the sublime ... Let us [now] transport ourselves to a very lonely region of boundless horizons, under a perfectly cloudless sky, trees and plants in the perfectly motionless air, no animals, no human beings, no moving masses of water, the profoundest silence. Such surroundings are as it were a summons to seriousness, to contemplation, with complete emancipation from all willing and its cravings; but it is just this that gives to such a scene of mere solitude ... a touch of the sublime. For, since it affords no objects ... to the will ... there is left only the state of pure contemplation, and whoever is incapable of this is abandoned with shameful ignominy to the emptiness of unoccupied will, to the torture and misery of boredom.[46]

Schopenhauer could never have heard *Tapiola*, of course, or indeed anything like it. But had he done so, it is impossible that he should not have thought it touched with sublimity, so prescient is his evocation. Whatever one makes of his metaphysics, in other words, I think that *Tapiola* shows much of what his remarks suggest here – and that the work emerges the deeper for it.

I return, though, to the two lines of thought I mentioned a moment ago. According to the first, *Tapiola* is to be heard as representational of Tapio's realm, the Nordic landscape, but from a perspective defined by the yearning loneliness of its beholder. The chilliness, the occasions for awe, ardour, terror, and even for levity, are all filtered through the loneliness, so that the landscape itself is saturated with it. Here, the perspective or attitude exhibited and the native bleakness of its purview are mutually reinforcing: the loneliness and the landscape etch each other's lines. Heard like this, *Tapiola*, in offering an exemplar of the so-called pathetic fallacy, and an extreme and comfortless one at that, has a claim to be considered epistemically profound, so long as it travesties neither the attitude, the landscape nor their interpenetration. And, for my money, it doesn't travesty them. But the potential force of this first line of thought is brought out better, I think, by the second.[47] According to this, *Tapiola* is to be heard as representational, not merely of the Nordic landscape, but of that landscape as it is embodied in Tapio himself, its god. Heard thus, the music tells us something about the anthropomorphising of nature. It tells us that if we read ourselves back into nature, and back into *that* landscape, specifically, and are as un-flinching as possible in our estimation of it, we conjure up a god whose heart must break; whose frozen, desolate solitude is, in the end, unbearable. It shows us, in showing us what it would *be* to be that landscape, what company, as anthropomorphising inhabitants of it, we would keep. It shows us, moreover, how the imaginative ensouling of the world, via a god, may constitute an act of the extremest imaginative cruelty, a cruelty whose (real) impact we, as actual inhabitants of that world, fear and suspect to be close at hand. Indeed it shows us, in an exemplary way, how our god-myths function to set up between ourselves and aspects of the world that we cannot quite face, or can face only by proxy, figures, spirits, gods who will absorb, suffer from, and buffer us from them. The attitude that we're now talking about, which is to say, the attitude evinced in the yearning loneliness that structures *Tapiola* when understood as a representation of Tapio, strikes me as potentially quite deep, even if the gloss I've just given of it – the best I can muster – is undeniably inadequate.

What is one to make of this suggestion? I don't really know. It is certainly true that what I've just written captures something of the impact that the piece has on me, something of the sense that (I find) I have that the profundity of *Tapiola* goes beyond the 'purely' musical. And I haven't any worries about Pugmire's 'alethic' requirement: as far as I can see, the attitude I've attempted to gloss travesties nothing. But then, in other frames of mind, I listen to *Tapiola* and am simply ravished by its 'purely' musical beauty (indeed its sublimity). So the answer must be – as it always must in aesthetic contexts, and as I've urged in one way or another throughout this book – that you've got to listen to it and see what you hear there. Is nature, is *Tapiola*, like that? I've just listened again, and (right now) I think that the answer is yes.

NOTES

1. See Chapter 3 for discussion of the notion of a 'text'. It follows from what was said there that a song which is profound in virtue of its text need not be a setting of a profound *poem*, since the text of a song and the poem it sets are not the same thing.
2. Here is a context in which it clearly *does* make sense to take purely instrumental music as primary. But, for the reasons I gave in Chapter 3, that is not because purely instrumental music is somehow more 'purely musical' than other kinds of music. It is because, in this context, purely instrumental music gives the question of musical profundity *bite*.
3. Arthur Schopenhauer, *The World as Will and Representation*, trans. E. F. J. Payne (New York, NY: Dover, 1969), vol. 1, pp. 256–63.
4. Consider a parallel: a newspaper article reporting a profound scientific discovery certainly has profound subject matter. But this does not make the article itself profound.
5. – what I have been calling 'autonomania.'
6. Peter Kivy, *Music Alone* (Ithaca, NY: Cornell University Press, 1990), p. 202.
7. *Ibid.*, p. 203.
8. *Ibid.*, p. 208.
9. For an exception to this point, see Stephen Davies, 'Profundity in Instrumental Music', *British Journal of Aesthetics* 42:4 (2002), pp. 343–56. Davies's idea is that some pieces of music are profound in virtue of the remarkable human capacities they reveal, that is, in virtue of the profound musicianship that went into making them.
10. Jerrold Levinson, 'Musical Profundity Misplaced', *Journal of Aesthetics and Art Criticism*, 50:1 (1992), pp. 59–60.
11. *Ibid.*, p. 58.
12. *Ibid.*, p. 59. For a different, and I have to say somewhat obscure, attempt to explicate musical profundity in terms of the connection between music and psychological states, see David A. White, 'Toward a Theory of Musical Profundity', *Journal of Aesthetics and Art Criticism* 50:1 (1992), pp. 23–34.
13. For Kivy's response to Levinson's critique, see his *Philosophies of Arts* (Cambridge: Cambridge University Press, 1997), pp. 162–76.
14. Levinson, p. 59 (see Note 10).
15. I first offered an account of this sort in 'Profundity in Music', in A. Neill and A. Ridley (eds), *Arguing about Art: Contemporary Philosophical Debates* (New York, NY: McGraw-Hill, 1995), 1st edn, pp. 260–71. The present account is a descendant of that earlier one. It is very similar in its overall thrust, but is free, I hope, of most of the infelicities and blunders that marred its predecessor. I am grateful to Maria Alvarez and David Pugmire for showing me just how much in my original argument needed to be fixed.
16. The structurally profound can in fact be understood in much the way that Quine suggests that the analytic nature of a judgement can be understood. Quine pictures judgements as forming a kind of net or web of interrelated propositions, in which some judgements are more centrally placed than others – more deeply enmeshed in the interrelations constituting the web. An analytic judgement is one which occupies a position close to the centre of the web, and so is deeply implicated in the web of judgements as a whole. On the present conception, then, an analytic judgement is a structurally profound judgement. See 'Two Dogmas of Empiricism', in W. V. O. Quine, *From a Logical Point of View* (Cambridge, MA: Harvard University Press, 1956).

17. With which, of course, we enter a grey area. Is chess, for example, of real interest or importance? Is cookery? Or engineering? Or the Rosetta Stone? Or Welsh culture? Clearly there is nothing general to be said. But my own answers, for what it's worth, would be: 'possibly'; 'probably not'; 'possibly'; 'probably'; and 'depends who's asking'.

18. Although of course, before its existence was known, the subject matter of electromagnetics could not have been significant *to* human beings. But its discovery allowed people to appreciate the fact that it was (and always had been) significant.

19. One concern's being deeper than another is, I take it, a matter of its structuring more of a person's mental life than the other does (which gives us, incidentally, an unsurprising connection between significance and depth).

20. A temptation succumbed to, I think, by David A. White, in 'Toward a Theory of Musical Profundity', *Journal of Aesthetics and Art Criticism* 50:1 (1992). See especially his discussion of the sadness of Beethoven's Quartet op. 131 (pp. 31–2).

21. Which is not of course to enter a criticism of Scarlatti's sonata: it is just to say that its virtues, though real, are not of *that* sort.

22. The scope of this point is important: from an expressive point of view, defiance is neither a virtue nor a vice, and so neither is (structurally) profound defiance. But this is not to say that the structural profundity of an expressive property – such as defiance – does not entail or presuppose features which might, from other points of view, be regarded as good-making. See section IV for discussion.

23. Ernst Bloch, *Essays on the Philosophy of Music* (Cambridge: Cambridge University Press, 1985), p. 38.

24. Although the presence of that word clearly *augments* whatever evaluative force is there anyway: it is worse, presumably, to be profoundly mean-spirited than just mean-spirited, and better, one would suppose, to be profoundly, rather than plainly or routinely, magnanimous.

25. There *is* a sense in which Bloch's insight might be considered, not merely valuable, but profound, even if *Elektra* itself is not plausibly to be regarded as of genuine significance. So, for instance, Bloch's insight might persuade us that *Elektra's* place in the tradition to which it appears to belong is either less secure or different than we had had reason to suppose. In a case such as this, however, the *object* of Bloch's insight is not, simply, *Elektra*. It is, rather, *Elektra* taken in the context of the tradition to which it appears to belong; and that tradition may well be plausibly to be regarded as genuinely significant, even if Strauss's putative contribution to it is not.

26. This kind of description is sometimes referred to as the 'formal object' of an emotion, and an event that is perceived to fit it as the 'material object' of a particular episode of that emotion. See, for example, Anthony Kenny, *Action, Emotion and Will* (London: Routledge and Kegan Paul, 1963), pp. 191–2.

27. One way to capture the intentionality of such an attitude is to regard 'things in general' or 'life' or 'the world' as the globalised material objects of a defiant disposition. See previous footnote.

28. The thought expressed here – a survivor from this argument's original incarnation in the 1995 edition of *Arguing about Art* (see Note 15) – is closely connected to some things that Jerrold Levinson says: see his 'Evaluating Music', in P. Alperson (ed.), *Musical Worlds* (Philadelphia, PA: Penn State Press, 1998), pp. 95–6 and 102–5. See also Martha Nussbaum, *Upheavals of Thought: the Intelligence of Emotions* (Cambridge: Cambridge University Press, 2001), p. 275.

29. That is, the emotion must answer to the world as it is.

30. David Pugmire, 'Profound Emotion: the Substance of the World and the Limits of the Individual Mind', typescript pp. 18–19.

31. *Ibid.*, p. 31.
32. It should be noted that Pugmire allows that some of these facts – facts about the way the world is – may be, in some measure, culturally constituted: *ibid.*, pp. 32–7.
33. Oscar Wilde, *De Profundis* (1905), Letter 501.
34. This is, in effect, one way of spelling out what the notion of 'insight' comes to in this context.
35. For further discussion of expressive uniqueness, see Aaron Ridley, *Music, Value and the Passions* (Ithica, NY: Cornell University Press, 1995), chapters 5 and 6.
36. And the gap that Schopenhauer left is thereby plugged, since, as I argued in section I, epistemic profundity attaches to the showing, or to the bringing to light, of features that are structurally profound for our understanding of matters that are of genuine significance to us – and in this case, what does the showing, the bringing to light, is, quite straightforwardly, the music.
37. Peter Kivy, *Philosophies of Arts*, pp. 146–62 (see Note 13).
38. *Ibid.*, p. 160. (The Latin might adequately be glossed – if not from a zoological point of view – as 'making a molehill out of a mountain'.)
39. *Ibid.*
40. See, for instance, his *Music Alone* (Ithaca, NY: Cornell University Press, 1990). See also the Background part of Chapter 3 of the present book.
41. For fuller discussion of this point, see *Music, Value and the Passions*, chapter 3 (see Note 35).
42. This is the sense, noted in Note 22, above, in which the structural profundity of an expressive property can entail or presuppose features which, from another – here a 'purely' musical – point of view, might plausibly be regarded as good-making.
43. Robert Layton, *Sibelius* (London: Dent, 1978), pp. 78–80.
44. *Ibid.*, p. 80.
45. This impression is especially compelling in a truly great performance. I have in mind Serge Koussevitsky's searing 1939 account with the Boston Symphony Orchestra.
46. Schopenhauer, *The World as Will and Representation*, vol. 1, pp. 203–4 (see Note 3).
47. – a line that will strike many readers as a stretch too far: lots of 'i's and 't's are left undotted and uncrossed in what follows, and while I'm clear how the gaps could, in principle, be filled, I am much less clear that explicitly filling them would be worth it. Those who have followed me this far will see how to do it for themselves. Those who haven't won't be convinced by chapter and verse in any case. I am content to regard the remainder of this paragraph as 'speculative'.

Conclusion

The Other Theme

> *End and goal.* – Not every end is a goal. The end of a melody is not its goal; but nonetheless, if the melody had not reached its end it would not have reached its goal either. A parable. (Friedrich Nietzsche, *Human, All Too Human*)

The theme upon which the chapters of this book have been variations is the failure of the autonomanic view – the view that music 'is a quasi-syntactical structure of sound understandable solely in musical terms … and making no reference to anything beyond itself'[1] – to capture some central facts about music and musical experience. I hope that I have said enough to establish that that failure is both systematic and severe. The autonomanic view mischaracterises and exaggerates the difference between musical and linguistic understanding; it begs the question against musical representation; it hopelessly and necessarily misconstrues the character of one major variety of music, namely, song; it shares with every other ontologically-driven position a total misapprehension of the role of evaluative issues in musical aesthetics; and it is altogether incapable of articulating the kind of value that some of the greatest pieces of music have for us. If I have started to chip away at the intuitions that can make autonomania seem so much as minimally plausible, I will have achieved most of what I wanted to. As the variations have unfolded, however, this principal theme has turned out to have a second theme running along-side it, a kind of counter-subject, also surfacing, in one form or another, in each of the five chapters. This second theme has been the way in which the notion of 'understanding' has been prone to a certain sort of misunderstanding. I want to conclude by bringing out this other theme more explicitly, and by offering a few thoughts about its connection to the principal theme that it seems so consistently to shadow.

The Other Theme

In Chapter 1 I invoked and defended Wittgenstein's distinction between two uses of the word 'understanding' – the internal and the external – and endorsed his view that together they make up the concept. My concern there was to show how external understanding, despite the prevalence and priority in musical contexts of internal understanding, is still, correctly construed, of genuine musical significance. The main point, though, was that you have to have both. If you can't offer a paraphrase or a gloss of something understandable – that is, if you cannot understand it externally – then you haven't understood it; equally, if your experience of an understandable sort of thing is never 'earthed' in a grasp of what an instance of it means – in an internal understanding, that is, of what an instance of it says – then you haven't understood it either. In Chapter 2, the arguments I reviewed against the possibility of musical representation seemed to grant this point, at least implicitly. Those arguments can be seen as (failed) attempts to show that an under-standing of putatively representational pieces of music never involves an internal understanding of them as depictions, even if certain 'matches' or 'fits' between a given piece of music and its alleged 'subject' may, as it were, be externally detectable. And had these arguments amounted to more than question-begging, their showing this would indeed have constituted a genuine case against music's ability to represent things.

By Chapter 3, though, the point seemed to have slipped out of focus, indeed to have gone missing entirely. There, it will be recalled, various philosophers were offering to account for the relation between a song's text and its music exclusively in terms of 'matching'. Had they succeeded, they would, in effect, have shown that that relation, because it cannot be understood internally, cannot feature in an understanding of song. It is true, of course, that they might have found this sceptical outcome congenial, at least at one level. But – if the scepticism were justified – they would surely have had trouble squaring it with their apparent conviction that the (degree of) 'match' between a song's music and its text is an evaluatively significant fact about it. If the relation between music and text is to *matter* in this way, after all, then it must also be part of what one understands when one understands a song; and in order to be that – in order, that is, to be understandable internally – it must consist in more than mere 'matching'. Nor were things in better shape in Chapter 4. Indeed, they were in much the same shape. The faithfulness – and, in that much, the value – of a performance of a piece of music was said to be a function of how well it 'matched' the work's content. But either faithfulness is indeed valuable, in which case it must go beyond 'matching' and be understandable internally; or else faithfulness really is a question, merely, of 'matching', in which case it cannot be the name of a value.

In the final chapter matters were somewhat less clear-cut, and it may be that no offences against the concept of understanding were conclusively diagnosed there. Certainly no new offences were diagnosed. But familiar worries did present themselves. It is possible, for instance, that the account of profundity offered by one writer depended, via the notion of 'adequacy', on there being a 'match' between the content of a putatively profound piece of music and the character of its profound subject matter. If so, then, for the reasons given in the previous paragraph, that account must be a failure, at least to the extent that it was intended to explain how profundity might be *valuable*. And the same writer's insistence that the content of something profound just cannot be glossed in a banality – and so that a banality can never indicate a grasp of what that profound content might have been – certainly gave the impression, to put it no higher, of a complete failure to understand the place of external understanding in understanding. In each chapter, then, including the last, Wittgenstein's analysis has had a part to play.

II

So how does the fact that the notion of 'understanding' is prone to a certain sort of misunderstanding go together with autonomania? I think that there are several ways. In Chapter 1 I noted that in contexts, for instance aesthetic contexts, where an internal understanding seems to be most naturally called for, it can be tempting to suppose that an external understanding has no place at all (a supposition that may be voiced, as a moment ago, in misgivings about the banality of the gloss through which such an understanding might be expressed). The supposition is mistaken, of course, and the temptation is to be resisted. By itself, however, there is nothing distinctively autonomanic about this way of thinking. The connection to autonomania gets closer, though, when the mistake is made, not merely in aesthetic contexts, but in contexts where intra-musical relations are what is at issue. Here, the mistake is to think that, because intra-musical relations call primarily to be understood internally, they *cannot* be understood externally. This, again, is just wrong. But if one makes the mistake, and if one is already committed to the autonomanic view that the essence of music lies precisely *in* such intra-musical relations, then one will be driven to conclude that an understanding of a piece of music is, and must be, *exhausted* by the (internal) understanding of the intra-musical relations it comprises. And with this step we arrive at exactly the conception of musical understanding that autonomanic philosophers of music almost always deploy – sometimes, as in Chapter 2, to blatantly question-begging effect.

A second sort of connection is this. To the autonomaniac, intra-musical relations are what matter. And yet, clearly, music does stand in relations to other things – for instance, to the words set in a song. So the question arises: what is involved in understanding such a relation? One possible answer is that the relevant form of understanding might (at least sometimes) be internal. But this is an answer that the autonomaniac cannot accept, or even, really, seriously entertain. If it were correct, after all, it would mean that an internal understanding of certain pieces of music might (at least sometimes) include and require an understanding of distinctively *non*-musical items (here, words); and that, clearly enough, is precisely what autonomania denies. So the autonomaniac is forced to construe the form of understanding relevant to the relation between a song's music and its text in wholly external terms, resulting, by no accident, in the kind of 'matching' talk discussed in Chapter 3. But there is no such thing as an exclusively external understanding. And, since there isn't, it is hardly surprising that the autonomaniac can get no evaluative work out of the idea.

A related pressure to think exclusively – if incoherently – in terms of external understanding arises from the autonomanic conviction that pieces of music are (essentially) structures of sound. If that is what pieces of music are like, the thought goes, then, for any given piece of music, the structure that is constitutive of it should be specifiable, and that structure should be what one understands when one understands a piece of music. And now we ask: what form of understanding of a work does a (valuable) performance of it evince? To which the autonomanic answer is again, and almost inevitably, 'an external understanding', since to concede that the understanding in question might, in some measure, be internal would be to concede that an understanding of a piece of music might include or require an understanding of something that was not itself part of the structure constituting that work, namely, the under-standing evinced by the performance. But autonomania denies that there *is* anything more to a piece of music than the structure of sound that constitutes it. And so, as we saw in Chapter 4, the pressure arises to construe the form of understanding relevant to performance as exclu-sively (if impossibly) external, and to cash out the relation between works and performances wholly in terms of 'matching' – thereby, as in the case of song, leaving nothing intelligible or helpful to be said about the value of any particular performance.

These connections between autonomania and the misunderstanding of understanding go quite deep, it seems to me, and certainly deep enough to account for the way in which the latter seems so reliably to shadow the former. Indeed, the autonomanic position is not only more or less incapable of acknowledging the co-necessity of the internal and external senses of understanding; it tends instead, as we have seen, to conflate the internal with the intra-musical, and to confine it to that, and to conflate the external with the extra-musical, and to confine that to that. And the upshot of this, as I have repeatedly said, is to render both the intra-musical and the extra-musical unintelligible. Autonomania *could* do better than this. It could, that is, distance itself explicitly from the first of the connections to the misunderstanding of understanding noted above, and acknowledge the possibility – indeed the necessity – of an external understanding of intra-musical relations, so rescuing the intelligibility of those, at least. But it can do nothing about the second two connections; and this guarantees that it must always find itself at a loss in the face of such evidently musical matters as songs and performances.

III

Anything understandable is capable of being understood internally *and* externally. This is a general point, equally true of pieces of music, of newspaper articles and of flat-pack assembly instructions. Some intelligible things, however, standardly call for one sense of understanding to predominate – pieces of music for the internal sense, for instance, assembly instructions for the external sense. And some intelligible things, pieces of music among them, call for a relative balance between the two that shifts with context. For the reasons given, autonomania is quite peculiarly bad at registering facts of this sort. It is also, for the same reasons, prone to leave itself with nothing worth saying about evaluative issues – concerning the appropriateness of a song-setting, for instance, or the faithfulness of a performance. It is this last point that I now want to revisit briefly.

Of the class of intelligible things that call for a balance between the internal and the external senses of understanding, one important member is the exemplar. When Aristotle urges us, in the *Nicomachean Ethics*, not merely to do as the just man does, but to do it as the just man does it, he is highlighting precisely this: to be able to do *what* the just man does is to understand his action externally; to be able to do it *as* the just man does it is to understand his action internally.[2] To be incapable of understanding in both ways, and of striking a proper balance between the two, is therefore, in Aristotle's plausible view, to be ethically ineducable.[3] But this isn't just a point about ethics. It is a point about value, and about the role of exemplars in inculcating a sense of it. To be able to recognise something as an exemplar is to grasp (at least something of) the value that it exemplifies. It is to see *what* value is present (or else one wouldn't recognise the exemplar as exemplifying anything) and to see it as present in just *this* form (or else one wouldn't recognise the exemplar as exemplary). It is, in short, to understand the exemplar both externally and internally; and this is the case whether the exemplar in question is a just man, a corkscrew, an e-mail programme or a song-setting. Anyone who couldn't do this would – again – be ineducable in the relevant value, indeed inaccessible to it.

This point should remove any lingering suspicion that the ineptitude of autonomania in assessing the appropriateness of song-settings, for instance, or the faithfulness of performances, is some sort of unhappy accident, avoidable, perhaps, by being a bit more careful. For the fact is that the autonomanic misunderstanding of understanding – the inability, in effect, to handle the internal/external distinction properly, certainly as that distinction applies to anything other than the understanding of intra-musical relations – is of a kind that *necessarily* cuts it off from an understanding of any sort of value that is not itself exclusively (and, one might add, question-beggingly) 'musical'. Unable to make room for or sense of the notion of exemplary instances of other kinds, it can acknowledge neither the values exemplified in them nor their exemplification; which must leave it either mute, or else babbling incoherently, in the face of every evaluative question that isn't arbitrarily restricted to sound structures and the intra-musical relations that they comprise. And this, one doesn't have to think very hard about it to see, is quite a serious shortcoming for a position in the philosophy of music to have. It is, however, and for the reasons that I have given, a shortcoming that is hard-wired into it from the start.

I said in the Introduction – and the chapters that followed should have borne me out – that no one is an autonomaniac all the way down. Even the quite severely afflicted have their moments of remission. I also noted that autonomania can sometimes be difficult to detect or to shake free of, and I think that the main body of the book should have shown why I said that, too. But my purposes weren't merely or entirely negative – even if they were, in at least two senses of that word, critical. What I hoped to do was to show, by attending (more or less) closely to a series of exemplary musical works, what a non-autonomanic philosophy of music might look like. So, for instance, I attempted to account for something of the special flavour of Ives's *Central Park in the Dark* by bringing a particular conception of understanding to bear on it; I tried to do justice to the effect of Debussy's bells in *La Cathédrale Engloutie* by refusing to beg the question against musical representation; I offered a way in which, once the hold of the 'purely' musical has been broken, one might assess the appropriateness of Delius's setting of *Cynara*; I attempted to show how some of the things that one might want to say about Busoni's transcription of Bach's *Chaconne*, things mistaken by autonomaniacs for ontological claims, were in fact *critical* remarks, of a sort relevant to an assessment of Busoni's achievement; and I tried, finally, to suggest what a non-autonomaniac might mean in attributing the very highest value to Sibelius's *Tapiola*, in calling it 'profound'. To the extent that I have succeeded – and I naturally have no view about what extent that is – I have done so by attending to what I have called the 'other' theme, the misunderstanding of understanding. In trying to stay clear about, or at least to keep an open mind about, what it might mean to understand a piece of music, I hope – certainly – to have avoided the more obvious pitfalls and implausibilities of autonomania. But I also hope to have done something subtler, and perhaps more important. I hope, in short, to have re-established a space, shut down by autonomania, for thinking responsibly about musical *value* – for explaining why, as I put it at the very beginning of this book, music *is* a part of life. And this, in effect, is to (try to) put the aesthetics back into the philosophy of music, where it belongs.

NOTES

1. Peter Kivy, *Music Alone* (Ithaca, NY: Cornell University Press, 1990), p. 202.
2. Aristotle, *Nicomachean Ethics*, Book II, chapter 4.
3. For a powerful and recent argument to this effect, see John McDowell, 'Virtue and Reason', in his *Mind, Value, and Reality* (Cambridge, MA: Harvard University Press, 1998), pp. 50–73.

Index

Index

Mozart, W. A., 32, 35, 38, 73
music, choral, 77
music, Martian, 1–15, 25, 44
music, purely instrumental, 14, 48,
    77–83, 91–2, 98, 101, 104n,
    132–3, 163n
Music for Strings, Percussion and Celeste,
    21
musicology, 10, 105
Mussorgsky, M., 131n
muzak, 1, 113, 115

nationalism, 4, 6
nature, 160–2
Neill, A., 69n, 163n
Newman, E., 103n
Nietzsche, F., 142
nightingale, 62
noise, 11, 17–18, 20, 53, 54, 56
notation, 8, 78, 107
novel, 7
Nussbaum, M., 164n

object, formal, 164n
object, material, 164n
objectivity, 3, 4, 6–7
Ode to Joy, 33, 113, 115–16
ontology, 13–14, 105, 107, 109, 111,
    113–29, 166
opera, 79, 80, 90, 103n, 132
organ, 109, 112, 128
organum, 51

painting, 35, 37, 52, 56, 58, 59, 62–4,
    65–6
paraphrase, 26–36, 41, 42–3, 95–7,
    154–5, 167
Paris: the Song of a Great City, 76
Pater, W., 7–8, 12, 16n
Pathétique, 12
Pavlov, I., 71
performance, 14, 88, 105–31, 169, 170
performance, authentic, 105, 109–11,
    126–8, 131n

performance, first, 121, 122–5
performance, revelatory, 110, 119–20
philosophy of mind, 15
piano, 1, 21, 42, 51, 52, 53, 54, 56, 58,
    66, 109, 112, 126
Pictures from an Exhibition, 131n
Pietà, 140, 141, 154
plainchant, 47
Plato, 67n
Platonism, 107–8, 129n, 130n
poetry, 7, 21, 31, 32, 34–5, 43, 59,
    75–6, 79, 80, 82, 83–5, 87–8,
    94–8, 99, 101, 119, 163n
power-drill, 17, 18, 19
Pratt, C., 74, 102n
Prime Minister, the, 54
profundity, 14, 132–65, 168, 172
profundity, epistemic, 140–5, 146,
    148, 149, 150–4, 157, 158,
    159–60
profundity, structural, 140–50, 152,
    153–4, 156–7, 158, 159–60
Pugmire, D., 150–3, 158, 162, 163n,
    164n, 165n
purism, 51, 52, 134
purity, 2, 3, 6–7, 11, 12, 18, 20, 51, 65,
    67, 77, 78–83, 89, 91, 102n,
    138, 158
Pythagoras, 2

quail, 62
Quine, W. V. O., 163n

radio, 54–5, 78
rag-time, 21, 42
Raphael, 65, 66
Ravel, M., 51, 131
relations, extra-musical, 12, 13, 44,
    170
relations, intra-musical, 12, 19, 20, 44,
    60, 168–9, 170, 171
relativism, 143–5
Rembrandt, 65
report, Kinsey, 6

Index

voice, 54–5, 86

Wagner, R., 133
water, 4, 6–7, 91
Watteau, 65
Webern, A., 89
White, D., 163n, 164n
Wilde, O., 151, 165n
William Tell, 12

Wittgenstein, L., 7, 22–7, 30–3, 34,
    41, 44, 45n, 167, 168
Wolfe, T., 155
Wolterstorff, N., 129n
wood-sprite, 139

xylophone, 85

Yankee Stadium, 2